RNITURE STYLES

CONTINUED ON INSIDE BACK COVER

MODERN, CASUAL AND ORIENTAL

Sheer draperies in seafoam draw open to reveal an attractive vista through a window wall. The "serene slab" benches, upholstered in yellow, form a striking grouping with the lacquer green corner table. A novel picture arrangement, hung on a deep burgundy wall, adds height to the grouping, while pink and dark green toss pillows add color. The cocktail table has a fashionable marble top, the all-rayon carpet a tweedy loop-pile texture. All together, the effect is dramatically Modern and casual, with overtones of elegance and a suggestion of the Orient.

TRADITIONAL RICHNESS

Traditional English furniture here blends exquisitely with contemporary sculptured carpeting in fashionable cinnamon brown. The fan-shaped firescreen complements the gilt trim of the fireplace, the luxurious chandelier the white of the fireplace and the dado. A pair of gilt tie-backs catch up the fullness of the festooned draperies. Slipcovers introduce a gay note of pattern. Lustered hurricane lamps and a fine wall candelabrum, as well as tiny figures and a decorative oil painting, carry out the traditional spirit of this rich setting.

New
CREATIVE HOME DECORATING

New CREATIVE HOME DECORATING

By

HAZEL KORY ROCKOW, Ph.D.

Senior Home Economist, Brooklyn College

And

JULIUS ROCKOW

Interior Decorator

Illustrated by

ROBERT J. CURRY

H. S. STUTTMAN COMPANY, *PUBLISHERS*

NEW YORK, N. Y.

PRINTED IN THE U.S.A.
By ROTARY GRAPHIC PRESS INC.
New York 10, N. Y.

INTRODUCTION

INTEREST IN HOME DECORATION is at a higher pitch today than ever before. More and more, conversation among women everywhere turns to this fascinating subject, and technical terms once reserved to the professional decorator are now widely current coins of speech. This is a good sign. It indicates that larger numbers of women intend to decorate or re-decorate their homes, drawing upon their own knowledge and good taste. It means that, as knowledge increases, standards in home decoration definitely will grow even higher. It enhances the likelihood that women, no longer content with drab and listless homes, will contribute new and interesting ideas to the art of decoration.

With growth in interest, there has come about a new attitude toward home decoration. The notion that a home is decorated only once to last for a lifetime, arose as a psychological reflection of earlier scarcity economies and is now outdated. Modern techniques of production have made home furnishings available to all persons and at all income levels. Accordingly, it is not surprising that many persons are re-decorating their homes periodically. True, they retain cherished pieces, but they alter color schemes, window treatment, slipcovers and accessories, and they add many new pieces of furniture. Since home decoration is usually a co-operative venture involving both man and wife, this new attitude may well be one of the healthiest developments in the field of present-day marital and family relationships. In any event, certain it is that the home is basic to the family, and that beautiful homes inculcate ideals and values that make for a decent, upright society.

Every book that is written with care expresses a point of view. The point of view underlying this book, the authors hope, is made explicit in the text. Our view is that home decoration is a creative activity. As such, it is guided by principles and esthetic values common to all the creative arts. Furthermore, fifteen years of active classroom and lecture experience has convinced one of the authors that practice not enlightened by a knowledge of principles is on the fringe of the trial and error method. Trial and error is uneconomical of money, time and effort and, all too often, never transcends error. For this reason, the authors have emphasized principles throughout the book, as well as their practical application.

the Rockows

In preparing this edition, THE PUBLISHERS wish to acknowledge their gratitude to the following organizations for supplying photographs and up-to-date information: Allied Stores Corp.; America House; Armstrong Cork Co.; Baker Furniture Co.; Bigelow Sanford Carpet Co.; Bloomingdale Bros., Inc.; Brooklyn Museum; Brunovan, Inc.; Cassard Romano Co., Inc.; Charak Furniture Co.; Cheney Brothers; Colonial Mfg. Co.; Comprehensive Fabrics, Inc.; Crawford Furniture; Dunbar Furniture Corp. of Indiana; E. I. du Pont de Nemours & Co.; Evans Products Co.; Ficks Reed Co.; Firth Carpet Co.; French & Co.: Inc.; Goodall Fabrics, Inc.; Grand Rapids Bookcase and Chair Co.; Greef Fabrics, Inc.; Grosfeld House; Hartford Textile Co.; The Heifetz Co.; Heywood-Wakefield Co.; Illuminating Engineering Society; Imperial Furniture Co.; International Business Machines Corp.; Intramural, Inc.; Robert W. Irwin Co.; Georg Jensen, Inc.; Johnson Carper Furniture Co.; A. & M. Karagheusian, Inc.; Karastan Rugs, Product of Fieldcrest Mills; Katzenbach and Warren, Inc.; Kentile, Inc.; Kindel Furniture Co.; Kling Factories; Knoll Associates, Inc.; Kroehler Manufacturing Co.; Lees-Cochrane Co., Inc.; James Lees and Sons Co.; Libbey-Owens-Ford Glass Co.; Lord & Taylor; R. H. Macy & Co.; James McCreery & Co.; The Mengel Co.; Mersman Brothers; Michaels & Co.; Molla, Inc.; Mueller Furniture Co.; Nye-Wait Co., Inc.; Onondaga Pottery Co.; Pine Shops; Pittsburgh Plate Glass Co.; St. Charles Manufacturing Co.; John B. Salterini Co., Inc.; F. Schumacher & Co.; Alexander Smith and Sons Carpet Co.; John Stuart, Inc.; Swedish Modern, Inc.; Sylvania Electric Products, Inc.; Richard E. Thibaut, Inc.; Towle Manufacturing Co.; Union National Furniture Co.; Valentine-Seaver; The Wall Paper Institute; Waverly Fabrics; John Wanamaker; Westinghouse Electric Corp.; Richard Wheelwright, Inc.; Widdicomb Furniture Co.; Youngstown Kitchens by Mullens Manufacturing Corp.; Ypsilanti Reed Furniture Co.; Zangerle and Peterson Co.

Especially do we wish to thank the following manufacturers for the full color illustrations of room settings which they graciously supplied us: Armstrong Cork Co.; The Bigelow-Sanford Carpet Co., Inc.; Goodall Fabrics, Inc.; Heywood-Wakefield Co.; A. & M. Karagheusian, Inc.; Karastan Rugs, Product of Fieldcrest Mills; Alexander Smith and Sons Carpet Co.; Sherwin Williams Co.; Waverly Fabrics Division of F. Schumacher & Co.

TABLE OF CONTENTS

COLOR ILLUSTRATIONS

New
CREATIVE HOME
DECORATING

A striking Modern home here indicates one of the leading trends in today's decorating — that to elegance. The enormous freeform cocktail table stands in front of — not the sofa — but three web and foam rubber armchairs. The window behind this grouping is undraped, with fluted glass to insure privacy while admitting light and an impression of vista. The long armless sofa, upholstered in a light color, stands opposite against a window curtained with sheer casement cloth. Latticework provides a divider to mark off the library section of this room.

Here authentic Chinese designs provide the theme for Modern furniture. The bone white walls contrast with the firecracker red of the drapery fabric which is also softened with soft green and gunmetal gray. The gunmetal is repeated in the textured sofa fabric, while a contrasting hand print covers the sofa cushions. A nubby texture, in avocado green, upholsters the club chair, a traditional patterned fabric covers the seats of the Chinese arm chair and Mandarin chair. Correlated fabrics such as these simplify decorating and make for an attractive result.

CHAPTER ONE

CREATING YOUR HOME

THERE IS a deep and abiding pleasure in creating a home. You take a dwelling and infuse it with beauty, comfort and charm. You transform the dwelling and endow it with the imprint of your personality. What was formerly a bare structure of walls, floors and ceilings, is now happily your home.

To the extent that you create well, you are guided, consciously or unconsciously, by the art of home decoration. This art is the distillation of human experience in the creation of homes. A knowledge of this art permits you to profit by its wealth of experience and achievement. It enables you to create an attractive home of your own.

For all its importance to you in creating your home, decoration is a simple, practical art. You will have no difficulty in mastering its principles and applying them surely and deftly. Color schemes, period furniture styles, spirit—all common topics of conversation today — will be an open book to you. These matters are essential in creating an attractive home. They are all phases of home decoration.

The home that you create your-

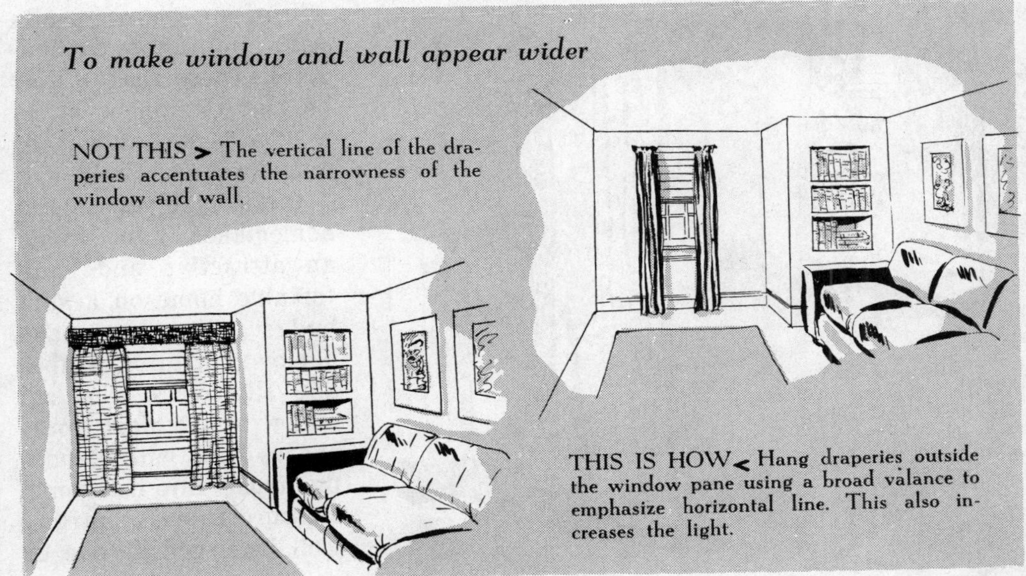

To make window and wall appear wider

NOT THIS > The vertical line of the draperies accentuates the narrowness of the window and wall.

THIS IS HOW < Hang draperies outside the window pane using a broad valance to emphasize horizontal line. This also increases the light.

self, through your own planning and doing, means more to you than a home you accept fully decorated by someone else. Decorating your home yourself is a genuine thrill. You will enjoy the process of creating your own home, and you will delight in the home that you have created.

In the home of your own making, each item will have a story behind it. You will know how you came to select your color scheme. You will know why you selected the particular style of furniture that you did and why you arranged your pieces as they are. You will know what spirit you wanted your home to express. All this is an essential part of the joy of creating a home. It is an experience you will always cherish.

Success in home decoration depends chiefly upon two qualities. First, it requires knowledge and pertinent information. Second, it requires good taste. Without knowledge, you cannot create well. Without good taste, your knowledge will not be put to its best use. Fortunately, both these qualities may be developed. Information can be acquired and good taste can be broadened. In fact, these qualities develop hand in hand.

You may think that other things are even more important than these qualities. You may believe that ample funds are the prime prerequisite. True, if you want to buy furniture, drapes and accessories, money is needed. But it is important to realize that the mere spending of large sums of money in decorating your home does not automatically make it a livable and pleasant one. Money is not a substitute for good taste. And knowledge will often secure results with a minimum expenditure. These results may be lost to one who has only a large amount of money to work with.

In fact, the resourceful homemaker can create an attractive and comfortable home on a slim budget. She can make her own curtains, drapes and slipcovers. She can make economical purchases that will fit harmoniously into her home. Resourcefulness might well be urged as one of

the basic qualities for the home decorator. It is, however, actually an aspect of knowledge. It is knowledge at work. The homemaker who has the knowledge is the one who can make resourceful use of it.

YOUR DECORATIVE PURPOSE

The home that you create expresses something. It expresses a spirit and an atmosphere that can be sensed. What it does express — whether formality or informality, comfort or luxury, welcome or aloofness, good cheer and gayety or reserve and serenity—we shall call your *decorative purpose.* Deciding upon a decorative purpose is an important step that you should take before you begin decorating your home. The effect you wish to achieve will determine how you go about it.

The mood or spirit that you want your home to express tells you what color schemes you may select, what type of furniture you should buy and how this furniture may be arranged. It will tell you what you should emphasize and what you should merge inconspicuously into the background. You should evaluate all your decisions in the light of your decorative purpose. It serves both as a goal that you want to attain and a guide that will lead you to achieve your goal.

A family that delights in quiet and comfort, that likes to read and listen to the radio, that prefers the simple to the ornate, the plain and reliable to the fancy and frivolous, will want a home keyed to the qualities it prefers. It would not welcome a home designed for formality and dignity, for ostentation and lavishness. A home that stressed sophistication or novelty and the passing vogue, would disappoint it.

The needs, desires and preferences of your family are therefore important in deciding upon a decorative purpose. In fact, unless your home answers its needs and meets its desires, your family will not be satisfied. It will not feel at home. You must, accordingly, evaluate these subjective matters. In doing so, you are actually

evaluating the personality of your family. The home that will please your family is one that is in keeping with its character and provides for its needs.

You will, of course, consider the size of your family as well as the age and sex of its members. A home with boys will want to take on a more masculine tone, especially in the living room and the boys' bedrooms. The furniture you choose for them must be sturdy and well able to withstand the hard buffeting of youthful spirit and activity. Girls would need sturdy furniture with a feminine touch. If infants are members of your family, you will want to include a nursery or a play area. Indeed, your family plans may envisage a newcomer. The actual selection of furniture in this event may then be different so as to allow for flexible readjustment in the future.

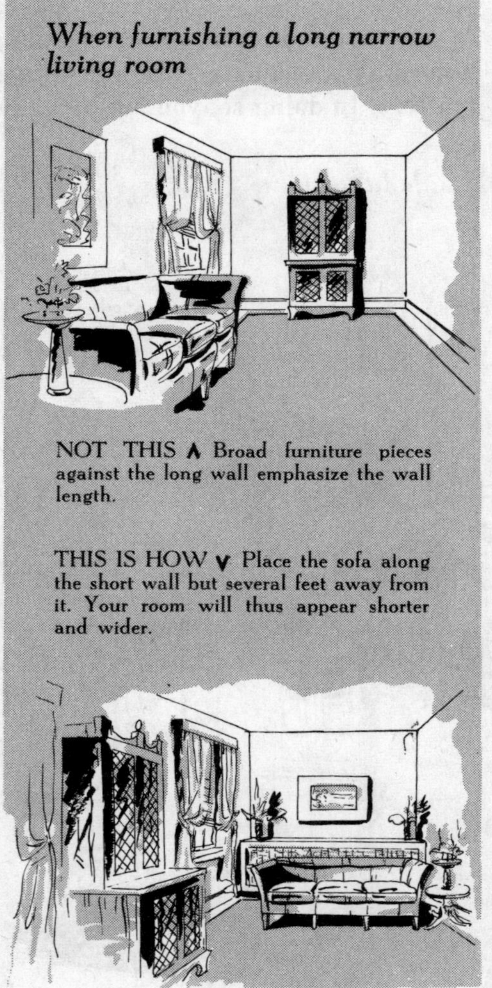

When furnishing a long narrow living room

NOT THIS ∧ Broad furniture pieces against the long wall emphasize the wall length.

THIS IS HOW ∨ Place the sofa along the short wall but several feet away from it. Your room will thus appear shorter and wider.

You have to take certain other factors into account in deciding upon your decorative purpose. You must consider the physical structure of the rooms that you intend to furnish. The size and shape of the room, the height of its ceiling, the number and placement of its openings, the amount of natural light and sun that enter the room—all these must figure in your calculations. If the room has certain features that you consider defects, you will have to decide how you may overcome or minimize them. You will, similarly, want to take advantage of the good points of your room and embody them in your final plan.

Where your home is located may matter too. A home at the seashore can be decorated and furnished quite differently from one in the mountains, while the home in the city will differ quite markedly from one in the country. Yet the general over-all effects that you want to achieve in any of these homes may be the same.

A TALE WITH A MORAL

The story of Jane is related here to impress you with the importance of choosing a decorative purpose and following it through in decorating your home. Jane owns a small home in one of the suburban developments of New York City. She had furnished this home over a period of years

Nature creates the background for this delightful informal living room which blends New England Colonial and Classic Modern Furniture. Inviting the out of doors within by means of huge picture windows is one of the significant contributions of present-day architecture. The comb-back Windsor chair, in the right foreground, the knotted plank walls and the fireplace add a note of distinction to the furnishings.

without skimping costs. Yet she was dissatisfied with the result.

She had tried hard to make her home pretty and inviting. She had furnished it with Georgian and Regency pieces. She had bought additional pieces, in a variety of styles, all lovely in themselves—end tables, lamps and easy chairs. She had repeatedly changed her draperies as well as her rugs, and she had tried several different patterns of wallpaper.

However, Jane and her husband realized they were not creating a home that pleased them. When they came to us for advice, we first asked them what spirit they wanted their home to embody. They had never asked themselves this question before. When they had juggled their furniture around, when they had added or replaced furniture and accessories, they had no clear notion of what they were attempting to achieve.

After analyzing their wants and needs, they were able to decide upon a good, clear-cut purpose. As Jane's husband is a lawyer, they both agreed on a formal home that would serve him as his office and would lend dignity and prestige to his professional standing. This purpose was in keeping with their personalities. And it was easily adaptable to their home.

They were able to judge their furniture, accessories and rooms in terms of this purpose. The living room was converted into an office. Its showily expensive wallpaper was replaced with a dignified one of quiet design. The bookcases, which contained his law library, were brought into the foreground. His desk became an important center of interest. The flamboyant carpet was dyed to match the formal tone of the room and the windows were draped to conform to this mood.

Their dining room was converted into a delightful Regency living room. They took advantage of their large breakfast nook so that it could serve when visitors came to dinner. They were able to combine their enclosed sun porch into both a waiting room for clients and a bedroom for the occasional overnight guest.

As a result of these changes, their home took on a new meaningfulness. It now brought deep satisfaction and pleasure. And the decoration cost them only a small fraction of the money they had literally squandered so ineffectually before. As Jane later said, decorating her home to achieve a purpose turned out to be one of the richest and most thrilling experiences of her life.

PLANNING YOUR HOME ON PAPER

Deciding upon a decorative purpose is not the whole story in creating your home. True, your purpose will guide you in selecting a color scheme. It will tell you whether the style of furniture you like will attain the effect you want. But you also must consider how you can arrange your furniture and accessories within your room so as to achieve comfort and order and create an attractive, harmonious whole.

To decide upon the furniture arrangement best suited for your room, you can resort to *paper planning.* Planning is an important step to you. It is a genuine timesaver. It is a tested money saver. It can teach you a great deal about furniture grouping and it can be thoroughly enjoyable.

Paper planning applies even if you want to add only a few more pieces of furniture to one of your rooms or want to re-arrange furniture you already have. In these instances, paper planning will show you what effects

you can retain or produce. You can see how all your pieces must be arranged to achieve harmony and comfort.

In paper planning your home, you make a miniature replica of your room. We have included a set of furniture figures and graph paper with which you can plot your room and furniture layout. The furniture silhouettes that we have included are in scale to the average sized pieces to which they correspond. Just be sure you measure your room carefully. Then, to maintain the same proportions as that of the furniture figures, allow each foot of room space to be represented by a corresponding line a quarter-inch in length.

With care you can draw a floor plan exactly like that of your room. You can maneuver the furniture figures on your floor plan. You will then be able to see, through actual trial, where your furniture should be placed to achieve the pleasing overall effect you want. By all odds this method is easier than moving full-sized sofas, tables, chests, chairs, lamps and everything else all around the room.

Planning your home on paper bridges the two aspects of home decoration — the mental planning and actually putting the plan into practice. In paper planning you try out your aim in miniature. Then you are prepared to translate it into actuality—on a full scale.

ABOUT THIS BOOK

This book contains many pictures. These pictures tell a great deal compactly. Many of them will offer you practical hints and workable suggestions that you may want to adopt in decorating your own home.

The *This is How* pictures show you exactly what to avoid and what to practice. They permit you to test your ideas and your home. "Is this what is wrong with my room?" you can ask yourself. If it is, the positive picture will show you how to correct the shortcoming.

The striated green of the walls, varied by branches of evergreen, combine with chartreuse rough-textured fabric to set the color scheme of this pleasing Modern dining room. The china cabinet is made up of a unit with three drawers and sliding glass panels covering two shelves. Another drawer unit is grouped with two cabinets to form a sideboard.

The pictures will suggest, very often, how a *minor change* in the arrangement of your furniture, in the choice of your draperies, in the hanging of a mirror, can bring about *major improvements* in your home. They will also show you how to take advantage of the opportunities and decorative possibilities that your home may offer. The difference between success and failure in home decoration is often a slender one. Doing it right does make a world of difference in the home.

In addition, this book contains twenty illustrations of color schemes. These color schemes are up-to-date and embody the latest trends in home decoration. They may supply precisely the information you require for your home. A color wheel is also provided. If you want to work out your own color schemes, the chapters on color will tell you how to do it.

This book will be practical in its outlook. It will not offer you advice based upon the transient vogue of the moment. Nor will it indulge in outlandish plans. This book is *not* designed for the rare individual who unhesitatingly builds the color scheme of her home to flatter and set off the color of her own hair. Nor is it designed for one who strains for the eccentric and novel by selecting her furniture so as to achieve startling effects.

Rather, this book intends to supply you with specific information and general knowledge that will assist you in meeting your particular problems and in answering your special questions. And, the authors sincerely hope, this book will open up new vistas for you. It will give you a new and finer appreciation of the possibilities that await you in decorating your home. It will give you a wider background and an enriched good taste. This background will permit you to evaluate your home and other homes. It will permit you to be a better judge of furnishings on display in shops from which you buy.

All this will aid you in planning your own home. It will help you to translate your plans into reality. It will assist you in actualizing your hopes, dreams and desires. And the home you create will please you today, tomorrow and through the years to come.

A 15th century polychrome Chinese figure in wood looks benignly upon a Modern room. The circular sectional sofa, versatile in its arrangement possibilities, is upholstered in dark green and forms the nucleus of a smart entertainment center. The beige rug is of cotton, the tables of blonde wood. The imposing mural behind the sofa offers a dramatic backdrop to the entire setting.

A sheer drapery on a ceiling track here separates the living room from the dining room. Patterned fabric at the windows of both areas also extends ceiling to floor and omits cornices. One club chair picks up the pattern of the window fabric. The lamp table at its side has a marble top and metal gallery. Marble is again found in the round cocktail table which is 18th century in style. The over-all effect is one of richness and formality, with a feeling of spaciousness.

A corner done in a dark color forms the background for a deep-tufted Madame Recamier sofa. The sofa is a part of the conversation center at the fireplace. A two-faced lady's desk, with its sides carved in a lyre motif, stands at right angles to the window. The drapery is a branching floral with a large repeat. The same fabric is also used in the deep cornice, shaped with a French Provincial curve outlined with fringe on the bottom. The luxurious carpet is woven with a sculptured Greek key motif, a design that is repeated in the shade of the lamp in the corner.

CHAPTER TWO

THE ELEMENTS OF BEAUTY

IF YOU consider the history of mankind, you will see two human impulses at work—the one to achieve beauty, the other to create a pleasing home. Both these impulses are rooted deep in human nature. They both give spiritual enrichment and true satisfaction. They both go hand in hand, for beauty is one of the qualities we want the home that we create to possess.

These two impulses existed even among the cavemen, the most primitive peoples of whom we have record. These peoples adopted natural caves or grottoes as their shelter. But they were not content merely to secure the creature comforts of life. They felt a need for beauty. They also felt a need to make their caves something more than dwellings. They wanted to transform them into homes.

The cavemen turned to beautifying their shelters. They scratched and painted pictures on the stone walls and clayey ground of their caves. These pictures of reindeer, bison and extinct mammoths were not mere decorations. They were genuine attempts to capture beauty and introduce it into their daily lives. Beauty was one of the qualities that the caveman sought in creating his home.

We today similarly seek beauty for

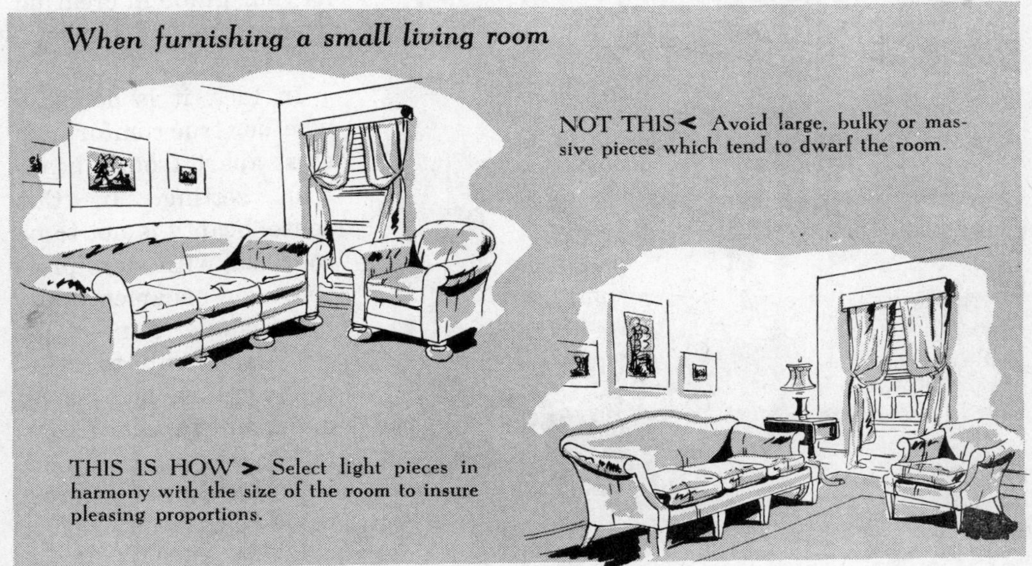

our home. We enjoy things of beauty, whether natural or man-made. We derive a satisfaction from viewing a beautiful scene, a graceful swan, a star-studded sky, a Rubens painting, a delightful home. We pride ourselves on our heritage of beauty, on the priceless works of art that have come down to us from bygone ages. Much of our present-day furniture reproduces the pleasing lines and forms created by the master designers of the past.

The impulse to beauty is one that leads us not only passively to enjoy the beautiful. It leads us to strive to create beauty and bring it more intimately into our lives. Of course, not all of us can create works of art. Only a da Vinci could have conceived and painted the Mona Lisa. But we all, nevertheless, have a need for beauty, a love for it. We have an urge to achieve it in creating our home.

In decorating your home, you have an opportunity to express your love of beauty and to satisfy your longing for the beautiful. You have an opportunity to place the stamp of your personality upon your home. You can create a home that will fulfill your needs and desires. In bringing beauty into your home, you enrich your life and that of your family.

Your purpose in decorating and furnishing your home will include a desire to attain both comfort and beauty. It will aim to produce an overall effect that is in keeping with the character of your family. If you are to achieve these objectives, you will have to know how to apply the principles of decoration. These principles can act as your guide in creating a beautiful and comfortable home.

In fact, it is doubtful whether true comfort can exist apart from a beautiful setting. In this sense, beauty is not to be confused with mere prettiness or ornamentation. Nor should comfort be restricted only to creature comfort. There is an important aspect of comfort that is psychological. It is this sort of comfort that stems from beauty

Treating the bay window

NOT THIS < Individual window treatment and rectangular furniture make bay windows a liability.

THIS IS HOW > Treat all 3 windows as one unit and accent with circular or sectional furniture.

and that is, actually, hardly distinguishable from beauty. Unless it is also beautiful, the room that is reputed to be comfortable is not wholly so, is not psychologically soothing, relaxing and pleasant.

Very often one hears the remark, "My shoes look like the dickens! But they're comfortable." We may agree that there is a justification for this remark. The comfort these shabby shoes may give is a physical comfort. But they do not give peace of mind. The wearer does not feel at ease. If he did, he would not have felt the need to rationalize his act. He would have worn them without comment, without defending them. In securing beauty, we should therefore assure comfort as well.

THE BASIC ELEMENTS

When we furnish our home, we take furniture, accessories and color and try to combine them so as to produce both beauty and comfort. But how do we judge whether a piece of furniture is beautiful? How can we determine which pieces of furniture will go well with one another? What accessories, what floor covering should we use for pleasing results with our furniture? What color scheme will suit our decorative purpose? How do we arrange our furnishings to form a coherent whole? How may we achieve the effect we desire, whether formal or informal, masculine or feminine, friendly and cheerful or dignified and restrained?

Some of these questions can be answered by considering the *basic elements* that enter into our room composition. These basic elements are only four in number. They are: line and form, color and texture. We shall find that they provide us with guides in evaluating a chair, a sofa, a table. They will aid us in grouping diverse pieces of furniture together. These four basic elements will tell us what effects we may hope to achieve and how we can achieve them. They will guide us in selecting our furnishings and our color schemes. They will help us in arranging our furniture, in choosing our fabrics and our floor covering.

These four basic elements are the members of our home decorating team. By teaming them together, we can produce a winning result. Through them we can attain beauty and the effects we desire.

PHYSICAL AND PSYCHOLOGICAL ROLES

These four elements each have a double value. They each play a dual role. The color red is a *physical* tool we may use. And equally important it has a *psychological* significance. Red is not merely a color used to tint a signal light. To the motorist who notices it, the red signal has meaning. It orders him, Stop! or Danger, proceed cautiously! Colors used in home furnishing also have a significance, even though in the home a tone of red does not command us to stop. Psychologic significance attaches not only to color, but to texture, line and form as well.

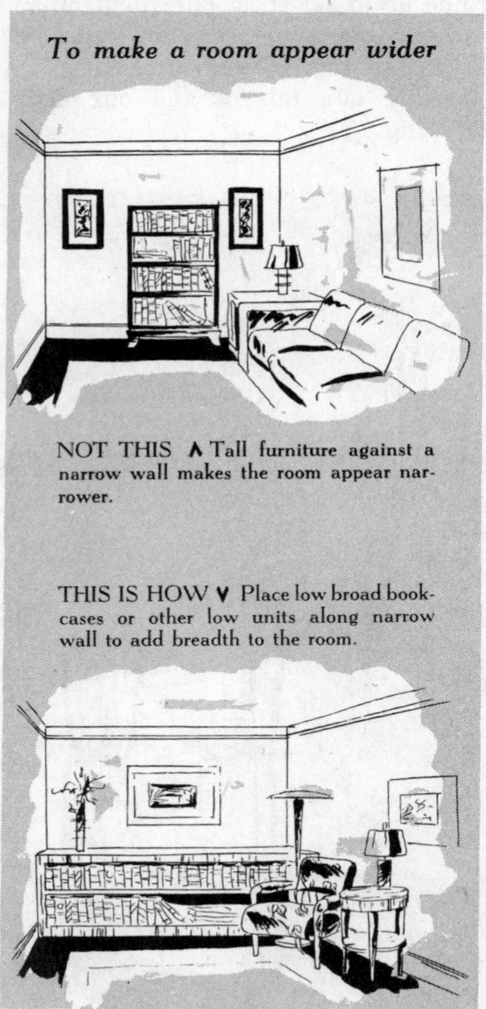

To make a room appear wider

NOT THIS ∧ Tall furniture against a narrow wall makes the room appear narrower.

THIS IS HOW ∨ Place low broad bookcases or other low units along narrow wall to add breadth to the room.

The fact that these four basic elements possess both physical and psychological characteristics is essential to us. We must consider not only the appearance that is produced by the physical aspects of these elements, but what these elements have to say as well. If we combine Hepplewhite furniture with homespun fabrics, the result may not quite satisfy us. If we realize, however, that the lines of the furniture are delicate while homespuns convey a feeling of coarseness, we can instantly appreciate what is amiss. Accordingly, in teaming together the four elements so as to produce a pleasing result, we must take account of both the physical and psychological properties.

If you are to use these basic elements to best advantage, it is necessary that you acquaint yourself with their physical and psychological potentialities. You are the coach of the team. You are the one who will decide how the team will act and respond together. The more you know of what your team members are able to do, the better you can direct them. And the better you can achieve your aim of producing an attractive home. We shall, therefore, consider briefly each of these elements and determine what their possibilities are.

LINE

You yourself have probably made

the remark that so-and-so "has good lines." This remark indicates the importance of line in designs of all sorts —in furniture, rooms, buildings, even clothes and automobiles.

Lines enclose space. They thus give the outline—or *contour*—of forms. Lines, accordingly, generate forms.

Lines are mainly of two types—straight or curved. Straight lines give the psychological impression of strength and steadiness, a feeling of manliness and simplicity. Their unsparing use may produce an impression of seriousness and even of austerity. Objects with straight line contours are simple and frank. Straight lines are characteristic of Colonial New England, Chinese Chippendale, Sheraton and Modern furniture. Used in decoration, straight lines form striped, checked, plaid and herringbone designs.

The prevailing direction that straight lines take varies the effects these lines produce psychologically.

Horizontal lines are especially reposeful and quiet, as befits the sleeping individual. Horizontal lines suggest rest and relaxation, as well as breadth. To achieve a restful room, then, you would stress the use of horizontal lines in your wallpaper, upholstery, drapes, lampshades, picture arrangement and furniture. And you would avoid the use of restless, dynamic diagonal lines. Horizontal lines would also predominate in a room keyed to informality.

Vertical lines appear strong and firm, adding height, dignity and stability. Vertical lines express masculinity and formality. They would, accordingly, be emphasized in a room keyed to express these traits, while their use would be minimized in a room that is intended to give the opposite effect. Thus, a boy's bedroom would stress vertical lines. A boudoir or a feminine bedroom would, however, avoid vertical lines in patterned or plain surfaces.

Diagonal lines suggest activity and movement. They are dynamic and restless. The backward slanting diagonal gives the feeling of instability. Diagonals lead the eye of the observer upward. For this reason, the herringbone design is preferable in patterned material, as it gives the effect of completed movement. Thus the herring-

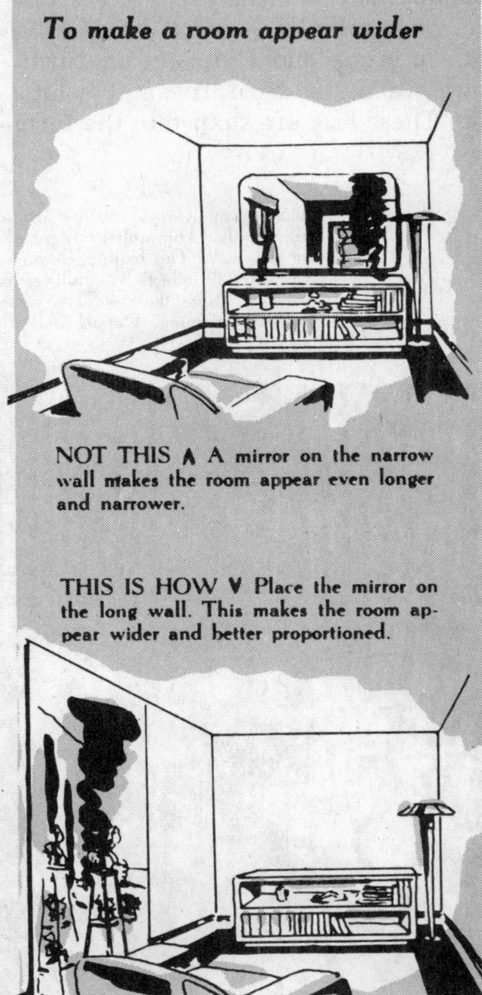

bone design conveys a feeling of balance.

Broken lines give the appearance of animation and gayety. If zigzag and uneven, broken lines indicate instability, disunity and confusion. Broken straight lines are often used, as with pillows or cushions on a sofa or davenport, to introduce pleasing variety.

Curved lines are graceful and feminine, soft and lighthearted in appearance, with an effect of relaxation and cheerfulness. Curved lines are rich. If overdone, however, curves become voluptuous and ornate. The gracefully curving cabriole legs of Louis XV, Queen Anne and Chippendale furniture are highly decorative and beautiful. These legs are shaped in the form of an S-curve. Duncan Phyfe and Victorian furniture also stress the use of curved lines.

Curved lines with an *obvious repeat,* as in a scalloped border, are associated with Colonial maple furniture. They are prim and precise. While graceful, they are lacking in subtlety and variety.

Curved lines with a *subtle repeat,* such as in the cabriole leg, are far more pleasing. Such curves are dignified yet lively. They are instinct with rhythm and movement.

From one point of view, forms or shapes are generated by lines. From the opposite point of view, all forms may be reduced to lines. This might

Contrasting vertical stripes contribute to the masculine character of this study. The upholstery of the Chippendale desk chair is keyed to the wall. The leather easy chair and the accessories are in key to the over-all effect. The allover pattern of the rug adds a feeling of richness. Note the use of a potted plant rather than delicate flowers in this grouping. Details like this illustrate the value of planning.

Straight and curved lines are pleasingly blended in this attractive dining alcove. A realistic tan wallpaper simulates a wood panel effect. The bleached oak chairs are upholstered in chartreuse, while the sculptured rug is a mint color. A slightly darker shade of tan is repeated in the coarse net curtains. The picture window overlooks a broad terrace furnished with weather proof garden tables and chairs.

lead you to think that the characteristics expressed by forms are those of their constituent lines. This is not wholly true, however, for a new factor must be considered in evaluating them. This factor is proportion.

FORM

Straight lines, in two dimensions as in plane geometry, form squares, triangles and oblongs, while curved lines form circles and ellipses or ovals. All these *forms* convey the feeling of completeness and fulfilment. But squares and circles add an overtone of mathematical precision. Their proportions are perfectly apparent and, in consequence, are sometimes uninteresting.

Usually, *square* rooms, wall areas and windows, square rugs, fireplaces, pictures, tables and bookcases are insipid and dull and should be avoided. For this reason, ability to alter the apparent dimensions of a room, a piece of furniture, a window or a grouping is important in home furnishing. We can make a ceiling appear higher or lower, or a wall look closer or farther away. What the actual physical qualities are is of less moment than what the qualities appear to be. The eye is the judge. And the eye perceives appearances, not actuality.

Triangles give the effect of unity and balance. The isosceles triangle, with its two sides of equal dimension, is widely employed with pleasing effect in home furnishing. It suggests balanced movement and is found in such diverse uses as lampshades and chair groupings as well as in decorative designs and in the arrangement of objects of art on shelves and mantels.

The *circle* is found in pictures, mirrors, pie-crust and round tilt-top tables and in much modern furniture. Circular pictures and mirrors are often effectively used to impart a pleasing contrast and variety, while circular sofas may be effectively employed as dominant elements in various groupings. They are especially pleasing about a radio or fireplace, or in the recesses of a bay window where they may conform to the shape of the area. To the extent that a curved piece of furniture or a furniture arrangement approximates a segment of a perfect circle, it is less interesting than *ovals* or more subtle and sinuous curves.

Oblong or rectangular surfaces and solids are far more popular in home furnishing than any other form. Oblongs are more interesting than squares as they permit greater variation. The more subtle the proportions are in an oblong, the more attractive it is.

THE RULE OF THE GOLDEN SECTION

The fact that *the oval is more pleasing than the circle and the oblong is more pleasing than the square* was discovered by the early Greeks. They conducted a sort of Gallup poll as to the preferences of observers. Then the pollsters measured the statues and buildings that observers had judged. From their studies, these students of esthetics found out which figures are considered the most pleasing.

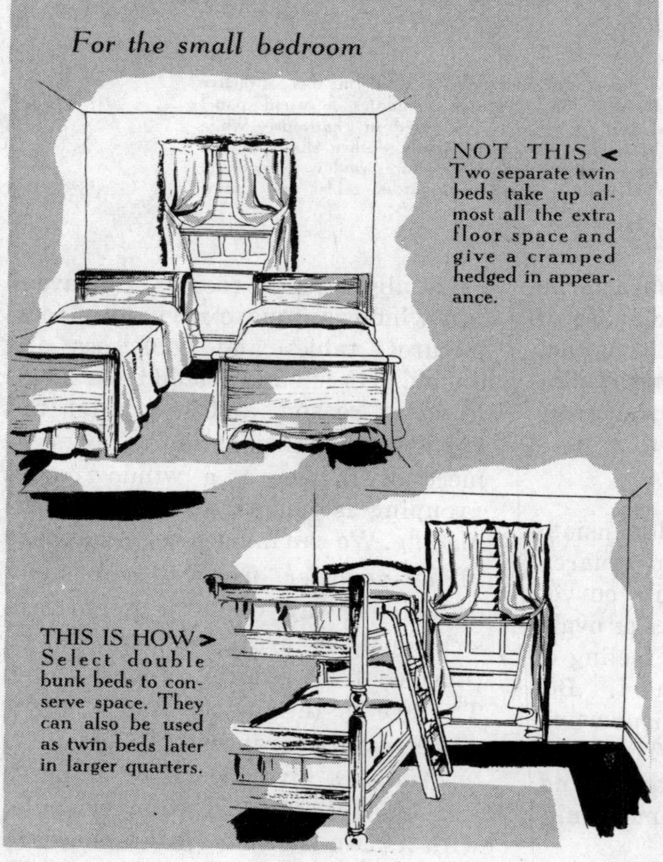

You may repeat their experiment in part and test your own preferences. Draw a three-inch square, an oblong five inches broad and one inch high, an oblong one inch wide and five inches high. Also draw an oblong two inches wide and three inches high and an oblong three inches by five inches. Which of these figures do you find pleasing? Which figures fail to arouse or retain your interest? The Greeks found that the last two figures are the ones that please most observers.

Being mathematicians, the Greeks placed the dimensions of width and height in the form of ratios. Thus, the square is in the ratio of one to one, for in every square the width is equal to the length. The four oblongs of your experiment are in the ratio of five to one, one to five, two to three, and three to five, respectively.

From this poll the Greeks were able to enunciate the *Rule of the Golden Section.* This rule states that, *among oblongs,* the most pleasing proportions are in the ratios of *two to three, three to five* and *five to eight.* This rule puts into mathematical form the proportions that please the eye and satisfy our sense of fitness. Accordingly, these ratios are mathematical guides by which we may attain pleasing proportions in our home.

A rug that is nine by fifteen feet in size is in the ratio of three to five. Its proportions are attractive. A room that is twelve by twenty feet is also in this ratio—and similarly in optimal proportion. The fact that the ratio of a square is one to one is the reason that square rooms lose interest for the onlooker.

An oblong divided into halves, thirds or quarters likewise lacks eye-appeal and subtlety. In these instances the ratios of the divisions are one to one, one to two and one to three, respectively. The Law of the Golden Section, in effect, abjures us not to divide our room or walls through placement of furniture, wall paneling or window openings into ratios that are simple and obvious.

You can apply this rule and its recommended ratios as a guide in setting up good proportions in your home. You will immediately notice that a two-foot mirror will go well over a bureau three feet wide, but less well over a six-foot sofa. In the latter instance the proportions are the obvious ratio of one to three. If you want interesting proportions, you will avoid the simple, precise ratios of halves, thirds and quarters.

Contrasting textures in upholstery and scatter rug add to the beauty of this room. The sectional sofa and the corner table combine to make a very comfortable corner arrangement. Curved lines are repeated in the circular coffee table, while the cheerful pattern of the wallpaper and the colorful prints contribute to this interesting grouping.

PROPORTION

Proportion is a matter of comparative size and shape and a matter of spacing. In our home, we want to secure pleasing proportions. We want our individual pieces to be attractive in size and shape. We want our pieces to be harmonious in relation to one another—that is, *in scale* with one another. We also want to space our furniture in our room and arrange it so as to produce an attractive ensemble.

We all have an eye for proportion. We ordinarily can sense whether a piece of furniture is in proportion or not. Our eye judges proportion through comparison with neighboring sizes and shapes. Thus our eye will tell us quickly if the shade of a lamp appears too large for its base or column. Such a lamp looks topheavy. A delicate Sheraton chair, with its slender, tapering legs, is altogether in scale. Its proportions please us. But try to imagine this chair with heavy bulbous legs! The incongruity is immediately noticeable. Yet heavy bulbous legs would be in scale in a Tudor refectory table.

Good proportion, accordingly, holds for the relationship among the parts of a single piece. Occasionally, defects in the proportion of a part may be overcome. If a chairback is out of

A FIREPLACE SETTING

This fireplace consists of marble framed by elaborately sculptured scroll work and surrounded by a mirrored wall. Gilt and red animate the green monochromatic color scheme of the room. Your main center of interest should similarly capitalize on the best feature of your room, whether fireplace, picture or bay window, or long, straight wall. Arranging furniture then in terms of centers of interest makes for room harmony and averts grouping pieces together by trial and error as in doing a jigsaw puzzle.

A BACKGROUND OF BOOKS

Books are considered decorative accessories. But in this study books provide the background treatment of the room as well. And if you remember Lord Bacon, conference is an ally of reading. Here provision for conference—and conversation—is made in a broad sofa and attractive Chippendale armchair. Studies like this one offer a luxurious yet masculine appeal.

proportion to the rest of the chair, the use of vertical lines in the upholstery will increase the apparent height of the chairback while horizontal lines will decrease the apparent height.

In grouping pieces of furniture together, the consideration of good proportion enjoins that the pieces should be in scale with one another. If we were to hang a small picture over a broad radio-phonograph combination, the disproportion between the two pieces would produce an incongruous effect. Two small pictures, which resembled each other in line, however, if hung side by side, would restore proper proportion.

The proportions of your furniture should be in keeping with the size of your room. Small rooms dictate the use of small pieces. Such pieces, scaled to the room, help to produce an effect of spaciousness. A large piano would dwarf a small room and any wall in such a room against which it could be placed. A console piano, however, would be in scale. As a rule, a small room should have light, delicate pieces, small patterns and subdued colors in moderate accent. Not only do small pieces fit the dimensions of a small room, but they prevent the room from becoming cluttered and impassable.

A large room can stand massive pieces, strong colors, large patterns and marked contrasts. But do not

Both types of balance are combined to produce a formal, luxurious effect in this Regency living room. The background, with its satin draperies, paired drum tables, lamps and mantel statues, exemplifies strict bisymmetric balance, while the sofa is in asymmetric balance with the two velvet easy chairs and library steps. The black lacquer coffee table with six bamboo legs is a popular Regency period piece.

smuggle an out-of-scale diminutive piece into a roomful of large furniture. If your room is narrow, avoid selecting wide pieces that may impede traffic. A broad dining table does not belong in a narrow dining room or alcove. A table of moderate size, with slender legs and lines, lends itself more pleasingly to such a room.

As the present-day home tends to smaller rooms than in the past, the trend today is toward the use of proportionately smaller pieces. The use of unit furniture and sectional pieces with increased flexibility of adaptation and utility is similarly a present-day tendency.

Proportions also produce varying psychological effects. Through experience, we have built up a feeling of fitness. In consequence, we feel that certain proportions are appropriate while others are not. For instance, we do not consider a throne a fit piece of furniture for the home, though we may admire its beauty. Not only would the throne be out of scale, but it would offend our sense of fitness. The same sense, however, would consider a throne wholly appropriate to a massive, dignified baronial hall.

Similarly, our sense of fitness requires that a large sofa be equipped with sturdy legs even though such legs do not add to the security of the sofa. The skyscraper bookcase, produced twenty years ago as the last word in modernity, was widely held to be eccentric. Its tall vertical lines were too drastically out of proportion

A Lazy Susan revolving table, a glass brick partition and specially designed linoleum feature this very practical and cheerful kitchen-dinette. The shelves for plants and flowers are particularly decorative, as is the efficient linoleum floor with its contrasting marbleized shadings. Linoleum also covers the table top, sink and desk. The webbed fabric of the chairs contributes to the attractive effect.

Bisymmetric balance and repetition of elements combine to tie this fireside grouping into a pleasant, integrated whole. The curved loveseats, covered in a soft amber fabric, are trimmed with dark green moss fringe. Both the amber and the green are repeated in the floral print of the draperies in combination with cinnamon and persimmon red. Tasteful accessories complete the grouping and make it an inviting spot for entertaining.

to the size and shape to which most persons are accustomed. A feeling of fitness is one of the imponderables that contribute to making up good taste.

Large sized pieces, of thick proportions, give the feeling of strength, durability and dignity. Small sized pieces, slight in proportion, give the effect of delicacy and grace. Your decorative purpose will help you determine the appropriate size and scale of your pieces. If, for example, you want to key your room to femininity, your pieces must carry out this purpose both in size and design.

Your home should grow out of the proportions of your rooms. It is through growth, plus the free play of imagination and personality as expressed in the character of your home, that beauty will ultimately come.

COLOR

Color is of first importance to you in decorating your home. Through color you can set the tone of your room. Color provides the background for your furniture groupings. Color is one means of creating consistency and harmony, and also of introducing variety and accent.

Like line and form, color contributes to unity through its dual role as physical and psychological tool. A room that is formal and dignified will use a color scheme that produces this effect. The colors will be subdued ones and pleasant. Bright, glaring colors would clash with this decorative purpose.

The psychological effects of color are especially marked. Color is often the means you will use in setting the mood of a room or of your entire home. Colors are warm or cool to the observer. The warm colors—red, yellow and orange—are stimulating, cheerful and energizing. These warm colors, further, give the impression of making a wall or a piece of furniture seem nearer to the onlooker, while the cool colors give the opposite impression of withdrawal.

Colors are consequently important in altering the apparent size and proportions of rooms. Colors may bring out the good points of a room or modify its bad points. A fresh coat of paint can conceal many a structural fault.

The cool colors are blue, blue-green and blue-violet, while green and violet are neither warm nor cool. The cool colors are restrained and restful. They are the soothing and quiet colors. We would use these colors if we wanted to produce the effect of a reposeful, comfortable room.

Bright colors enliven a room, make it light-hearted, youthful and gay. Dark, dull colors exert a depressing effect. They grow monotonous. We should thus violate harmony were we to decorate a nursery in dull colors. Harmony requires that there be unity of effect. The background must be consistent with our furniture grouping and with the mood and spirit our room is to express.

Bright colors excel in attracting attention, while drab colors evoke little attention. Lively colors do add fillip to a room. They give it zest and snap. They introduce accent, variety and contrast. If appropriate, colors can intensify the effects of line, form and texture. The colors in your room must blend together for harmony. They must go well with one another. Color can give charm, or take it way.

Hanging 2 pictures vertically

NOT THIS < The smaller picture hung above the larger seems to float off into space.

THIS IS HOW — The larger picture hung above the smaller integrates the grouping.

Proportion is applicable to color when we think in terms of amounts of color used throughout a room. The proportions of different colors that we may use **in our room for its furnishings should not be the obvious halves, thirds** and quarters. In general, the purer and stronger the color, the smaller the area on which it may be used. The less intense the color, the greater the area to which it may be applied. Hence, strong colors may be used in accessories and accent, but backgrounds usually should use the subdued, quiet colors.

Your choice of colors forms your color scheme. Color schemes may be built up from a color wheel, or adopted from the colors in a painting, a piece of fabric or a natural scene. You will find out more about color and how to choose pleasing color schemes in the next two chapters. These chapters deal fully with this important question.

TEXTURE

Texture is the last of our four basic elements. While we ordinarily associate texture chiefly with textiles, fabrics and woven material, it is a quality of all materials. Texture is the quality of roughness or smoothness, coarseness or fineness that we detect through our sense of touch and our sense of sight.

We can usually look at a surface and tell, even without touching or handling it, whether it is pliable or rigid, hard or soft, smooth or fine. Sometimes, however, a surface may appear more resilient to our touch than it appears to our sight. But it is only our sight that can distinguish a surface as lustrous, shiny and rich or dark, dull and weak.

Textures have more than physical properties. As do the other basic elements, textures have a psychological effect. Rough textures appear rugged and masculine. Rough textures are informal, while smooth textures and tight-woven fabrics give a feeling of formality. Along with vertical lines, rough textures are suitable in decorating a boy's bedroom.

Oak gives us, in texture, a feeling of strength and sturdiness. Denim, corduroy and leather arouse the same feeling-tone. An oak Morris chair, with its leather seat, large yet simple form and its plain color, is in perfect harmony. But alter any one of these elements, change the wood to rich mahogany, or change the leather to soft mohair, and the effect becomes incongruous. Textures no less than the other basic elements must be in keeping with the whole.

Coarse textures contrast with fine ones. A rough plaster surface reduces

the apparent height of a ceiling, while relatively smooth texture will increase its apparent height. Rough surfaces make colors look darker. A smooth surface, however, reflects more light and thus makes the color appear lighter.

Oak and mahogany do not go well together because of their marked difference in texture. Walnut will go well with either mahogany or light oak. We would use coarse materials like homespun, jute, crash or denim with oak, or materials medium in texture like printed linen, tapestry, cretonnes, rep and certain chintzes. But silks, satins, velvets, taffetas, brocades and Oriental rugs we associate with mahogany.

The psychological overtones of textures, no less than their physical properties, indicate what we shall put together. Colonial maple and pine instantly suggest hooked rugs, pewter, copper and pottery, with homespun effects and patterned chintzes. A modern room invites the use of blocked linens, colorfully printed cottons, homespuns, rough and novelty textured fabrics.

The textures of our materials should be appropriate both to their function and to the decorative effect we wish to produce. Brocaded silks will go well in a formal setting, but not in an informal setting. Brass, iron and pottery will harmonize with a fireplace setting in which crystal glass and richly designed glazed china will be out of place. Textures are an important tool at our disposal. We must therefore give careful consideration to them in furnishing our home.

UNITY

To achieve beauty in our home, we must team together the four basic elements. *Beauty requires both unity and variety.* In furnishing our home, we must first secure unity. Our furniture, accessories, and color scheme must team up with one another to form a coherent organization. We must combine the basic elements into a harmonious unified whole. And we must inject vitality and interest into our organization.

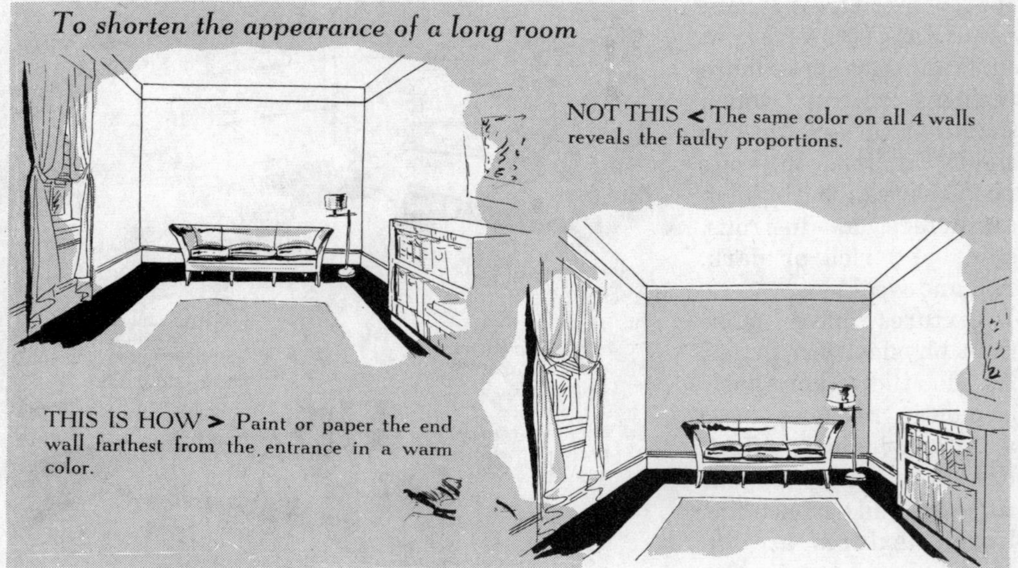

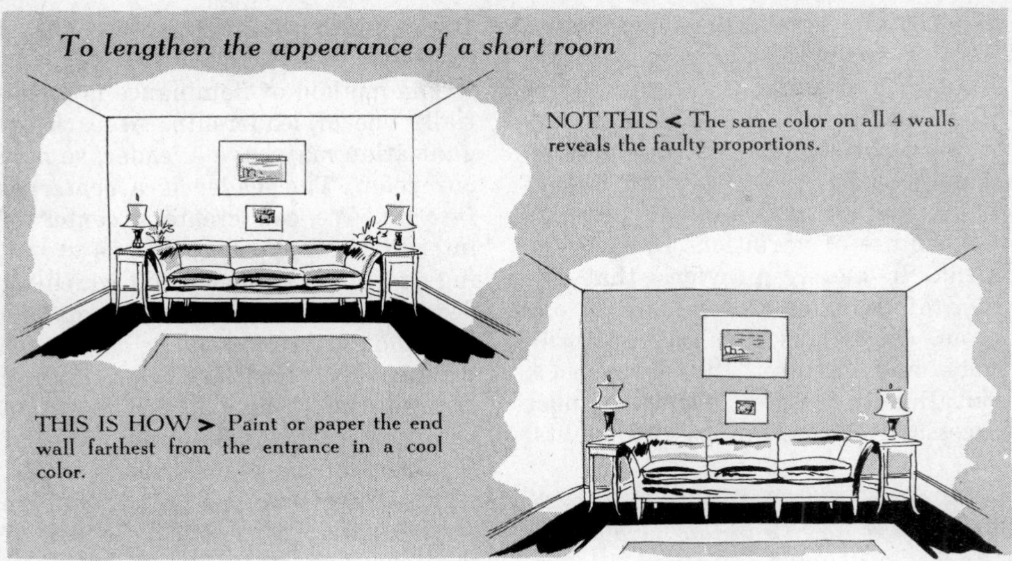

Fundamentally, unity is nothing more than teaming together the basic elements. As these elements each have a dual value, our team must have both physical and psychological unity. Our room must have a unified physical appearance and it must express a unified psychological effect. Our room must avoid the confusion of too great a variety in line, form, color and texture. A room whose lines express quiet and repose, whose colors express gayety and liveliness, whose textures emphasize richness and luxury, says too much to say any one thing clearly.

We can attain unity in our home through two methods—*repetition* and *dominance*. Repetition achieves unity through physical likeness and reiterated expression, while dominance achieves unity through making one element or furniture grouping the center of attraction and subordinating everything else to it. We use both repetition and dominance in creating a beautiful home.

Repetition consists in using lines, forms, colors and textures that are respectively alike and in having each of these elements express the same theme. The lines that we repeat must resemble one another perceptibly. If not, we would not actually be repeating the same sort of line. Similarly, the resemblances in the sort of color, form and texture that we use must be apparent to the eye.

Equally important, what each of the elements expresses must be the same. When we repeat horizontal lines, large low shapes and soft cool colors in a room, we attain a unified physical and psychological effect. Our room appears restful and quiet. If, however, we were to introduce furniture with long horizontal lines into a room painted a brilliant red-orange, our walls would conflict with our furniture. We would get disunity. For unity, we not only repeat a particular element but we must assure that all the elements work together to produce the same over-all effect.

In practice we can hardly restrict ourselves to one sort of line. We not only require horizontal lines but we also require vertical lines and curves. This is so because our furnishings must serve certain human needs. However, we still can achieve beauty if we resort to the method of dominance.

The method of dominance provides for the use of variations in each element. It merely provides that one kind of line should dominate in our room, as well as one kind of form, color and texture. In consequence, variations of these elements must necessarily be used in lesser amounts.

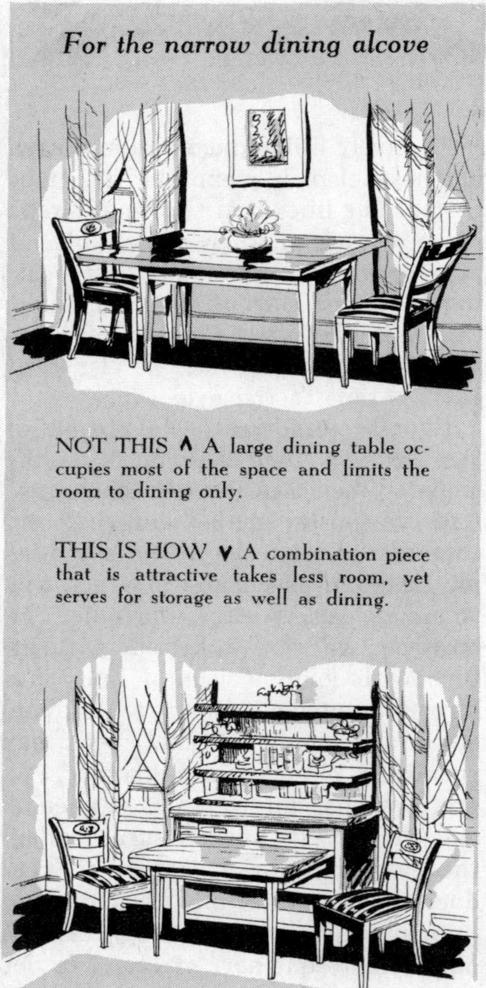

For the narrow dining alcove

NOT THIS ∧ A large dining table occupies most of the space and limits the room to dining only.

THIS IS HOW ∨ A combination piece that is attractive takes less room, yet serves for storage as well as dining.

They are subordinated or even omitted entirely.

The method of dominance is essentially one of leadership. As each organization may have a leader, so may our room. The leader is a *center of interest*. We can create a center of interest through selecting one grouping as a focal point around which we decorate and furnish our room. The center of interest is made important through size, position, color, texture or ornament. It may attract attention because it contains the main pieces of furniture in the room—a sofa, radio, piano, table. Or it may take advantage of the main architectural feature of the room—the windows, a fireplace, a long straight wall, or a corner.

Our center of interest must be in keeping with the room as a whole. The lines, colors and textures that characterize it must be repeated elsewhere in the room. The effect it expresses must be in tune with the overall effect of the entire room. We thus repeat the physical and psychological qualities of our center of interest throughout the room, while keeping the center dominant. The two methods of repetition and dominance are, in consequence, actually allied.

If we want our living room to radiate good cheer and welcome, we can create a center of interest that sets this mood. Our pieces of furniture will be gay and vivacious. Our entire room will look pleasant and inviting. Our accessories will contribute to this effect. If, however, we use a wallpaper that is dark and cheerless, we do not have unity. The wallpaper has upset the effect we intended.

If, on the other hand, we want our living room to express formality and reserve, our center of interest must conform to this effect. A center of interest that is informal, with coarse textured reclining chairs, a table strewn with reading material and a cabinet of records featuring "hot licks," would be out of key with the rest of our room. Such a center, however, might serve admirably in an informal room.

BALANCE

We can create a center of interest through the use of a balanced grouping. The notion of *balance* is one that is familiar to us all. Balance is exemplified in a scale or a seesaw—as well as in a furniture grouping. A scale or seesaw is in balance when it is in a state of equilibrium. It then gives a feeling of completion and of harmony. A room or grouping is in balance when it also evinces these qualities.

Another example of balance is a mathematical equation. The simple equation, 10=10, is complete as both its members are equal and alike. It is an instance of repetition. The method of repetition uses *formal* or *bisymmetric* balance when it is used to group pieces of furniture. A furniture grouping is in formal balance when all the pieces on one side of a central line are repeated on the other side while the space relationships are maintained for each similar piece. The two halves of the grouping are then identical.

Place two soft cushions at either end of a sofa. If the cushions are alike and are similarly placed, you have a simple illustration of formal balance. You have in no way upset the unity that the sofa itself possesses. Or, hang a mirror above a chest and flank the mirror on each side with a vase. If the vases are alike and placed at corresponding positions, you again have formal balance and a unified arrangement. But move one of the vases out of position and you have introduced a disturbing element. You no longer have balance. The sense of completion is gone.

Formal balance gives the feeling of restfulness and stability, order and restraint. As its name suggests, it yields a formal effect. This type of balance is repeated in many parts of a room. Like a division into obvious ratios, it has the effect of precision.

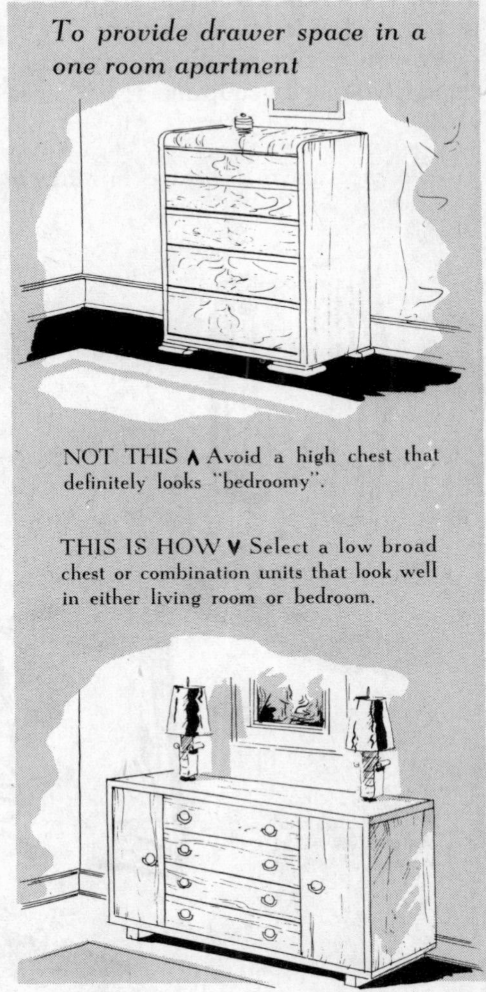

It may consequently lack the warmth we seek in a home. It may be cold, remote, aloof. We may, however, use a balance that secures both unity and variety. This type of balance is *informal* or *asymmetric* balance.

Asymmetric balance is achieved when the elements on one side are not repeated on the other side. To achieve balance, however, the elements must exert the same weight of attraction. The equation, 3+7=6+4, is still in balance, for it is equivalent to 10=10. But the left-hand and right-hand members both differ. This difference in the two sides is the very factor that introduces variety.

We can easily create an asymmetrically balanced grouping. If we place a pair of easy chairs on either side of a fireplace, with a low coffee table between them, we would have bisymmetric balance. Substitute a sofa for one of the easy chairs and our grouping is out of balance. Now place the pair of chairs with a small tier table between them opposite the sofa. The group will now give the effect of balance. We have achieved asymmetric balance. We have also attained unified grouping set off by variety in the pieces. If our pieces individually are in good taste, with pleasing color and proportion, the over-all effect will be beautiful.

Asymmetric balance is more subtle than simple bisymmetric balance. Both types of balance serve to secure unity and create a center of interest. But asymmetric balance also serves to inject the factor of variety. Though more difficult to achieve, its results are far more pleasing.

Though bisymmetric balance is considered to be formal in effect and asymmetric balance informal in effect, these characterizations are not literally true. The former may find use to good effect in an informal room, while a formal room may use both types of balance very effectively. Bisymmetric balance is, however, emphasized in formal rooms.

Balance applies to all the basic elements. Our homes, if they are to present a feeling of completion and harmony, must be balanced. We must secure a balance in line and form, a balance in color and texture. A room in which only one color was used, while unified, would be tiresome and uninteresting. A room that used only plain textures would seem flat and poor. The introduction of a small amount of contrasting patterned texture would give the feeling of balance. And also give the spice of variety.

CONTRAST

Besides the use of informal balance, we may introduce variety into a unified grouping through the use of *contrast*. Contrast serves to make one feature stand out and thus draw attention to itself. If introduced into a center of interest, contrast can serve to lend emphasis to the grouping. It can also diversify the grouping and make it truly an interesting one. All the factors that enter into giving dominance to a center of interest — size, position, color, texture and ornament—may serve as contrasting qualities.

To the extent that the sizes and shapes in our center of interest are unusual, we may introduce variety. The position of the pieces in a grouping, if unusual, will also add contrast. Color contrast is of especial importance in securing variety. Bright colors will, if used as accent, excite attention. Dark colors against a light background or light colors against a dark background, produce a pleasing diversity.

Variety may be obtained through the use of varying plain or patterned textures. Unusual ornamentation will similarly gain variety.

We can introduce contrast, not only to diversify a grouping, but an entire room. A room limited to horizontal lines and cool colors might become monotonous. A dash of warm colors and curved lines would give the room variety. It would make the room interesting and alive. It should be remembered that a large room can stand more contrast than can a small one.

Contrasts, of course, must be used with moderation. Unless our contrasts are restrained, our room may become a riot of conflicting items of attention. When too many items demand atten-

tion, we are likely to pay attention to none. Our mind simply rebels at the many demands made upon it. Our contrasts, therefore, must be used sparingly and in small amounts.

The possibilities for variety in home furnishing are practically endless. All that is required is resourcefulness and temperate good taste. With variety our homes will have just that dash of difference that makes a home beautiful and distinctively one's own.

Accent on the horizontal endows this library-living room with a reposeful air. The modern homespun-type draperied wall, with shaggy fringes that repeat the high piled texture of the rug, is distinctive. The formal balance of the background is matched in the furniture arrangement. Light and dark woods add interest, while the white of the wood trim and fireplace is reiterated in the lampshades and pottery.

CHAPTER THREE

What colors say

HAVE YOU ever admired the beauty of the sky, with its myriad soft colors blending magically into one another, accented here and there but all forming a miraculous pattern? There are few wonders in this world which can equal the miracle of color.

It is our purpose, in this chapter, to give you an appreciation of this vast symphony of color. It is our purpose to quicken your senses to the color which surrounds you and which unconsciously shapes your moods and spirit. Without irreverence, we shall try to take this complex subject out of the sky and present it in a fashion that will enable you to use the rich palette of color in decorating your home.

Color is one of the prime means through which you can bring beauty into your home. It is one of the chief means you will use in expressing your decorative purpose. With color you can create a mood, an atmosphere. **Color can give your home grace and** charm, an air of restfulness and contentment. Color is a powerful tool at your disposal. Through its wise use you can achieve much. Misused, color will mock all your efforts. Your home then will be uninteresting and drab,

To highlight a piece of furniture

NOT THIS < Furniture placed against a dark background seems smaller and less colorful.

THIS IS HOW > Place furniture against a light background to make it seem larger and more colorful.

or garish and unpleasant, restless and uncomfortable.

YOU MUST BE AWARE OF COLOR

Words cannot do justice to color. To one who unfortunately is blind from birth, no amount of description can convey the drama and experience of color. If you want to know color, it is absolutely necessary to experience it. Try, if you can, to describe the color *red.* You have to perceive color, live through the experience of a rainbow or of a beautiful autumn woodland scene, fully to appreciate the glory and splendor of color.

As a prerequisite to a full appreciation and understanding of color, you must become alive to its beauty. You must develop a genuine color awareness. Look at colorful paintings which delight you. Notice the colors that the artist employs and how deftly they blend with one another. Do the same with pieces of fabric, with colorfully designed pottery, with Nature. Only then can you begin to understand the power of color. Our world teems with color. To develop your tastes, to broaden and enrich them, you must revel in colors and steep yourself in their lore.

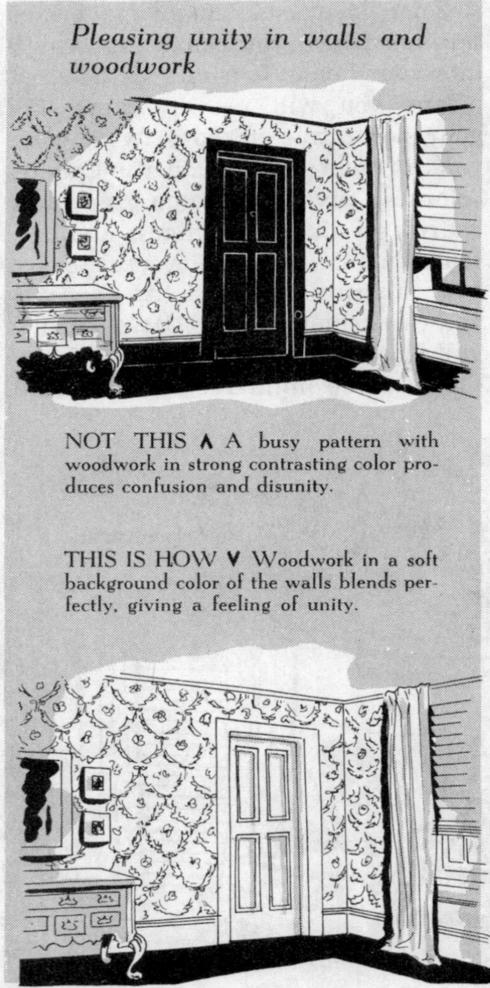

Pleasing unity in walls and woodwork

NOT THIS ∧ A busy pattern with woodwork in strong contrasting color produces confusion and disunity.

THIS IS HOW ∨ Woodwork in a soft background color of the walls blends perfectly, giving a feeling of unity.

In this chapter we shall present the rudiments of color. We shall describe how the universe of color grows out of three primary, irreducible colors. We shall describe how colors are tinged and softened, making them pleasant and easy to live with. You will find out what colors say, so that you can have your colors express the mood and atmosphere you desire to create.

THE RUDIMENTS OF COLOR

We all are more or less familiar with colors. But simply knowing the names of a few colors is not enough. It may, as a matter of fact, lead to confusion. Suppose that you and your husband decide that the chairs in your dinette should be painted red. You call in a painter and order that they be painted this color.

In this instance three different persons are thinking of the one color red. Yet each may be thinking of a very different red. One may be thinking of a deep shade of red with a lot of black in it. The second may be visualizing a vivid scarlet while the third person may be recalling a pale rose tint.

Each of these three colors—or hues, as they may be called—has red in it. To that extent they are members of the one family. But how differently each of these reds lends itself to decoration! The deep red or the pale rose may be used with pleasing result for large areas. The vivid scarlet, however, should be restricted to small areas, limited to accessories as an accent, or used in a room such as a breakfast room which is not occupied for long periods of time at a stretch. The scarlet is not an easy color to live with. A little of it in decoration goes a long way.

The vivid scarlet is a *pure* color—strong, unmitigated and loud. It expresses a fiery warmth, the hot blood of temper. The pale rose tint has so much white added to it that its nature has been subdued. While it still yields some warmth, the addition of white has made it far more pleasant and amenable. Pale rose has a note of lightness and delicacy. The dark shade of red, produced by the addition of black, gives a feeling of strength. It has a masculine effect. This shade may be used for pleasing contrast or to add a note of dignity.

The pure colors are the colors which Newton obtained when he broke up the rays of sunlight by means of a prism. The band of colors which are thus obtained form the spectrum. The colorless rays of sunlight are separated into all the colors which compose it. Whenever we view a rainbow, with its band of colors, we see a natural reproduction of the spectrum. The prism merely duplicates this phenomenon.

Pure colors are those undiluted with white, black or gray. Because of their very purity, these colors do not lend themselves happily to lavish use in home decoration. They tend to tire us and grow monotonous, owing to their lack of variety and subtlety. They may, however, be used with good result as touches of contrast and accent. They may be used as the color in accessories or as part of a patterned material in upholstery, drapes, rugs and wallpaper.

THE PRIMARY COLORS

It is a remarkable quality of pig-

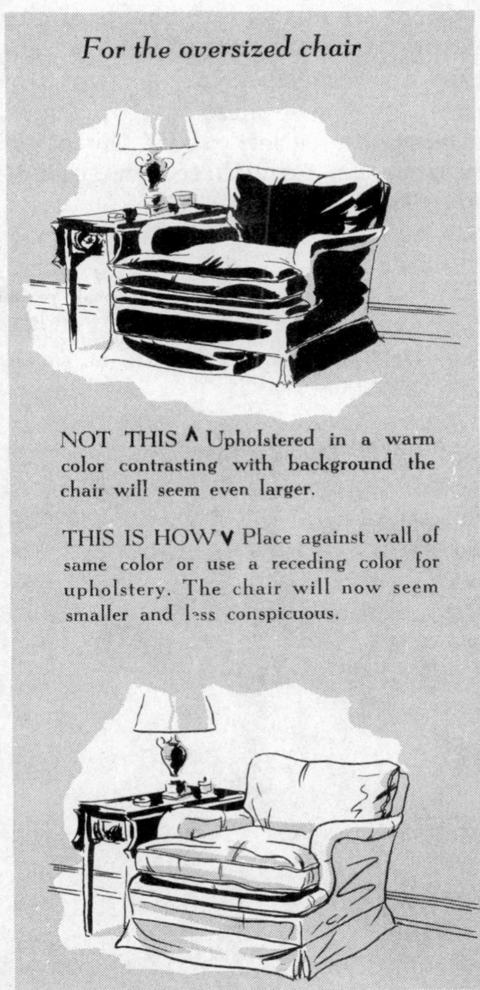

ments and paints that we can build up all our hues from as few as three of these pigments. These three pigments are the colors red, yellow and blue. Very aptly, they are called the three *primary* colors. They themselves cannot be formed by mixing other colors or pigments. They cannot be reduced into any component hues. They themselves, however, can produce all the other pure colors! When they are mixed together in various proportions, they give us the basis of our whole palette of color.

THE SECONDARY COLORS

When we mix equal amounts of any two of these primary colors, we obtain a *secondary* color. As we may mix any one of these three primary colors with either one of the other two, we can form three new secondary colors. Each primary color has a hand in thus forming two secondary colors. These secondary colors are new, pure hues. They differ from any of the three primary colors. They have an individuality of their own. Unlike the primary hues, however, the secondary colors are derivative and may be broken down into the primary hues which compose them.

If we mix equal amounts of yellow and blue, we obtain green. A mixture of equal parts of yellow and red will result in orange, while an equal mixture of red and blue will yield violet. The three secondary colors, then, are green, orange and violet. When produced by a mixture of equal amounts of the primary hues, they are at their sharpest, in the strength in which they appear in the spectrum.

A wallpaper that seems to undulate affords a striking background for this exceptional master bedroom. The bleached oak headboard of the studio bed is functional, providing cabinets and shelves. The bedspread is a green rayon taffeta, the curtains a beige rayon and cotton net and the wallpaper is a pale green with dark green patterns. The chest is soft green, the carved broadloom rug is in forest green.

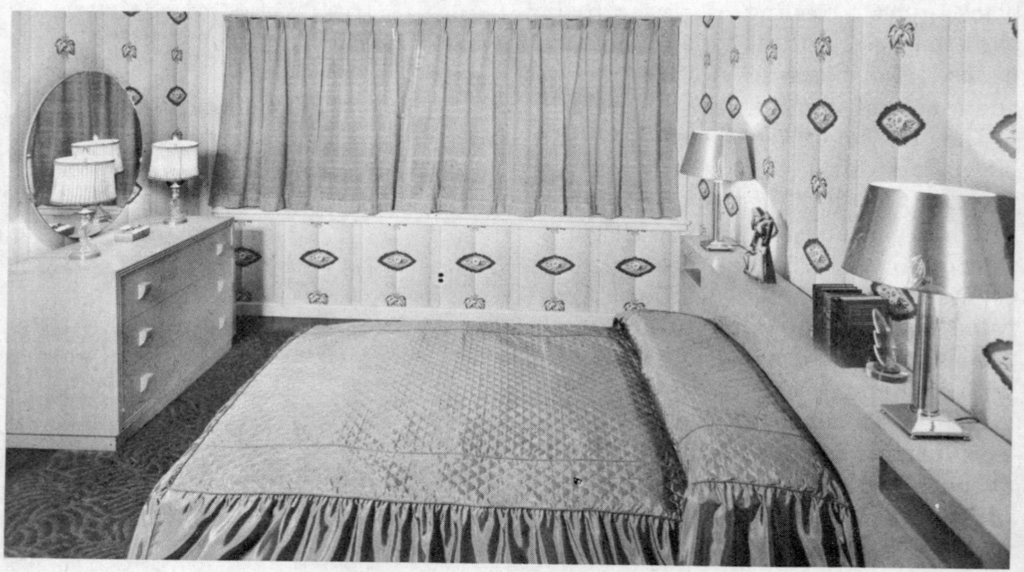

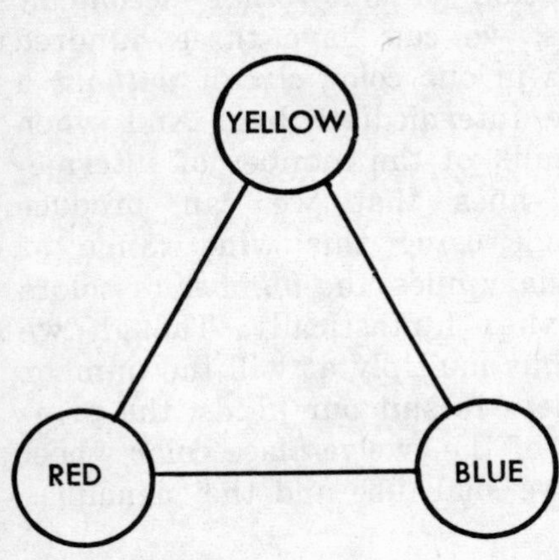

DIAGRAM 1
The Primary Colors

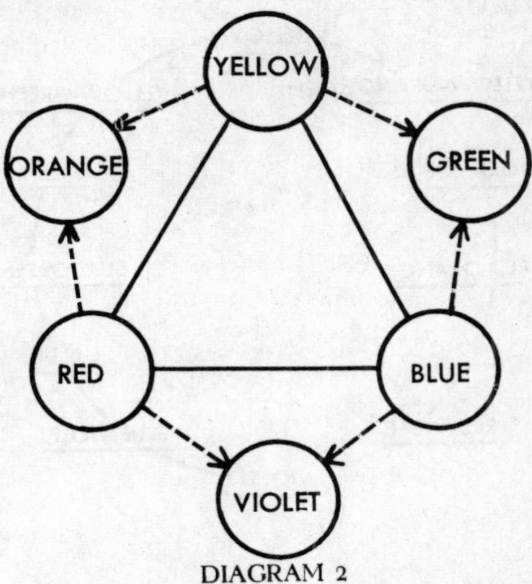

DIAGRAM 2
The Standard Colors

If we arrange the three primary colors and the three secondary colors as illustrated in *diagrams* 1 and 2, we so place the colors that we can see at a glance which primary hues go into forming each secondary color. In each instance the secondary color results from the mixture of the two primary colors which flank it. Thus orange, in *diagram* 2, falls between yellow and red and these two primary colors form orange. The primary and secondary colors together comprise the six *standard colors.*

THE INTERMEDIATE COLORS

We can, furthermore, mix any two colors in *diagram* 2 that are adjacent to each other. The six colors that result are the *intermediate* colors or hues. The process of forming these six intermediate hues is as follows:

Yellow plus green............**yellow-green**
Blue plus green.....................**blue-green**
Blue plus violet......................**blue-violet**
Red plus violet..........................**red-violet**
Red plus orange....................**red-orange**
Yellow plus orange........**yellow-orange**

In each instance of this process we combine a primary with one of the secondary colors which the primary helped originally to form and which lies next to the primary in our diagram. For convenience, we usually place the name of the primary color first in designating these six intermediate hues. With these six intermediate hues, we now have the twelve colors upon which we shall base our color wheel. Prepared in this way, these twelve hues are each at their purest. They have not been tinged. For this reason, these twelve hues are known as *normal* hues.

THE COLOR CIRCUIT

Arranged in the color circuit as in *diagram* 3, the family relationships of the twelve hues are readily apparent. Yellow and blue, both primary hues, upon combination, form the secondary hue green. Yellow and green produce the intermediate hue yellow-green. Similarly, yellow and the secondary hue orange form yellow-

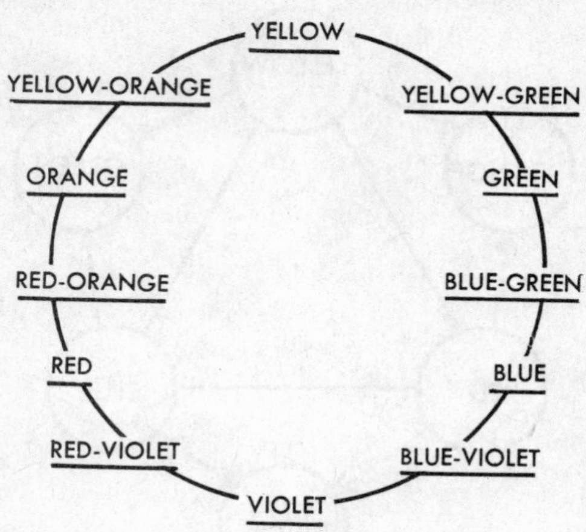

DIAGRAM 3
The Color Circuit

orange upon mixture. With three primary colors, we have obtained a total of twelve colors. This color circuit is the basis of our color wheel.

We can readily imagine still other colors falling between any two hues that are adjacent to each other in the color circuit. In fact, the number of colors which in practice can be produced from the three primary colors is simply amazing. Thus we have seen that equal parts of red and yellow produce orange. But we can obtain *gradations* of orange through using one part of red and ninety-nine parts of yellow. True, the orange that we obtain from this proportion is much closer to yellow than to red.

We can continue this process of manufacturing colors. We can increase the amount of red progressively by one part while decreasing the amount of yellow by a corresponding part. In this way we can produce one hundred gradations of orange between red and yellow!

By continuing this process in the formation of our other secondary colors, we can have three hundred colors in our color circuit *without* a single intermediate hue. And when we think of the number of intermediate hues that we can produce through using this wide range of secondary hues, the number of colors multiplies fantastically. Though we can thus multiply at will the number of colors to suit our needs, the principles of the twelve-place color wheel that we shall use and the principles

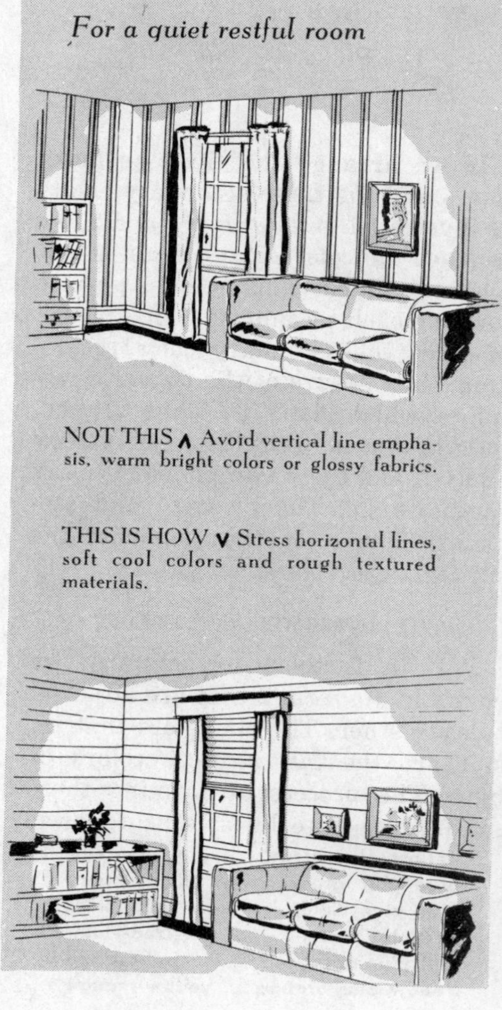

For a quiet restful room

NOT THIS ∧ Avoid vertical line emphasis, warm bright colors or glossy fabrics.

THIS IS HOW ∨ Stress horizontal lines, soft cool colors and rough textured materials.

underlying the effective use of color remain the same.

VALUE

We can produce other kinds of variations in the twelve colors of the color circuit. We all have noticed that sometimes, when writing with a pen, we get some lines that are darker or lighter than other lines. The color of these lines, however, remains the same, for we are using the same ink. This difference in color is a variation in *lightness* or *darkness* of the color. Such variations are differences in the *value* of a hue.

A *tint* of a color, therefore, is a color value that is lighter than the normal value of the pure color, while a *shade* of a color is a value that is darker than the normal value of the pure color. Tints and shades are produced in paints and pigments through the addition of white or black respectively to the color. Not only are we able to achieve gradations in hues but we are thus able to produce gradations in value within any one hue.

We may darken any hue in our color circuit until it approaches black in its shade. Or we may lighten any

WHITE	BLUISH WHITE
TINT	BLUE TINT
GRAY	BLUE
SHADE	BLUE SHADE
BLACK	BLUISH BLACK

DIAGRAM 4
Scale and
Corresponding Values of Blue

hue until it approaches white in its tint. Any hue, therefore, may be put into a scale going from its deepest shade through its normal value to its lightest tint. This scale corresponds to the progressive changes of black through gray to white. *Diagram* 4 shows this comparison in value between blue and the scale. While we here present a five-place scale for simplicity, the eye can register differences equal to ten distinctions in value.

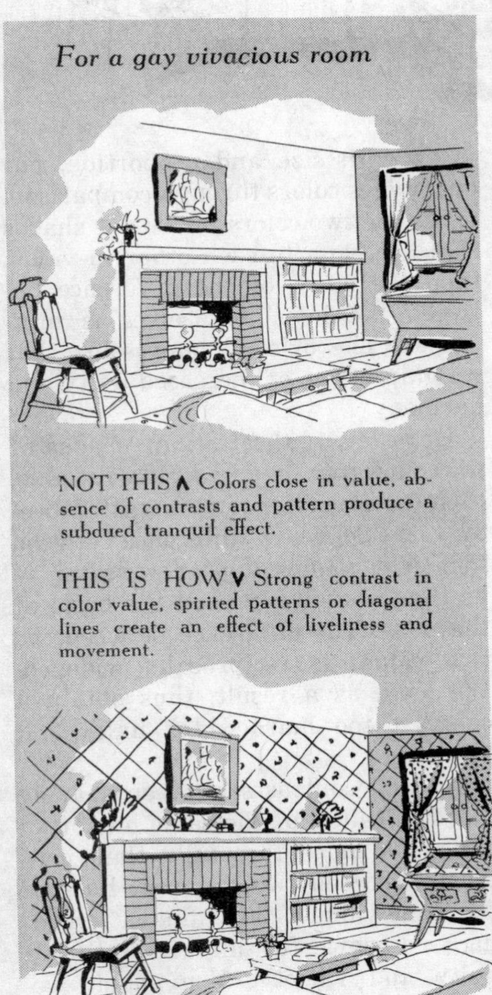

For a gay vivacious room

NOT THIS ∧ Colors close in value, absence of contrasts and pattern produce a subdued tranquil effect.

THIS IS HOW ∨ Strong contrast in color value, spirited patterns or diagonal lines create an effect of liveliness and movement.

In *diagram* 4 the scale goes from black, at the bottom, to a shade of gray, to full gray in the middle. It then passes through a tint of gray to white. The corresponding values of blue progress from a bluish-black to a medium blue shade. The normal value of blue is at the center. The blue then goes upwards to a medium blue tint and ends in a very faint bluish-white. If you look at the color wheel on page 65, you will see examples of tints and shades of each of the twelve colors. The tints and shades are arranged on the outer rim of the circle, beyond the pure colors to which they respectively refer.

EFFECTS OF VALUE

Tints and shades are widely used in home decoration. They make it possible to repeat a hue while at the same time altering it subtly yet perceptibly. Through the use of varying values which we obtain by tinting and shading, we can insure unity and secure contrast, emphasis and variety in our color scheme.

As with size and proportion, our eye judges colors through comparison. If we use two colors in tints or shades that are close to each other in value, then the effect of the difference between the hues themselves is minimized. The over-all impression that we gain is one of increased unity and harmony.

However, if the tints or shades of the colors we use vary widely in value, then the eye notes the contrast. Moreover, the degree of difference between the color values appears greater to us than actually it is on the basis of the scale. The difference between the two values is reciprocally widened. We may, as a result, thus obtain a contrast too marked for unity and harmony.

In fact, contrasts between sharply varying values of the same hue often strike us more forcefully than contrasts between two different hues of the same value. Color value is accordingly a powerful ally in securing unity and variety. You should remember and observe these facts when deciding upon the color scheme for your home. Simply because you select two kinds of red for your color scheme does not automatically insure that these reds will go well with each other or with the other colors in your scheme. If one red is a light tint and the other a medium shade, the two reds may clash.

Through choosing colors alike in value, whether the colors are the same hue or not, you increase the harmony between them. When done skilfully, variations in value can produce very interesting and effective contrasts. In each instance, however, you have to get the proper values for your color scheme!

When a tint is used as a background, through contrast a shade would look still darker when placed against it. Colors likewise appear darker than they actually are against a white background, while against a dark background or black, colors appear lighter.

Objects also appear to differ in size as a result of the value of their coloring. Light values and white give the impression of greater size. Dark values and black, on the other hand, appear to decrease the size of an object. This applies to both room and furniture. To increase the apparent size of a room or of a piece of furniture, you would paint it a light tint or even white. And you would paint the room or furniture a dark shade if you wanted to reduce its apparent size.

In home decoration you secure an effect of unity, quietness, restfulness and reserve by keeping all your color values nearly uniform. The greater the contrast in value the greater is the effect of gayety, liveliness and movement. The light color values go best with a light background, the dark values best with a dark background. Such close values may produce beautiful effects, but may also tend to monotony. Light tints add to the femininity of curved lines, while dark shades emphasize the masculine effect of straight lines.

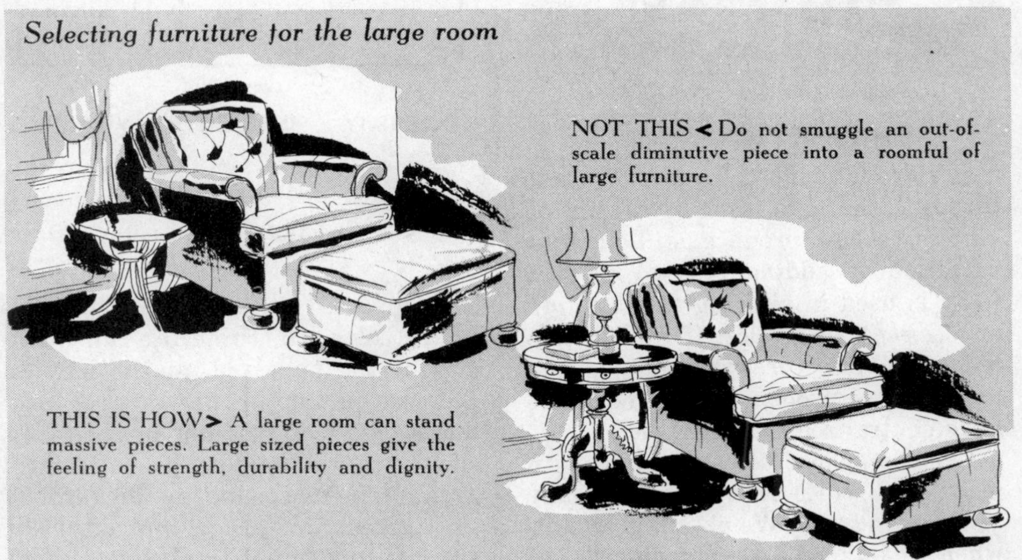

Selecting furniture for the large room

NOT THIS < Do not smuggle an out-of-scale diminutive piece into a roomful of large furniture.

THIS IS HOW > A large room can stand massive pieces. Large sized pieces give the feeling of strength, durability and dignity.

Books as colorful accessories

NOT THIS ▲ Books scattered about haphazardly are no decorative asset.

THIS IS HOW — Books add color, pattern and warmth when kept as a group. Build a reading group around them.

INTENSITY OR GRAYING

Besides altering the value of a hue through the addition of white or black, we can produce still another variation by adding gray to a color. Gray is used in altering the *strength* or *weakness* of a color. If we mix pigments of the three primary colors together, we produce gray. The colors have neutralized one another.

Gray is a *neutral* color along with black and white from which it may also be produced. We obtain gray also when we mix yellow and violet. Violet consists of red and blue. By adding yellow to violet, we actually are mixing together the three primary colors. We produce gray whenever we mix a primary color with the one secondary color in which the primary is not originally a constituent.

The addition of gray reduces the *intensity* of a color. The pure colors of the spectrum or the normal colors of the color wheel are at their fullest strength of intensity. They are saturated. We can weaken these colors progressively by the addition of increasing amounts of gray until finally we neutralize the colors entirely. The colors are then indistinguishable from gray.

Intensity is thus the degree of grayness that a color possesses. It is the comparative strength or weakness of a color. The smaller the amount of gray in a color, the greater the intensity of that color; and vice versa. Colors which have been grayed are referred to as *muted* colors.

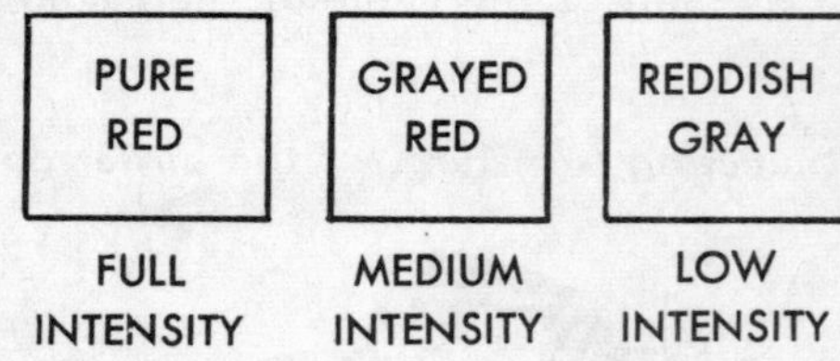

DIAGRAM 5

Variations In Intensity

Diagram 5 shows three intensities of the color red. From the full intensity of the pure red, at the left, an increase in the amount of gray produces a red of medium intensity, as shown in the middle block. A still greater increase in the amount of gray gives a red of low intensity. The red of full intensity, being a pure color, contains no gray in its composition. Both the other reds have, however, been grayed. If you refer to the color wheel on page 65, you can see examples of varying intensities of each of the twelve colors. The intensities are within the circle of the normal colors, running toward the center of the wheel.

Multiple-duty headboards for a small apartment

NOT THIS ∧ This headboard serves only one purpose, which hardly does for the small apartment.

THIS IS HOW ∨ Select a decorative headboard designed to provide cabinet, shelf and table facilities.

EFFECTS OF INTENSITY

The strength or weakness of a color is equivalent to its brightness or dullness. A dull finish is one that has been grayed. It is a soft color, of low intensity. A pure color is at its full intensity. It is exerting its fullest individual psychological effect. The pure normal colors of the color wheel, accordingly, are strident, garish, unrestrained.

For this reason colors at full intensity can only be used in moderate amounts if we want to avoid the effect of loudness and vulgarity. In moderation, colors at full intensity introduce accent and interest. Bright, intense colors should be used only in small areas and as elements of a pattern. For in large doses they tire us out. The grayed colors are less bold and startling. In exchange for their loss of intensity they have gained in subtlety, quietness and good taste. The grayed colors, therefore, invite use for large areas.

When we use two or more colors in a room, we should avoid too great a difference in the intensity of these colors except for accent and contrast. We should likewise avoid too great a correspondence in their intensity. The intensity of colors is heightened by contrast. A patch of bright blue stands out more sharply when it is surrounded by an area of blue lower in intensity. A grayed green placed against a green background of stronger intensity appears grayer. It looks less intense than it does when alone. In each of these instances the contrast in intensity has heightened the particular effect.

Against a gray background, the intensity of a hue is increased. Still greater emphasis will be secured, however, when a hue is set in contrast to a background of either white or black. White and black strengthen contrasts in both value and intensity. Against a dark red background, pure red appears both lighter in value and grayed in intensity. The differences of both value and intensity have been deepened by the contrast.

In dealing with color, it is accordingly possible to alter both the intensity and the value of hues at the same time. When we vary colors in both these respects, we achieve the richest and most subtle effects. In practice, of course, you are not called upon to determine the precise degree of variation in one or both of these qualities. As a home decorator, you merely designate or select colors which already possess these variations. But in appraising a color scheme for your own use you will assure more pleasing results if you can answer the question, "Will this color gain in effectiveness if it is tinted or shaded or if its grayness is increased or reduced?" A knowledge of the facts governing these variations will prove of value to you in attaining the very best results.

WHAT COLORS EXPRESS

Now that you are familiar with the rudiments of color, you should become acquainted with what colors express. What the intermediate colors say depends on the primary and secondary colors that enter into their composition. If you know, therefore, what the six basic colors say, you will know what colors express. These six colors say what they have to say most emphatically when they are pure. They are then bold, outspoken and unsubdued.

Of course, colors themselves don't actually talk. They do, however, arouse a reaction in human beings who are alive to them. In this sense, accordingly, colors do say something. What they say is the feelings which they produce in us. And these feelings are not to be brushed aside in your effort to secure a pleasing and tasteful color scheme in your home.

WARM AND COOL COLORS

Certain colors have already been referred to as *warm,* while others have been said to be *cool.* To complete this classification, we may call still other colors neither warm nor cool. The

Teaming basic elements together

NOT THIS < If you combine delicate furniture with homespun fabrics, the results are not pleasing.

THIS IS HOW — Delicate furniture teams well with smooth, delicate fabrics. Gives pleasing over-all effect.

warm colors are red, orange and yellow. All the hues in our color wheel which contain these colors share in this warmth. The colors grouped around blue in the color wheel are the cool colors.

Green, which contains equal amounts of yellow and blue, is neither warm nor cool. And violet which contains equal amounts of red and blue resembles green in this respect. As the greens and violets go toward the warm colors, they gain in warmth, while they partake of coolness as they approach blue. Thus, yellow-green grows warm in expression as its gradations contain increasing amounts of yellow. As blue-green increases in blueness, it grows cool.

Warm colors are important to the decorator who is concerned with the exposure of a room. A northern exposure, with little sun, can be cheered up with warm colors. A sunny southern or western exposure, however, may produce a feeling of coolness through use of the cool blues. In a very sunny room, yellows in large areas will result in glare.

The amount of light that a room receives is usually, in this day of **towering buildings, of more importance than the fact of geographic exposure.** If your room lacks light, then the use of light tints rather than dark shades is indicated. A light room, however, may use the shaded colors without serious diminution of natural light.

The warm colors *advance,* while the cool colors *recede.* Red and orange, the warmest of the colors, seem to go toward the observer. Blue, blue-green and blue-violet give the effect of withdrawing. Warm colors, in consequence, increase the apparent size of objects while they decrease the apparent size of a room. They can create the effect of greater intimacy in a room. Cool colors act in the opposite fashion and produce the effect of diminishing apparent size of objects while they create an effect of spaciousness in a room. This power of advancing or receding applies equally to a wall, a ceiling, a chair or a picture.

Together with the use of horizontal lines, warm colors may therefore serve to lower the apparent height of a ceiling or increase the size of a piece of furniture. Cool colors and vertical lines increase the apparent height of a ceiling or decrease the apparent size of a piece of furniture. These effects of color are of importance in restoring or creating proper proportions.

Warm colors are not only exciting and cheerful, but they give an effect of buoyancy, liveliness and activity. By their power of bringing an object nearer to the observer, warm colors lend added emphasis and significance. They tend to give a room a note of intimacy. Warm colors blend well with one another and thus assist in producing unity. Used in touches in a room that is predominantly cool, warm colors introduce a note of contrast. They accent a grouping or an object.

The cool colors have the opposite effect. They are restful, soothing, quiet colors. They produce an effect of aloofness and reserve. Through their power of withdrawal, cool colors give an effect of spaciousness. Cool colors may, if used exclusively, result in disunity. They tend to emphasize the distinctiveness of individual pieces of furniture and of accessories. As a result, the room will not seem to hold together. Too much cool color in a room, also, makes for somberness. The effect is a depressing one.

These general effects hold, not only for the related intermediate hues, but for the tints, shades and grayed intensities of the colors in the color wheel. Changes in value and intensity from the pure color modify these effects. Such changes introduce subtlety sophistication and charm. And changes in value and intensity do make it easier to gain both harmony and contrast with colors. Besides these general effects of warmth and coolness, advancement and recession, we associate more specific feelings with each of the colors themselves. We shall consider the feelings we associate with each of the six standard colors.

WHAT THE STANDARD COLORS SAY

Yellow, a warm color, is the sunniest and brightest of colors. The most cheerful of the colors, it suggests light and gayety. In home decoration, we may use yellow glass curtains to in-

For walls in poor condition

NOT THIS ∧ Plain wallpaper accentuates the underlying blemishes.

THIS IS HOW ∨ Conceal the blemishes with a wallpaper that has an all-over pattern.

troduce a feeling of sunniness in a dark room. For large areas we may also use tan, sand, bisque, beige and champagne, as well as pale yellows.

Red, the badge of courage, is full of vigor and fire. It is the most highly stimulating and exciting of the colors. But red is also associated with restlessness and violence. For these latter reasons red should be used with restraint. The shades of red—crimson, for instance—tend to darken a room and impart a somber effect. Red does carry a feeling of richness, hospitality and warmth, however. It makes an excellent contrasting color. In the red family, the pastels are very pleasing. Rose, coral, shrimp, raspberry, currant, cherry red and burgundy are all widely used.

Blue, the coolest of the colors, suggests a feeling of serenity and restfulness. It induces a feeling of unruffled dignity and tranquility. Blue-green and blue-violet are widely used in home decoration. Avoid cold blues. Tinted blues, such as Wedgwood and robin's-egg, are good background colors. Turquoise, delft, delphinium, slate-blue, navy and iris find popular favor.

Green has a calm and restful effect. It is one of the least strident of the six standard colors. More than any other color, green is the color of Nature. With increased blue, green is cool. With more yellow in it, green becomes lighter, gayer and warmer. Green, in home decoration, profits by addition of an accent. Soft apple, lime, chartreuse, mint, leaf and moss greens are widely used for walls and floor covering. Emerald, hunter, olive, and malachite are popular for accent and contrast.

Orange combines the sunny cheerfulness of yellow with the vigor and warmth of red. Very intense orange, however, crackles with heat and may become irritating. Among the oranges, rust, copper, apricot, rosewood, peach and henna especially recommend themselves for use in home decoration.

Violet is a rich, aloof and dignified color. It is not an intimate color. As the blue in it is increased, violet tends to express coolness. With more red, violet becomes warm. Mauve, mulberry, pansy-purple, fuschia and eggplant find ready use in home decora-

For children's bedrooms

NOT THIS ∧ Avoid adult patterns or plain backgrounds in children's rooms.

THIS IS HOW ∨ Select a patterned paper of interest to the child or use stencils and decals on plain painted walls.

tion while lavender or lilac are feminine colors reserved for bedroom and boudoir.

THE NEUTRAL COLORS

In addition to the colors of the color wheel, white, gray and black are frequently employed in home decoration. White embodies a feeling of delicacy and quiet. White goes best with cool colors. Black, the lowest of the colors in value, is frequently used in smart, sophisticated backgrounds. It has an air of modernity which seems to mock at the cares and travails of life. Black serves as an excellent contrasting field for colors, besides lending a touch of opulence. Black goes best with the warm colors. Black lacquer is much used together with bleached woods in modern rooms and is also widely used in rooms featuring Regency style.

Gray is neutral in its expression. The blue and green grays are cool, the yellow and red grays are warm. Battleship gray—made through the admixture of black and white—is a depressing color. A blue-gray or green-gray is soothing and goes well in a room with a dominantly warm color scheme. A rose toned gray is very pleasing in a room in which cool colors dominate. Gray goes well with the pure colors. It gives the effect of neutralizing them and toning them down.

Gray is growing more and more popular in home decoration, being widely used for walls, rugs, upholstery and drapery. Gray combines very effectively with both tints and shades of many colors, especially the warm ones. Gray and beige are used very effectively together. The one caution that need be observed is to avoid the dull, drab, listless grays.

Grays vary from pale silvery tones to deep gray-browns. The browns are formed by mixing any hue from red-violet to yellow-orange with dark gray until the hue itself is hardly distinguishable. The light browns, tan and beige are very interesting background colors, offering the home decorator wide opportunity. Like the grays, these colors are enjoying widespread popularity.

You are now acquainted with what colors say. In the following chapter we shall tell you how you may originate color schemes of your own. We also give you twenty complete color plans for various rooms and period styles of furniture. These plans are illustrated in full color. They are for formal and informal rooms in both traditional and modern styles. If you want to adopt any of these schemes for your home, a chart lists the full details of the first sixteen of these rooms.

CHAPTER FOUR

COLOR SCHEMES FOR YOUR HOME

THE BEAUTY that we find and cherish in Nature is very largely the beauty of color. We all enjoy color. We are attracted and stimulated by it. We want our home to share in the beauty of color. The choice of a pleasing color scheme will bring beauty and distinction into our home.

In going about the selection of a color scheme for our home, we may resort to either one of two methods. We may choose color combinations that we admire and that already exist, awaiting our use. Such a combination we may find in a flower, in a painting, a colorful piece of china or in a piece of fabric. Or we may devise our color scheme through the use of a color wheel.

Either method can give very pleasing results. What is essential to success with either method is an inner feeling for color. This feeling can be acquired only through developing a consciousness of color. If you wish to attain good results with color, no quality is so basic to you as this quality of color consciousness.

You can develop a feeling for color through noticing colors more analytically and carefully. When you observe a sunset, try to distinguish the various

To unify connecting rooms

NOT THIS < Varied wall treatment and separate rugs make rooms look smaller and emphasize their separateness.

THIS IS HOW > Use at least one color in common. Same wall treatment or continuous floor carpeting achieves unity most effectively.

colors. See which colors blend together. Notice how the contrasts are achieved. Try especially to determine how the colors have been tinted, shaded and muted. With a little practice, you will be able to distinguish these variations. You will find a new pleasure in colors, and an increased confidence in your ability to express your moods, convey your feelings and attain your decorative purpose through them.

Your first question in arriving at a color scheme for yourself is the decision as to which colors you will use. This decision will rest upon your individual color preferences. It will depend on the use to which the room will be put. It will be tempered by the decorative purpose which you desire to achieve. And it will depend upon the style of furniture which you use in decorating your home.

To restore proper scale

NOT THIS ∧ A small picture over a broad piece of furniture produces an incongruous effect.

THIS IS HOW ∨ Two small pictures hung side by side will restore proper proportion.

COLORS FOR YOUR PURPOSE

The decorative purpose you select as your own may be any one of several general kinds. You may want your home to express formality, or you may prefer it to express informality. If you want *formality,* you will use either subdued colors or rich fullbodied colors with rich textured materials. With subdued colors, you will also express reserve and quiet, while the fullbodied colors will be rich and gracious. Either of these two effects are compatible with formality. Black and gold will also help you to carry out the feeling for formality.

Pewter and copper are restricted to the informal room, while silver is a formal accessory. For *informality,* you will usually select clear, bright colors. But if your furniture style is Colonial New England, you may select turkey and cranberry reds, with light browns and yellows like saffron and mustard. The colors for this style are vigorous, forceful and strong, the colors that we find in Nature.

You may want to have a room that is feminine or masculine in tone. For the *feminine* room you will use soft, delicate pastels, with smooth textures. You will stress curved and horizontal lines. Tints of lavender or lilac are distinctly feminine. The keynote of the feminine room and of the masculine room as well, is set by its colors, accessories and textures. In the

Color contributes to the beauty of this pleasant Modern living room. The table-desk and triangular end table are decorative space-saving pieces of furniture.

Wallpaper	dusty rose pink pineapple pattern with green sprigs against a cocoa brown field
Draperies	bottle green
Rug	raisin
Sofa fabric	pink and brown tweed weave
Lounge chairs	one olive green; the other copper
Leather	on sofa, end tables and pull-up chair is light shell pink
Furniture wood	amber mahogany
Coffee table	gold and silver lacquer flecked on black lacquer

A Monochromatic Color Scheme uses only one hue of the color wheel. This hue is usually varied in value and in intensity to achieve an interesting, smart effect.

An Adjacent Color Scheme uses any two or more colors that lie side by side on the color wheel, varying them in value and in intensity to attain pleasing harmony.

A Complementary Color Scheme adopts any pair of hues that lie directly opposite each other on the color wheel. One hue dominates, the second provides contrast.

A Split Complementary Scheme consists of a combination of three colors—a primary or intermediate color plus the two hues that lie on each side of its complement.

A Triad Color Scheme is a combination of three hues that divide the color wheel into three equal parts; a 12-place wheel contains four different triad harmonies.

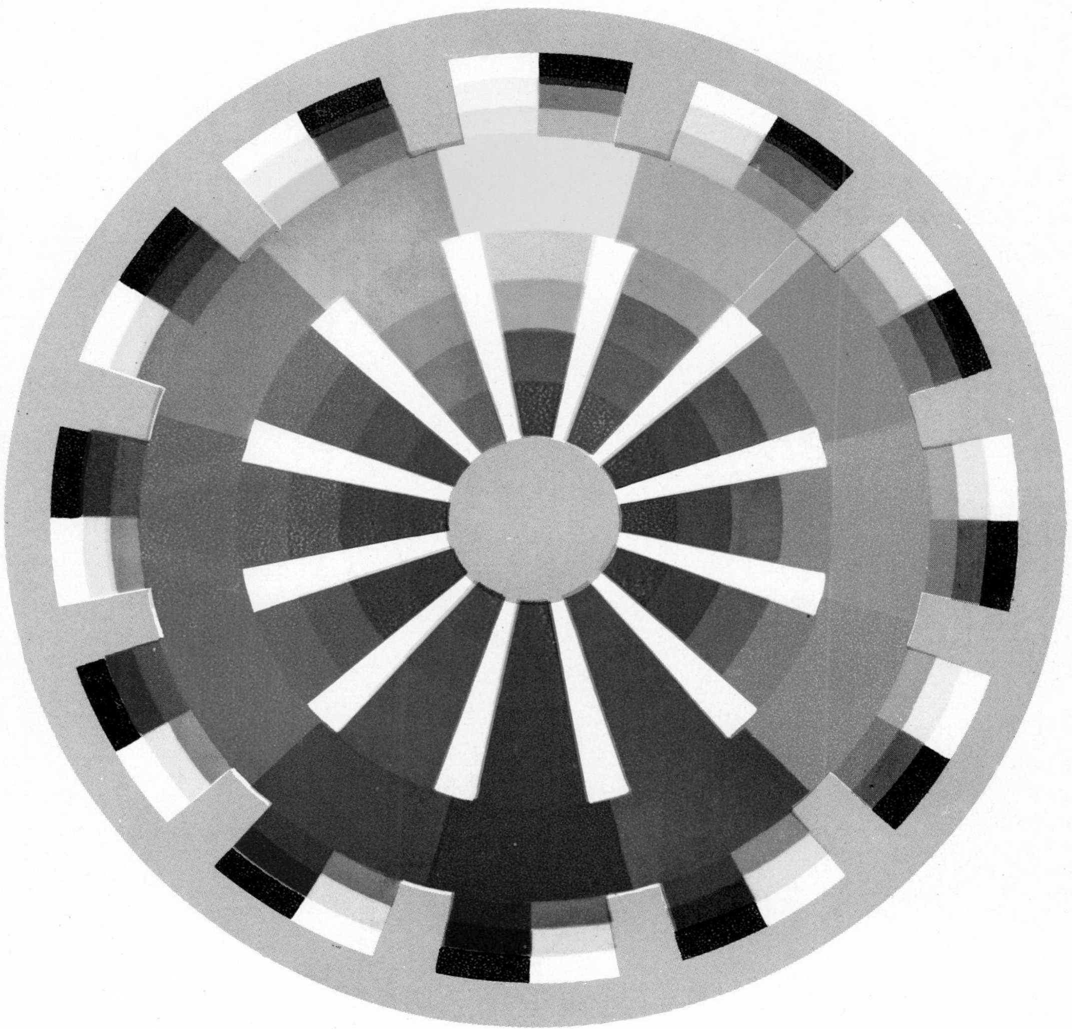

COLOR WHEEL

This color wheel consists of the twelve normal, pure hues and their gradations in value and in intensity. The tints and shades which constitute values of each color are arranged in scale on the rim outside the pure colors of which they are gradations. The muted, grayed, intensities of the pure colors fall within the circle of normal colors, running toward the neutral gray center of the color wheel. With this color wheel you can devise any of the five types of schemes shown on page 64 for your home. Chapters 3 and 4 describe how you can do this.

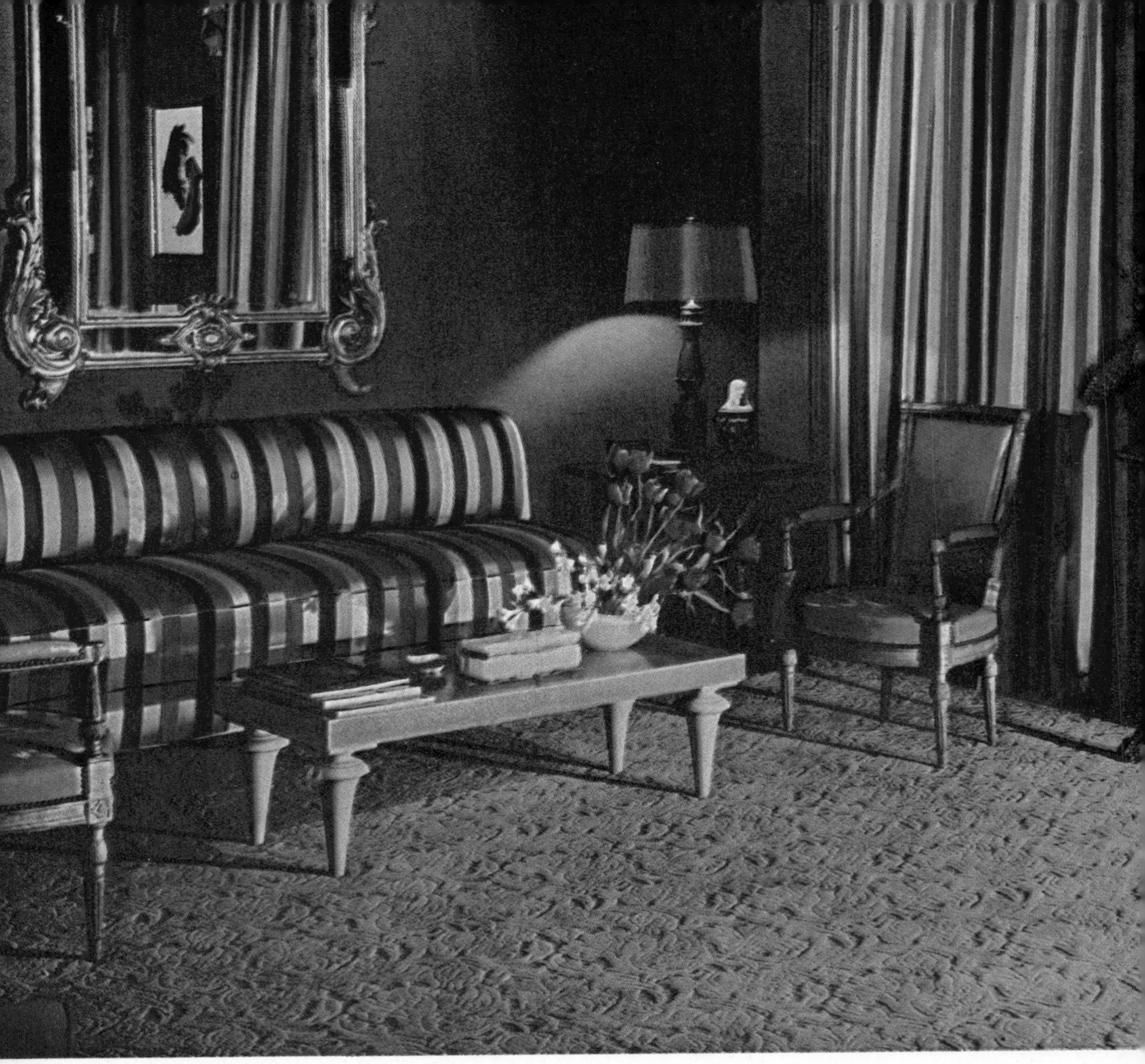

TRADITIONAL—YET CONTEMPORARY

Elegance and formality characterize this traditional yet contemporary room. The deep color of the walls and the gray of the sculptured carpet afford a perfect foil for the bisymmetric balance of the entertainment group. The gilt and white of the coffee table not only endow the piece with importance but serve to tie together the colors of the entire grouping. The pair of Louis XVI chairs contrast effectively with the contemporary sofa set off by the traditional gilt framed mirror.

A SPACIOUS BAY

A pair of curved loveseats capitalize on the bay windows which look out on a beautiful vista in the distance. The ceiling to floor draw draperies, with a deep cartridge-pleated heading, open up to reveal the broad expanse of windows. The classic square pilaster at the edge of the bay incorporates an unusual period note as does the decorative frieze at the ceiling line. Tall table lamps impart height as does the dramatic sculpture of the head.

Color Scheme 1

A formal Georgian room in an adjacent color scheme of blue, blue-green, a plum blue-violet and neutral dull gold gives an effect of dignity and richness.

Color Scheme 2

Red with its two split complements, blue-green and yellow-green, sets the color harmony for this luxuriously formal English Regency room which deviates from tradition in its treatment of walls and trim.

Color Scheme 3

A French Provincial city style room with an adjacent scheme of soft faded pastel blue, grayed pale Wedgwood and accessories in gilt, soft green and pastel prints creates an atmosphere of feminine grace and formality.

Color Scheme 4

Faithful to the Victorian era is this formal living room done in an adjacent scheme of mauve and violet-tinged rose with a deep blue-green as complement.

For details of these four color schemes see chart on page 88.

Color Scheme 5

The charm and simplicity of Colonial New England furniture here receive a triad treatment that adopts the cranberry red and mustard yellow so typical of this quaint, informal style.

Color Scheme 6

Brilliantly colored stencils highlight the complementary and adjacent scheme of this informal, carefree room decorated in the Pennsylvania Dutch style.

Color Scheme 7

Gayety and cheerfulness mark this French Provincial country styled room which uses blue-violet, medium blue and faded gray-blue with bright red as accent in an adjacent scheme.

Color Scheme 8

The natural finish of knotted wood furniture in the Modern country cottage style lends a spirit of informality and comfort to this room decorated in triadic red, yellow and blue.

For details of these four color schemes see chart on page 89.

Color Scheme 9

A monochromatic beige combined with complementary tones of red and green assures a pleasant setting for this Modern living room which conveys a hint of formality and a spirit of ease.

Color Scheme 10

This Modern living-study room achieves livable sophistication through a yellow monochromatic scheme relieved by contrasts of green in accessories and chair.

Color Scheme 11

A raspberry wall that contrasts with the soft blue-gray of the other three walls distinguishes this fine semi-formal room in the Classic Modern style and illustrates the variability of the primary triad color scheme.

Color Scheme 12

Light wood contemporary furniture of traditional lineage joins with complementary tones of red and green to produce a gracious, pleasant formality.

For details of these four color schemes see chart on page 90.

Color Scheme 13

Coral, seafoam and chartreuse, a split complementary scheme, contribute to this attractive informal room furnished with Modern light and dark pieces.

Color Scheme 14

This Modern blonde wood dining room, keyed to delightful informal entertainment, chooses a monochromatic scheme in coral and neutral colors with green leaves as a piquant accent.

Color Scheme 15

A Classic Modern combination room, which stresses comfort and informality, selects a complementary harmony of dominant green and a deep red-violet.

Color Scheme 16

The gay flowered print of the draperies forms the basis of this triad color scheme that gives this Classic Modern room a cozy, livable appeal with a charming semi-formal quality.

For details of these four color schemes see chart on page 91.

Color Scheme 17

Quiet femininity is the note of this formal bedroom which unites traditional and Modern furniture in a complementary plan of rose, pink and green.

Color Scheme 18

Very pale shrimp pink and turquoise with soft white and gray are the complementary colors of this rich feminine bedroom in semi-formal French Provincial.

Color Scheme 19

Tones of green in an adjacent scheme with complementary tints of pink introduce a restful charm into this delightfully sunny informal Modern bedroom.

Color Scheme 20

The primary triad appears again in blue pastel walls, dull red linoleum, yellow curtains, pink beige wood with red knobs, a yellow bedspread with a navy blue and vivid red design, red leather chair and accessories in white, red and deep blue.

COLORS FOR YOUR PURPOSE

PURPOSE	MAIN COLOR CHARACTER	ACCENTS	COMBINE WITH
FORMALITY	Subdued cool colors or rich full bodied colors.	Black Gold Silver	Vertical lines Smooth textures Formal balance
INFORMALITY	Clear bright colors. Warm colors.	White Pewter Copper	Horizontal lines Rough textures Informal balance
HOSPITALITY	Warm colors. Deep reds. Rich browns.	White Gold Copper	Curved lines Rich textures Soft lighting
SOPHISTICATION AND MODERNITY	Subdued background colors. Marked contrasts in value and intensity.	Black White Strong color	Straight lines Varied textures Cove lighting
QUIET AND RESTFUL	Colors close in value. Soft muted colors. Cool colors.	Gray Tinged gradations of color	Horizontal lines Little pattern Dull or rough textures Indirect illumination
GAY AND VIVACIOUS	Warm colors. Clear bright colors. Marked contrasts in value.	White Vivid colors	Diagonal lines Spirited patterns Rough or shiny textures Direct lighting Informal balance
FEMININE	Soft delicate pastels. Dusty tints. Tints of lilac and lavender.	White Grays Gilt	Curved and horizontal lines Smooth textures Floral patterns
MASCULINE	Strong deep shades. Browns. Tans.	Vivid colors	Straight vertical lines. Plaids and stripes Rough textures, leather

masculine room, you will feature muted colors or strong, deep shades, with coarse, rough textures and straight vertical lines. Vivid colors are used for relief. Tans, browns, deep reds, moss and olive greens may be used to further your decorative purpose.

If you want a *quiet, restful* room, you will keep the colors that you select close in value. Cool colors, especially soft blues and greens, enhance the feeling of repose. The colors will be soft and muted. Pattern will appear only sparingly in such a room. And horizontal lines will be stressed. For the *gay, vivacious* room, however, you may use clearer, brighter colors. Its colors will be the warm clear yellows and the bright reds. And there will be marked contrasts in value.

To achieve *sophistication* and *modernity,* you may select a subdued background with strong color accents in the foreground. Blacks and whites may be used for contrast. And you will secure added variety through contrasts in value and intensity. Sophisticated rooms may be built around one single color, with novel effect through tinging this color or through introduction of a strong color accent.

The room designed to bespeak *hospitality* will use warm colors. In formal rooms with this effect you may use the deep rich colors, but in informal rooms the colors selected may be clear and bright.

Your decorative purpose will accordingly tell you which colors will best fulfill your aim. By selecting suitable colors your room will speak with one voice. You will then translate your plans into reality. And you will achieve your plan and purpose.

Your preferences will be broadened and enriched through a growing consciousness of the beauty of colors and an awareness of the precise expressiveness which you may attain through the use of tinged colors. For the tinged colors carry the significance of the pure colors along with all the subtle overtones which variations in value and in intensity give.

Creating unity through lighting

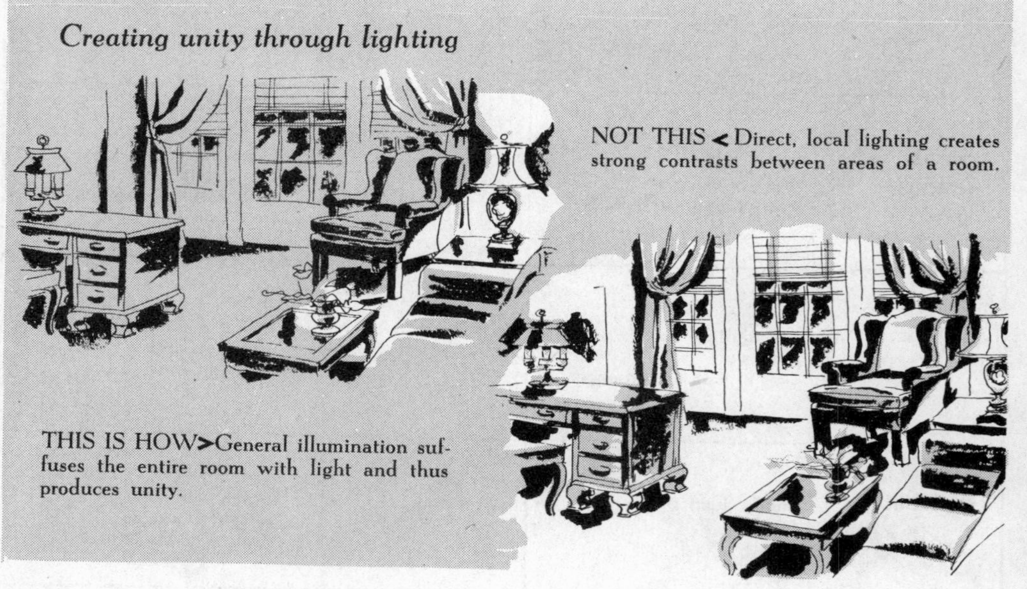

NOT THIS < Direct, local lighting creates strong contrasts between areas of a room.

THIS IS HOW > General illumination suffuses the entire room with light and thus produces unity.

COLOR AND FURNITURE STYLES

How your choice of furniture styles will influence the color scheme you finally adopt will be fully treated in subsequent chapters. Chapter 9 deals with the problem of harmonizing your furniture with its background. A chart clearly indicates what goes with what. The kind of furniture you select will be based on the use to which the room will be put. The style of the furniture will rest in part on your preferences. In part it will rest on the mood you wish to achieve and the decorative purpose you wish to express. Before you have a knowledge of the characteristics of different styles, it would hardly be enlightening to discuss this question in detail.

MONOCHROMATIC COLOR SCHEME

The color schemes which we can produce through the aid of the color wheel are in general of two types, the *related* and the *contrasting*. The monochromatic and the adjacent color schemes are both of the related type. The complementary, split complementary and triad color schemes belong to the contrasting type.

A *monochromatic* scheme is based on the use of one underlying color. Variations are obtained in this scheme through the resourceful use of blending and contrasting values and intensities of this color. This method is a difficult one to handle. The danger that it faces is, of course, the ever-present one of lack of variety. The use of one main color does insure unity. But the achievement of variation is tricky. And without variation, we sacrifice interest and liveliness. We get monotony and boredom.

Monochromatic schemes have, however, been very deftly used in modern interiors. The values and the intensities have been successfully adapted to express the purpose of the decorator. Textures attain an extremely important place in monochromatic schemes. The use of varied textures achieves variety through differences in the reflection of light and in the casting of shadows. Occasionally, one piece of furniture or accessories in a different hue are used to provide a desirable accent.

Color Scheme 10 gives one such room done in monochromatic colors. This modern room uses various values and intensities of yellow. For accent it has a deep green chair. This contrast secures a pleasing variety. The over-all effect is a smart and sophisticated one, while the yellow radiates hospitality and good cheer and the subdued tones of the background provide a restful, easy feeling.

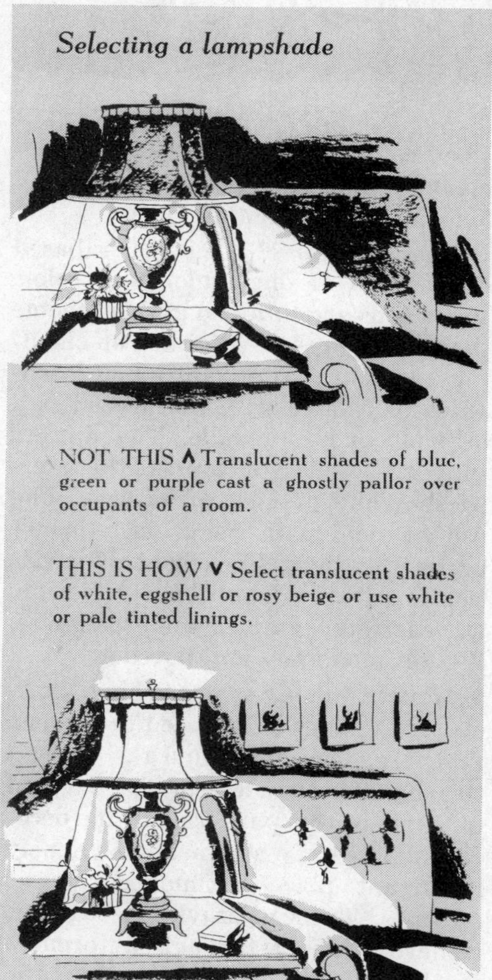

Selecting a lampshade

NOT THIS ∧ Translucent shades of blue, green or purple cast a ghostly pallor over occupants of a room.

THIS IS HOW ∨ Select translucent shades of white, eggshell or rosy beige or use white or pale tinted linings.

ADJACENT COLOR SCHEME

The second type of related color scheme is the *adjacent*. Very often, in fact, adjacent schemes are referred to as related schemes. Adjacent color schemes simply select colors which lie side by side on the color wheel as illustrated on page 64. They thus secure unity. Unity is also gained through *keying*.

Colors are keyed together when they are related to one another by a common bond. The colors of an adjacent scheme have a common element through their position on the color wheel. This common element is strengthened in keying.

Colors may be keyed in several ways. One way is by graying them. Their relatedness is then strengthened through their neutrality. Glazing a color is another method. In glazing, one color is painted over another and the mixture serves to mediate both colors. Or we may glaze colors through coating them with a varnish. Rough textures serve to key colors together through the interplay of light and shadow. Colors are also united through the use of neutral colors—white, black, gray, silver and gold. These neutral colors act as a tie between colors which might otherwise contrast rather sharply. Finally, we may add one color to each of the other colors in our scheme. By adding green to yellow and blue, we can key both these colors.

Color Scheme 1 pictures a formal Georgian room with an adjacent color scheme. The colors here employed are mainly blue, blue-green, a plum blue-violet and neutral dull gold. The effect is gracious, tranquil and dignified, rich and pleasant.

Color Schemes 3 and 7 are also examples of adjacent color schemes.

Here, through a difference in color and texture, one room is definitely formal, the other definitely informal—this despite the fact that both rooms have a French Provincial style of furniture. The color contributes to the difference and expresses the varying moods. The former of these rooms uses a background of pale green Wedgwood blue and soft faded blue pastel. The accessories are in gilt, soft greens and printed pastels. All this gives the room an air of formality, richness and delicate lightness.

The latter of these rooms uses blue-violet, medium blue and a faded gray blue, with bright red as accent. Other accents are in grayed blue-violet. Pieces of copper are also used decoratively in this room. The effect is very informal, as befits its country style, with a feeling of simple gayety and cheerfulness.

Adjacent color schemes usually are quiet and soothing, for strong, disquieting contrasts are lacking. Their beauty often relies upon skilful keying. The subdued colors give an effect of spaciousness and repose. Unless the colors selected differ in value and intensity, zest and snap may be wanting.

The colors best adapted for adjacent schemes are those which fall between the primary colors on the color wheel. With green and yellow-green, yellow may be used as accent, while with green and blue-green, blue suggests itself.

COMPLEMENTARY COLOR SCHEME

One method of enlivening adjacent color schemes is through the use of *complementary* colors. Complementary colors are those which lie exactly opposite each other on our color wheel. The colors opposite each other fall at either end of a line as shown on page 64. The colors of any such pair are complementary to each other.

The greatest degree of contrast between hues exists between the complementaries. Thus yellow and violet, green and red, blue and orange are all pairs of complementary colors. They are thus contrasting colors. While colors that lie side by side on the color wheel are related through a common element in their makeup, complementary colors are not related. When blended together, complementary col-

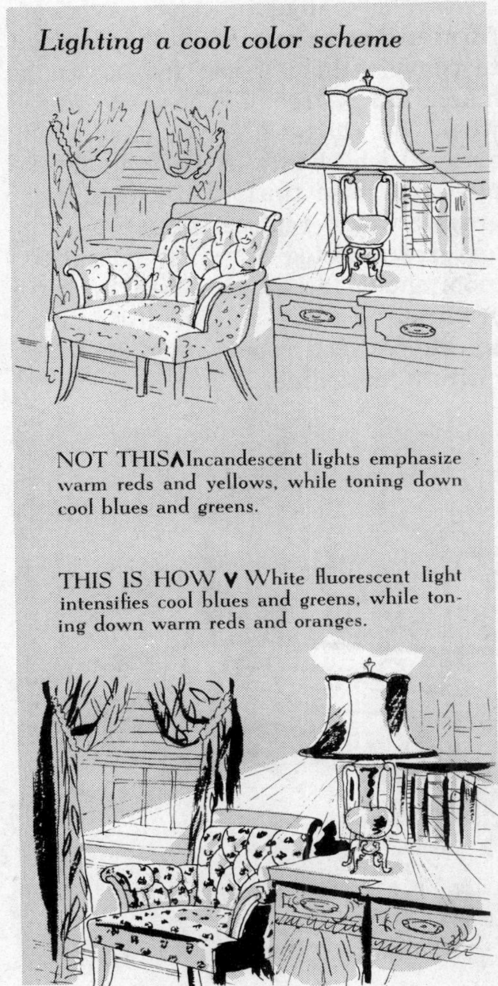

Lighting a cool color scheme

NOT THIS ∧ Incandescent lights emphasize warm reds and yellows, while toning down cool blues and greens.

THIS IS HOW ∨ White fluorescent light intensifies cool blues and greens, while toning down warm reds and oranges.

ors neutralize each other and produce gray. Thus we may gray a color, not only through adding gray itself, but by mixing it with its complementary.

Color Scheme 17 presents a pleasing complementary color scheme for a bedroom. The dominant color is red, with green as its complement. The soft green bench and drapes add a quiet contrast to the reds. The soft rose tone used in this scheme is a color which is flattering to most persons. The general effect is quiet and feminine, with a note of formality and reserve.

With a change in colors, type of furniture and accessories, it is simple to convert this scheme for use in a masculine bedroom. The soft green would be changed for a dark, dull green. Rich shades of red would replace the rose tints, while tans and browns would replace the beige. The textures selected for the masculine room should be rough. With the appropriate change in furniture and accessories, the room would then be entirely masculine.

Oftentimes, adjacent and complementary color schemes are used together in decorating a room. As *Color Scheme* 4 indicates, such a combination of two schemes may be used with successful effect. In this room, the mauve and violet-tinged rose are related colors, while the deep blue-green is the complementary. Used with ornate Victorian furniture, the general expression is one of luxury and richness. Altogether this room appears florid and showy, a modern room in the traditional manner.

SPLIT COMPLEMENTARY COLOR SCHEME

When two hues are used side by side, the contrast between them is strengthened. The degree of difference is made more pronounced. This is especially true of complementary colors. For this reason, contrasting color schemes are more brilliant and colorful than are the related schemes. They are more vibrant.

True complementary colors often produce a too sharp and disagreeable contrast. The contrast can be softened

For the double-duty bedroom

NOT THIS < This arrangement complicates bed making and looks ungainly.

THIS IS HOW > A convenient corner table affords an attractive solution.

somewhat through using, not the complementary color itself, but the related colors which lie to either side of it. Thus, if we were to select yellow, rather than use its direct opposite on the color wheel, we could use the two colors on either side of violet—blue-violet and red-violet. Red, similarly, goes better with blue-green and yellow-green than it does with its complementary green. Such a contrasting color scheme is called a *split complementary*.

If in forming our split complementary we select a primary or an intermediate color, we can use the two colors which lie on either side of its complementary. Thus, on our color wheel, if we select the primary blue, the complementary color is orange. By using the blue with the colors on either side of its complementary, we get a split complementary scheme consisting of blue, red-orange and yellow-orange.

If we select the intermediate hue, yellow-orange, the split complementaries are violet and blue, while for yellow-green the split complementaries are red and violet. The basis for use of split complementaries lies in the fact that the two split complementaries upon mixing form the complementary itself.

This fact, however, limits us in selecting the starting color from which we can build up our split complementary scheme. We are limited to primary and intermediate colors as our starting point. We cannot begin our split complementary scheme from a secondary color.

The reason for this is that secondary hues have primary colors as their complementaries. Thus, green has red, violet has yellow and orange has blue. The complementary primary color, however, cannot be formed by any other colors. In other words, the split complementary of a secondary color cannot give the complement, as this latter is a primary color. Therefore, we are restricted to primary and intermediate hues as our starting point in forming a split complementary color scheme. This does not, however, forbid using either secondary or primary colors within the scheme itself. This stricture holds only for the planning of such a scheme from an initial color.

One example of a split complementary scheme is given in *Color Scheme* 13. The blue-green and yellow-green of this modern room are the split complements of the coral. The over-all effect is one of informality or semiformality, a quiet, cheerful room with a note of gayety and warmth.

To lower a high ceiling

NOT THIS ∧ Shun vertical lines and small sized furniture.

THIS IS HOW ∨ Use a warm tone in ceiling. Stress horizontal lines throughout room. Large sized furniture will do this trick too.

TRIAD COLOR SCHEME

The remaining method of selecting a color scheme from the color wheel is through selecting the colors at the points of an equilateral triangle. These colors, on our color wheel, are exactly three colors apart from one another and divide the color wheel into three equal divisions. Thus, starting at yellow, we would get the other two primary colors. The three primary colors thus form one of the possible *triad* color schemes. This may be seen by referring to page 64.

Altogether, we can get four such triads on our twelve-interval color wheel. One triad consists of the three primary colors, the second triad consists of the three secondary colors. The remaining two triads consist of the six intermediate hues. Yellow-orange, blue-green and red-violet comprise one of these triads; and yellow-green, blue-violet and red-orange make up the other.

Color Scheme 5 pictures an Early Colonial room in the New England style. This room is decorated in a triad scheme. The effect in this instance is informal, with the charm and simplicity which characterize this style.

PRINCIPLES OF COLOR

In translating your color scheme into reality, the problems which you face are the same regardless of the manner in which you arrived at your scheme. The color wheel is an important ally of yours in working out your color schemes. The use of the color wheel can help you to select the specific colors in your color scheme. It can also help you to determine which colors go well together. You can similarly determine this through use of the alternate general method that was already recommended—that of adopting your color scheme from a flower, a natural scene, a painting or a piece of printed material. In each case you can see for yourself whether your colors will blend or clash.

With a knowledge of what the colors themselves may say, you can select a color that will harmonize with your decorative purpose. And select one which will express your own tastes and preferences. Color, while important, is not the only element you have with which to secure your aim. Your choice of furniture is also of importance. And your furniture will possess certain lines and textures. These two qualities, consequently, must also be ingredients in your recipe.

The problems that you face, therefore, do not arise from the selection of any specific color. Specific colors may easily be determined. You simply select the colors that you prefer, that will go well with one another and that contribute to the decorative plan you intend. But you still have a problem.

COLOR DISTRIBUTION

The problem is one that applies to both related and contrasting color schemes. It is the problem of determining the *distribution* of colors so as to secure both unity and variety. If you can decide upon a color for your large areas, such as the walls, ceiling and floor, then you have taken the step that will contribute toward unity. Contrast can be attained through using contrasting colors or tinged colors in the accessories.

The principles that apply to the distribution of color are, consequently, mainly matters of scale or proportion. The general principle has been noted in several variant contexts. It is this: *The stronger the intensity and the higher the value of a color, the smaller the area this color should occupy.* And the converse applies as well. *The weaker the intensity and the lower the value of a color, the greater area the color may occupy.*

The apparent size of a room, we have already noted, may be increased or diminished through the use of receding or advancing colors respectively. The effect of spaciousness may be enhanced through treating walls

Decorating Junior's Room

NOT THIS ∧ Avoid pastel colors and daintiness in curves, materials or patterns.

THIS IS HOW ∨ For a more masculine tone use sturdy furniture, rough textures, strong colors. Stress vertical lines.

and woodwork, walls and floor covering, or walls and furniture in the same color. In small rooms, the use of light tints will also give the effect of greater space.

If the colors that you select for your scheme are close in value and intensity, then you need observe only the Greek rule of the Golden Section. This rule, you may recall, tells us to avoid precise, obvious divisions. We should preferably use divisions in the ratios of two to three, three to five, or five to eight. This insures added interest and also serves to make one color in your scheme the leader—the *dominant* hue.

If you select a triad color scheme for your room, you will violate this rule if you use each one of your colors in equal amounts. Instead, you should make one color dominant, use the second in moderate amount, while reserving the third for accent and contrast.

With all types of color schemes, it is necessary that one color be dominant. It is through dominance that the mood of a room is fixed. But dominating is not domineering. The brightest, most intense colors are usually reserved for emphasis and accent. In all color schemes, the neutral colors—white, gray, black, silver and gold—may be used. These colors are not considered in classifying the schemes as related or contrasting.

You need not, furthermore, follow any of the five types slavishly in using the color wheel. Each of the methods is flexible. Types of color schemes may be combined. And mention has been made of the enormously complicated color wheels that are possible. These wheels allow greater freedom and variety. Freedom may also be secured through adopting your scheme from Nature or a work of art.

BALANCE AND EMPHASIS

In apportioning the areas, it is especially important to take account of the tinged colors, of the values and intensities of colors. We have already seen how contrasts in value or in in-

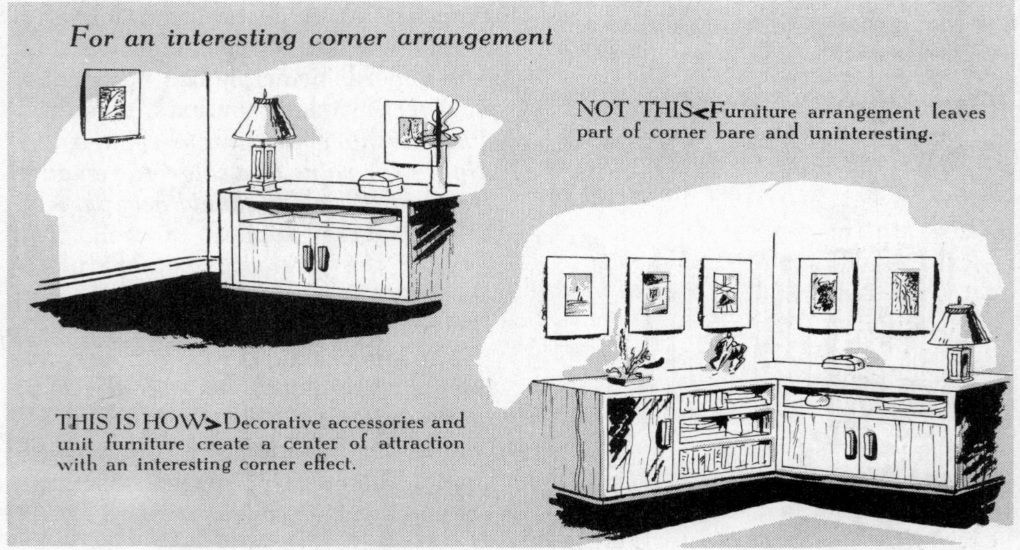

tensity are heightened. A small amount of warm color will serve as contrast to large areas of cool colors. A small amount of shaded color will stand out in contrast with large areas of tinted colors, while a touch of pure or brilliant color will accent large areas of muted colors.

The pure colors of the color wheel are not themselves well suited for wide use in a room. They must be varied in value and intensity. What they have to say is very strident. And it is said in an uninteresting manner. Pure colors, however, are often used effectively as accents. If we wish to secure accent, we must be sure not to relegate the accenting color to an isolated corner of the room. The accent should set off your more important groupings.

If we apportion our colors so as to make one color dominant, we still may have concern over securing balance among the subordinate colors. We achieve balance with colors through repeating the colors in different areas of our room. In a room in which only the drapes are blue-green, the room may seem somewhat out of balance. It is necessary, if this is so, only to repeat this blue-green in another accessory somewhere else in the room. And *for balance, colors should be distributed throughout the entire room, not concentrated in a single area.*

Emphasis is introduced through the use of contrasting hues, values or intensities. It is for this reason that the contrasting color schemes are important. Before we can achieve contrast, we first must have unity. For unity, we must select one color as the principal color of our scheme. The principal color need not be the background, however, even though the background covers the largest area. The background is the field against which objects that we want to emphasize will stand out.

We must remember that backgrounds are exactly what they are called. They must not obtrude. They should serve to set off the foreground. They should not distract attention.

Nor should the background be one that is hard to live with.

What is to be emphasized belongs in the foreground. The background, therefore, while dominant in area, is actually subordinate to the foreground in decorative importance. The emphasis that we secure through contrast will in consequence be given to colors that are used in lesser amounts.

This contrast may be secured through hue, value or intensity. But it is this contrast, this emphasis, which will enliven your room and give your room just that bit of difference so important to individuality and distinction.

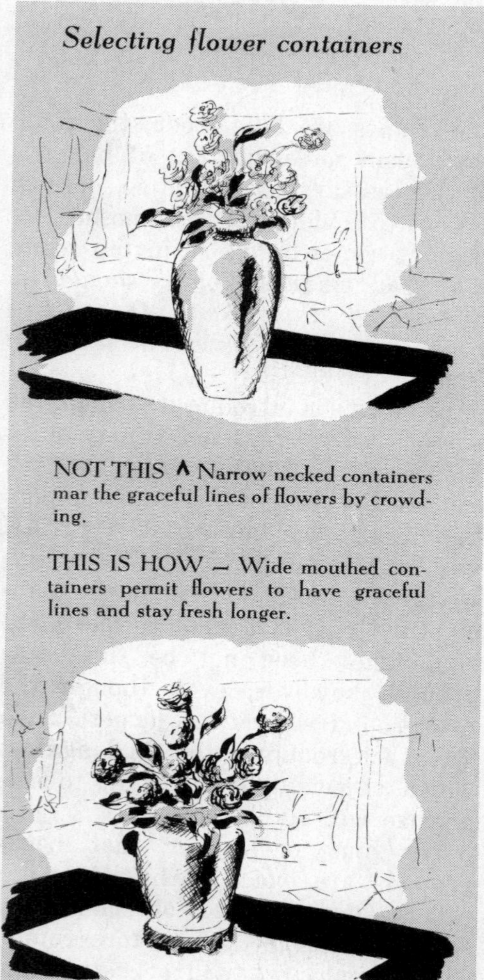

Selecting flower containers

NOT THIS ∧ Narrow necked containers mar the graceful lines of flowers by crowding.

THIS IS HOW – Wide mouthed containers permit flowers to have graceful lines and stay fresh longer.

TREATMENT OF CONNECTING ROOMS

If two adjoining rooms in your home are connected by a wide doorway or other architectural opening so that an observer can see from one directly into the other, you will have to give these rooms especial attention. For best decorative effect, these rooms ought to be considered as a unit. The color schemes that you adopt for these rooms should blend with each other. There should be at least one color in common between these rooms. This unity is most effectively achieved if the same wall treatment is used throughout both rooms. Continuous floor covering—carpeting, linoleum or similar rugs—will also serve the same purpose.

It will make for even greater unity if you use two colors in common. The two colors, in this instance, need not, however, be used extensively in each of the rooms. As is so often true, the factor that will finally determine the treatment is that of unity. And the way in which you attain this quality will depend upon the architectural features of your home. It will depend upon how much of each room is visible from the other, as well as upon the size of the rooms. If the rooms are small, it is advisable to use the same wall coloring throughout. If the rooms are large, greater variation is possible.

The simplest method of treatment is to begin with the more important room first. If your two connecting rooms are living room and entrance hall, then you will begin your plan with the color scheme for your living room. While here your problem is to combine both unity and variety in interesting proportions, the selection of a common color or colors will serve to secure unity. The use of a common color will result in producing the effect of greater spaciousness, as well as greater restfulness. If you emphasize the contrast in the colors of the two rooms, you will produce the opposite effect.

If your two connecting rooms are kitchen and dinette, both rooms may be treated in the same manner. Your kitchen will then take on some of the quality of cheerfulness, lightness and gayety that you want for your dinette. The present trend in home decoration is in line with your decorative purpose. Kitchens today no longer are the solid whites of ten years ago. Frequently the only white areas in kitchens are those of the mechanical units—the stove and the refrigerator. You can therefore repeat the scheme of your dinette in the kitchen.

In planning your color scheme, it is necessary to take account of the fixed decorations of the room. You must give thought to the walls, woodwork and floor. If the room is already partially furnished, you must consider these furnishings as well. To apply your color scheme requires consideration of only a few principles. These principles are those of proportion, balance and emphasis. You must also plan your color scheme to express the effects that you wish to achieve. With careful planning and forethought, you will achieve beauty and good taste in your home.

WORKING OUT A COLOR SCHEME

Now that we know the principles underlying the use of color, let us see how we would go about working out a color scheme for a room. If you want a modern, distinctive room, you might adopt a monochromatic scheme. The color you select will be one you like and believe is well adapted to express your decorative purpose. Let us say that this color is green.

For a monochromatic scheme, you will vary this one color in your room in accordance with your purpose. If you want a quiet, subdued room, masculine in tone, then you know that you will employ shades of green,

grayed greens and deep grays. You will, furthermore, use tans and browns. The tints of green which suggest lightness and femininity, if used at all in this room, will be restricted to accent only. All this is directed by the mood and atmosphere that you want to express and that colors and their tinges convey.

You may, accordingly, decide upon a dark green rug with chairs upholstered in moss green. For the background, you may use tan—tan walls with drapes that are tan in background and have a brown and green geometric plaid or striped pattern. We may feel assured that these colors will go well together. If you fear that the over-all effect may be somewhat somber, you may add a rich red leather chair and picture for vivacious contrast.

Suppose, however, you want to secure delicacy and femininity through a green monochromatic room. You will then use soft, pale tints, while limiting the use of dark greens and deep tans and browns. Your greens will be used with whites, pinkish grays or rosy beiges. You may do your background in white or in a pleasant pale green muted tint. The drapes, then, may be somewhat darker than the walls or white with a dainty leaf green pattern. For the rug you may select any one of a wide variety of hues. It may be moss green, a rosy beige, or a pinkish gray. It may even be a rich brown color. You may repeat the drapery material in the upholstery. Or, instead, you may select other soft green shades or light tints of green. And you might use white accessories with a small amount of green trimming. Your room will then reflect your purpose.

These are only suggestions for your guidance in working out just one type of color scheme for your home. We have by no means exhausted all the possibilities of a green monochromatic scheme. Regardless of the details of your final plan, this is the method by which you can work out such a scheme.

Let us see how we might build up a contrasting color scheme. The mono-

NOT THIS < The broken line arrangement fails to unify pictures or relate pictures to furniture.

THIS IS HOW > Aligning bottom edges relates pictures of uneven size, unifying pictures and furniture.

chromatic schemes are difficult ones, resting as they do for effectiveness upon the subtle interplay of variations in value and in intensity. Complementary schemes do avoid the danger of succumbing to monotony.

The color wheel shows that red and green form a complementary pair. We shall use this pair, with green as the dominant color. In contrasting schemes you will recall, it is important that we clearly decide upon our dominant color. And our purpose will be to decorate a bedroom which will be quiet and restful, feminine and reserved in tone.

The reds that we may select will be soft dusty rose tones of pale pinks, for these are feminine colors. Our greens similarly will be light, pale and soft. The walls may be done in a very pale pink, a rosy beige or a light dusty rose. Any one of these will give a pleasant, soothing background with a touch of warmth and intimacy.

For the floor we may select a pinkish-gray carpet or we may use a pale-tinted gray-green. The bedspread and drapes may be a soft green with a pink and dark green floral pattern. The chair may be a solid green, slightly darker than the drapes and the bedspread. The accessories might be in white and very pale pink.

You may want to work out your color scheme from a piece of printed fabric that you like. Adopting your scheme from such a source is one of the two general methods of deriving a color scheme, you will recall. Let us imagine that the fabric consists of a white background with a pretty floral design largely in claret red and that it uses yellow and pale blue in small amounts. This is actually a triad color scheme. The fabric looks cheerful and gay, warm and bright. And these are the qualities that we want our room to possess.

As we have the colors that we shall use, we must now consider how we shall distribute them in our room. How shall we allocate our dominant red and our subordinate blue and yellow? What colors shall we use for the walls, what for the floor covering and draperies? We must also decide upon the colors we shall use in our upholstery and accessories.

Since the room is large, we may use the laughing yellow of the print for the background color of our room. Had our room been small, we would have chosen the pale blue as the color of the wall. Using the print as our basis, we distribute the colors as follows:

Wall	pale yellow with white woodwork
Floor Covering	claret red
Draperies	the floral print
Upholstery	
sofa	pale blue
large easy chair	the floral print
side chair	golden yellow
chair	grayed Wedgwood blue
Accessories	white plus bright red and touches of deep blue

With Classic Modern furniture, the over-all effect that we have secured is informal or semi-formal, depending upon the textures of the materials selected and the arrangement of furniture throughout the room. Our room now welcomes us with a cozy and livable quality. It is illustrated in *Color Scheme* **16.**

The steps that we follow in working out a color scheme are now apparent. We decide upon our decorative purpose, the effect that we intend to secure. The use to which the room will be put determines the furniture and accessories that we shall use. We then select the colors for the room. We choose as our colors those that will carry out our decorative purpose and express our personal preferences. We assure that we achieve harmonious unity and pleasing contrast. We determine that one color will be dominant. The rest is simply a matter of allotting areas for distribution of color. If you follow the order in the example immediately above, you will find that this can be done very easily.

The colored illustrations of twenty color schemes that accompany this chapter may serve you as a guide or offer suggestions to you for other

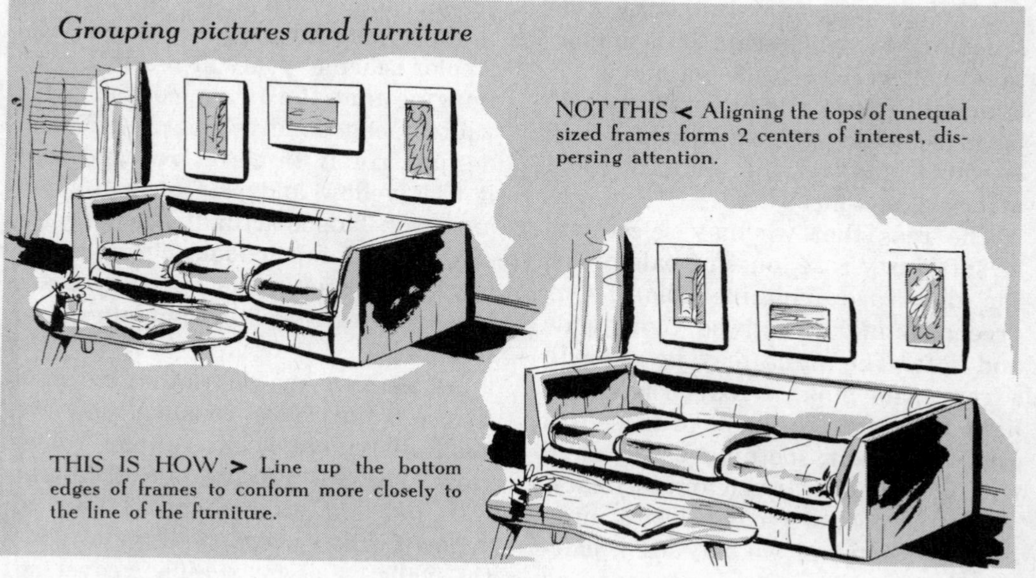

color schemes. The charts give you all the color details of sixteen of these illustrated rooms. Practice with these color schemes. See how you may vary them. Ask yourself what colors you would prefer to use in place of those already selected. Try to decide what effect your variations will produce. Working out color schemes is real fun.

Once you grow conscious of colors and their effects, you will find your life enriched and broadened. You will know beauty. You will gain deeper, finer experiences and a keener expressiveness. The study of color is deeply rewarding in its own right.

Vivacious colored and patterned draperies, repeated in the bedspread, highlight the sunshine corner windows of this bedroom. The pattern is in chartreuse and black on a white background. The pebble twist rug is a Sequoia tan, while the corner chair is covered in gray textured fabric. The light wood of the twin dressers contrasts with the tier table and a spacious mirror picks up the gay pattern of the bed.

DEFINITELY FORMAL			
Color Scheme 1	Color Scheme 2	Color Scheme 3	Color Scheme 4
GEORGIAN English, 18th Cent.	**ENGLISH REGENCY**	**FRENCH PROVINCIAL** (City Style)	**VICTORIAN**
FURNITURE WOODS Mahogany and walnut	**FURNITURE WOODS** Dark woods with black and gold	**FURNITURE WOODS** Walnut Natural fruitwoods	**FURNITURE WOODS** Dark with gilt trim
WALLS Creamy gold	**WALLS** Wallpaper—pale gray in striped satin effect	**WALLS** Pale grayed Wedgwood blue	**WALLS** Mauve
FLOOR COVERING Oriental — gold background with design in deep and light blue, bluegreen and plum	**FLOOR COVERING** Very deep bluegreen	**FLOOR COVERING** Aubusson (beige and pastel florals) or Broadloom in soft faded blue tint	**FLOOR COVERING** Yellow brown floral rug
DRAPERIES Floral print—gray gold background and blue, green, plum	**DRAPERIES** Grayed soft yellow green	**DRAPERIES** Striped satin damask, blue, bluegreen, and green and gold	**DRAPERIES** Deep bluegreen with gold tassels
UPHOLSTERY SOFA — soft medium blue frieze WING CHAIR — gray gold damask CLUB CHAIR — plum mohair SIDE CHAIR — needle point	**UPHOLSTERY** SOFA—rich red mohair CHAIR — champagne damask CHAIR — deep blue green but lighter than rug striped with gray	**UPHOLSTERY** SOFA — light turquoise CHAIR — petit point — gold and pastels CHAIR — soft deeper blue than walls or rug.	**UPHOLSTERY** SOFA — brilliant rose, violet tinge CHAIR — deep bluegreen floral damask with gilt trim CHAIR — plum
ACCESSORIES Lamp shades — cream, cream and green Bases — White alabaster, bluegreen alabaster Green leaves	**ACCESSORIES** Black Gold White	**ACCESSORIES** Gilt Pastel green French prints in pastels	**ACCESSORIES** Bright rose Gilt Dark brown
TYPE OF COLOR SCHEME Adjacent	**TYPE OF COLOR SCHEME** Split complementary	**TYPE OF COLOR SCHEME** Adjacent	**TYPE OF COLOR SCHEME** Adjacent and Complementary

DEFINITELY INFORMAL			
Color Scheme 5	Color Scheme 6	Color Scheme 7	Color Scheme 8
COLONIAL **New England**	**PENNSYLVANIA DUTCH**	**FRENCH PROVINCIAL** **(Country Style)**	**MODERN** **Country Cottage**
FURNITURE WOODS Maple Pine Fruitwoods	**FURNITURE WOODS** Walnut, pine and painted with stencils in brilliant colors	**FURNITURE WOODS** Natural fruitwoods	**FURNITURE WOODS** Natural finish Knotted woods
WALLS Light green blue with white wood trim	**WALLS** Pinkish white with terra cotta wood trim	**WALLS** White paint	**WALLS** Pale yellow
FLOOR COVERING Oval hooked rugs in beige and soft colors	**FLOOR COVERING** Braided or flat weave terra cotta and yellowish mixture	**FLOOR COVERING** Rag rug or any flat weave faded gray blue	**FLOOR COVERING** Braided or Mexican serapes Dark blue borders with tan, red, blue, white
DRAPERIES Mustard yellow—small calico print with deep blue and bright red	**DRAPERIES** Gay Dutch blue	**DRAPERIES** Toile de Jouy type light and dark blue print on white	**DRAPERIES** Red and white gingham with navy blue edging
UPHOLSTERY SOFA — brown CHAIR—cranberry red CHAIR — print, deep green blue on white	**UPHOLSTERY** SETTEE—small print of copper tans on Dutch blue Medium blue painted chairs with stenciled hearts and tulips in bright yellows, blues and lavenders CHAIR — burnt orange	**UPHOLSTERY** SETTEE — blue violet cushions CHAIR—red CHAIR—medium blue Chair cushions — same as drapes	**UPHOLSTERY** SOFA OR DAYBED Strong medium blue with yellow corded edges Chair—same blue Chair—grayed red
ACCESSORIES Cranberry red White Pewter	**ACCESSORIES** Deep blue glass Earth brown pottery	**ACCESSORIES** Copper Bright red Blue violet (grayed)	**ACCESSORIES** Yellow lamp shades Deep blue bases Deep blue and gray pottery
TYPE OF COLOR SCHEME Triad	**TYPE OF COLOR SCHEME** Complementary and Adjacent	**TYPE OF COLOR SCHEME** Adjacent	**TYPE OF COLOR SCHEME** Triad

FORMAL OR SEMI-FORMAL			
Color Scheme 9	Color Scheme 10	Color Scheme 11	Color Scheme 12
MODERN	**MODERN**	**CONTEMPORARY (Classic Modern)**	**CONTEMPORARY (Classic Modern)**
FURNITURE WOODS Bleached woods and lacquer	**FURNITURE WOODS** Light and dark (cream and brown)	**FURNITURE WOODS** Dark woods	**FURNITURE WOODS** Light woods
WALLS Gray beige	**WALLS** Old ivory	**WALLS** 1 wall raspberry 3 walls soft blue gray	**WALLS** Pale soft yellow green
FLOOR COVERING Very dark green	**FLOOR COVERING** Brown	**FLOOR COVERING** Soft blue gray of walls	**FLOOR COVERING** Gray beige
DRAPERIES Deep tan coarse net	**DRAPERIES** Deep yellow (mandarin)	**DRAPERIES** Patterned-gray background with yellow formalized leaf design	**DRAPERIES** Soft Green
UPHOLSTERY SOFA — gray beige darker than walls CHAIRS 1 red— clear, medium shade 1 green — same intensity 1 beige	**UPHOLSTERY** SOFA— deeper sand color than walls DESK CHAIR— deep green CHAIR — taupe CHAIR — yellow	**UPHOLSTERY** SOFA — gray (against raspberry wall) 2 CHAIRS—solid wine DESK CHAIR — yellow leather CHAIR — medium gray blue	**UPHOLSTERY** SOFA — grayed rose CHAIR — soft yellow green, deeper than walls CHAIR — topaz
ACCESSORIES Dark green leaves as accents Lamp shades soft rose beige Coffee table or vases and small accessories — vivid Chinese red lacquer	**ACCESSORIES** Dark green color of chair Daffodil yellow White	**ACCESSORIES** Lamp shades — white and raspberry binding Pottery—Wedgwood blue and bluegreen argenta	**ACCESSORIES** Rose red and dull gold
TYPE OF COLOR SCHEME Monochromatic background with Complementary	**TYPE OF COLOR SCHEME** Monochromatic with green accent	**TYPE OF COLOR SCHEME** Triad	**TYPE OF COLOR SCHEME** Complementary

INFORMAL OR SEMI-FORMAL			
Color Scheme 13	Color Scheme 14	Color Scheme 15	Color Scheme 16
MODERN	**MODERN**	**CONTEMPORARY (Classic Modern)**	**CONTEMPORARY (Classic Modern)**
FURNITURE WOODS Light and dark	**FURNITURE WOODS** Light	**FURNITURE WOODS** Medium tones	**FURNITURE WOODS** Light and dark
WALLS Soft warm gray	**WALLS** Coral	**WALLS** Green	**WALLS** Pale yellow with white woodwork
FLOOR COVERING Sea-foam, a soft tint of bluegreen	**FLOOR COVERING** Gray brown	**FLOOR COVERING** Warm gray	**FLOOR COVERING** Claret red
DRAPERIES Chartreuse (grayed) with coral binding on edges toward center	**DRAPERIES** Soft slate gray	**DRAPERIES** Gray with deep violet red pattern	**DRAPERIES** Floral print—white with red, yellow and soft blue
UPHOLSTERY SOFA — coral CHAIR — chartreuse slightly darker than drapes CHAIR — print, white with green and egg-plant	**UPHOLSTERY** Beige Brown	**UPHOLSTERY** SOFA—brown and tan mixture CHAIR — gray with green corded edge CHAIR—same as drapes	**UPHOLSTERY** SOFA — soft pale blue CHAIR — deeper gray blue CHAIR — same as drapes CHAIR — yellow
ACCESSORIES Chartreuse and rose	**ACCESSORIES** White and dark green leaves	**ACCESSORIES** Green and dull gold	**ACCESSORIES** Poppy red White Deep blue
TYPE OF COLOR SCHEME Split Complementary	**TYPE OF COLOR SCHEME** Monochromatic with color accent	**TYPE OF COLOR SCHEME** Complementary	**TYPE OF COLOR SCHEME** Triad

MIXING FURNITURE STYLES

STYLE	SPIRIT	MIXES WELL WITH —
QUEEN ANNE (Simple) (More elaborate)	Comfort, Simplicity, Usually Informal Formal	Colonial New England. Early Chippendale. Cottage type furniture. Formal Georgian.
CHIPPENDALE (Early) Chinese and Smaller Pieces	Sturdy, Masculine, Informal Formal or Informal	Queen Anne. Hepplewhite. Sheraton. Duncan Phyfe. Modern.
HEPPLEWHITE	Classic, Elegant, Delicate, Feminine, Formal	Adam. Sheraton. Chinese Chippendale. Smaller Chippendale pieces. Louis XVI. Duncan Phyfe. Classic Modern.
SHERATON	Classic, Simple, Delicate, Formal	Adam. Hepplewhite. Chinese Chippendale. Smaller Chippendale pieces. Louis XVI. Duncan Phyfe. French Empire. Directoire. English Regency. Classic Modern.
FRENCH PROVINCIAL (City Style)	Feminine, Delicate, Gay, Graceful, Usually Formal	Louis XV. Louis XVI. Queen Anne. Simpler Georgian pieces. Duncan Phyfe. Classic Modern.
FRENCH PROVINCIAL (Country Style)	Simple, Sturdy, Quaint, Countrified, Informal	Colonial New England. Pennsylvania Dutch. Informal Queen Anne. Cottage & Farm House types.
DIRECTOIRE	Classic, Graceful, Formal	Sheraton. Duncan Phyfe. Federal American. English Regency.
FRENCH EMPIRE	Classic, Dignified, Imposing, Formal	Duncan Phyfe. Federal American. English Regency. Victorian.
COLONIAL NEW ENGLAND	Quaint, Picturesque, Simple, Sincere, Informal	Simpler Queen Anne. Early Chippendale. Pennsylvania Dutch. French Provincial—country style.
PENNSYLVANIA DUTCH	Quaint, Gay, Friendly, Sturdy, Informal	Colonial New England. French Provincial—country style. Informal Modern.
DUNCAN PHYFE FEDERAL AMERICAN	Classic, Elegant, Formal	Adam. Hepplewhite. Sheraton. Louis XVI. Directoire. French Empire. English Regency. Classic Modern.
ENGLISH REGENCY	Sophisticated, Rich, Elegant, Formal	Chinese Chippendale. Sheraton. Hepplewhite. French Empire. Duncan Phyfe. Federal American. Classic Modern.
VICTORIAN	Homey, Elaborate, Usually Formal	French Empire. English Regency. Federal American.
CLASSIC MODERN	Sophisticated Formal or Informal	Chinese Chippendale. Sheraton. Duncan Phyfe. English Regency. French Provincial. Organic Modern.
ORGANIC MODERN	Comfort, Restful, Simple, Flexible Informal	Some Classic Modern.

CHAPTER FIVE

KNOWING PERIOD STYLES

IF YOU had lived in the rollicking England of Shakespeare's day, you would have had great difficulty in furnishing your home. Furniture was made only by hand. In consequence it was extremely scarce and costly. You would have had to improvise. You would have been limited to the few pieces of furniture known at that time. You would have been restricted to the style of furniture of the Elizabethan period. You would have had to use the woods and materials available in your immediate locality.

Your floor would have been of dirt, pounded down and carpeted with rushes that you would have gathered yourself. You would have thrown your refuse in kitchen middens located in the lane outside your door. Your furniture would have been crude and unpainted. You would have sat on hard benches without backs. These benches were called *forms.* Or you might have used *joint stools,* so named because they were products of joiners or carpenters. Hand hewn planks spread across trestles would have served as your table. And at night you would have placed your pallet on top of the chest, snuffed out your candle and you would have gone wearily to bed.

The few pieces of furniture that did

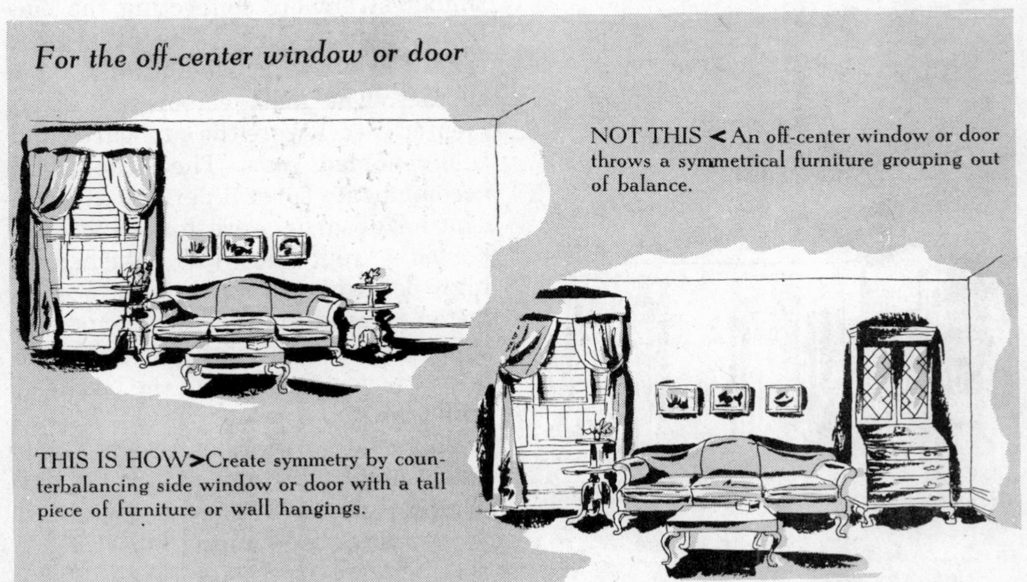

For the off-center window or door

NOT THIS < An off-center window or door throws a symmetrical furniture grouping out of balance.

THIS IS HOW > Create symmetry by counterbalancing side window or door with a tall piece of furniture or wall hangings.

exist in that age of Queen Elizabeth were reserved for the nobility. Only they could afford to hire the foreign craftsmen who made furniture. So scarce was furniture that the Queen herself, when going to visit one of her liege lords, used to have pieces of her furniture transported with her.

Elizabethan furniture was massive in size, straight in its lines, elaborate in ornamentation and built of solid oak. It looked imposing. It was meant to inspire awe and proclaim the standing of its owner. Comfort was practically unthought of. And beauty was sought through intricate carvings, inlaid and turned wood, elaborate crests and ornamental panels.

The chairs of that day were regarded as thrones. Some of the chairs had arms, but these were hardly serviceable as arm rests. The backs of the chairs usually consisted of solid wood panels decorated with a strapwork design surmounted with a carved crest. The panels resembled wall wainscoting in their treatment. For this reason one type of chair of this period was known as the *wainscot chair*. The chair backs were seldom tilted but were perpendicular to the floor. Few of the chairs were upholstered though some were provided with stuffed cushions called *squabs*. The seats consisted of solid flat wood, narrowing toward the back. The legs of the chairs were straight. Occasionally the front legs boasted of bulbous melon ornamentation and were connected by low stretchers that served as foot rests.

The tables were of the ponderous refectory or draw type with heavy timber stretchers connecting the bulbous, columnar legs. The draw type table permitted enlarging the table surface. The most elaborately ornamented pieces were the cupboards and the canopied beds. The beds could accommodate several persons at once. The headboards were high and supported a roof that was attached to high posts at the foot of the bed. A tester covered the roof while curtains shrouded the sides of the bed. The mattress was fastened to the bedstead with ropes.

These pieces of Elizabethan furniture would hardly appeal to you today or meet your needs. They were clumsy, poorly designed and proportioned,

Curved valances for the formal room

NOT THIS ∧ Curved lines with an obvious repeat, as in a scalloped border, are associated with Colonial maple furniture.

THIS IS HOW ∨ Curved lines with a subtle repeat are more pleasing and dignified.

crudely executed. Their scale was much too massive for present-day use. They lacked comfort. Though costly, they would hardly strike you as beautiful. Yet they were the modern furniture of their day.

Many of the pieces of furniture that we use today evolved from this early furniture. The contribution of the 16th century to modern furniture making, despite the shortcomings of its individual pieces, was a great one. It was during this century that furniture was separated from the floors and walls of buildings to which previously it had been attached. Thus movable furniture came into being. Necessarily, the movable furniture was coarse and crude, judged by modern standards. The craftsmen of that day had little experience and tradition upon which to draw. They were further limited by the materials and processes of manufacture that were available to them.

Today we can select furniture in a wide variety of styles. We too have our modern style of furniture, a product of our own day. In addition, we have the rich heritage of past styles upon which to draw. Unlike the Elizabethan, you are faced with a wealth of styles from which you may choose. Which style will it be? What will guide you in making your decision?

CHOOSING A FURNITURE STYLE

The style of furniture you choose should be one that appeals to you. You need not, however, reproduce any one style down to its last detail. In fact, you may achieve very interesting results through mixing styles. Blending styles may make your home more personal and individual. But mixing should be done carefully. It is important to select styles that have the same flavor or spirit. If you want to mix styles, you will find the chart at the beginning of this chapter helpful.

You should choose a style that appeals not only to you but to the members of your family. You should similarly choose the color scheme and accessories that you like. If you choose what you really do like, you will be expressing yourself. Your home will embody your personality.

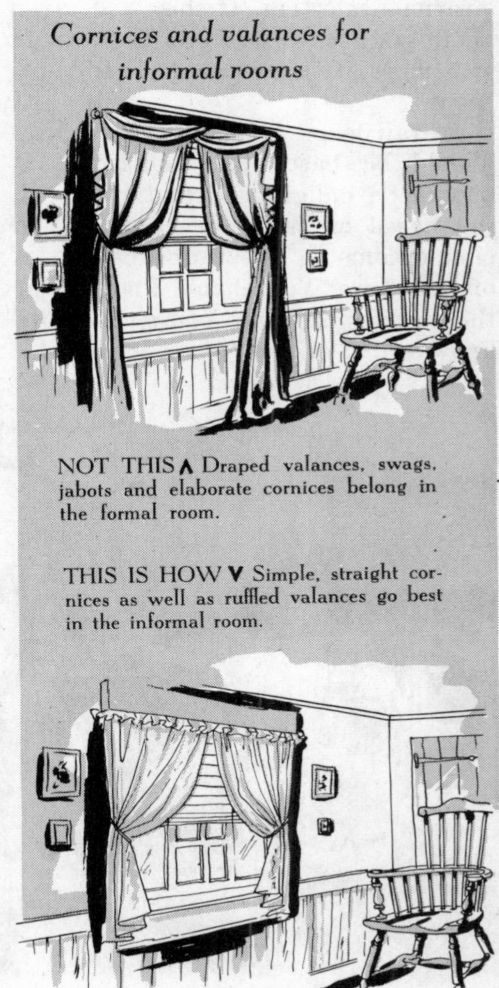

Cornices and valances for informal rooms

NOT THIS ∧ Draped valances, swags, jabots and elaborate cornices belong in the formal room.

THIS IS HOW ∨ Simple, straight cornices as well as ruffled valances go best in the informal room.

There is nothing wrong with having likes and dislikes. In fact, unless your home is decorated and furnished in accordance with your feelings, it won't satisfy you. Nor will your home please the members of your family if it does not suit their taste.

If you are acquainted with different styles of furniture, your preferences will have full play. You can then decide what you really like and will continue to like. Too many persons select one style because it is the only style with which they are familiar. Later on, when they see another style that they admire, they regret their previous selection. If they had given their taste a fair chance, they would not meet with eventual disappointment.

In fairness to yourself, your taste should be based on knowledge. It should be enlightened and reasoned, not based on whim or caprice. You should come to know different styles of furniture. You should know what these styles express. You should also know which effects can be expressed, which cannot, with these styles. What any style says is quite definite. If this were not so, then the style could not accurately be called a style. It would be saying everything and anything and, as a result, not saying any one thing clearly.

Styles that express the same things go well together. You can mix such styles. Hepplewhite and Sheraton go well with certain Chippendale pieces, with some Louis XVI pieces and with some Duncan Phyfe. English Regency blends with Sheraton, Hepplewhite, Chinese Chippendale and Duncan Phyfe. Mixing gives you greater freedom and variety, a greater chance to express your personality and create the kind of home you desire. But you must be familiar with the characteristics of different styles in order to mix pieces with good results.

Styles that are similar in scale, line and texture go well together. Woods need not be identical to mix well. You can mix light woods with dark and so achieve very pleasing contrast. All that is necessary is that these elements

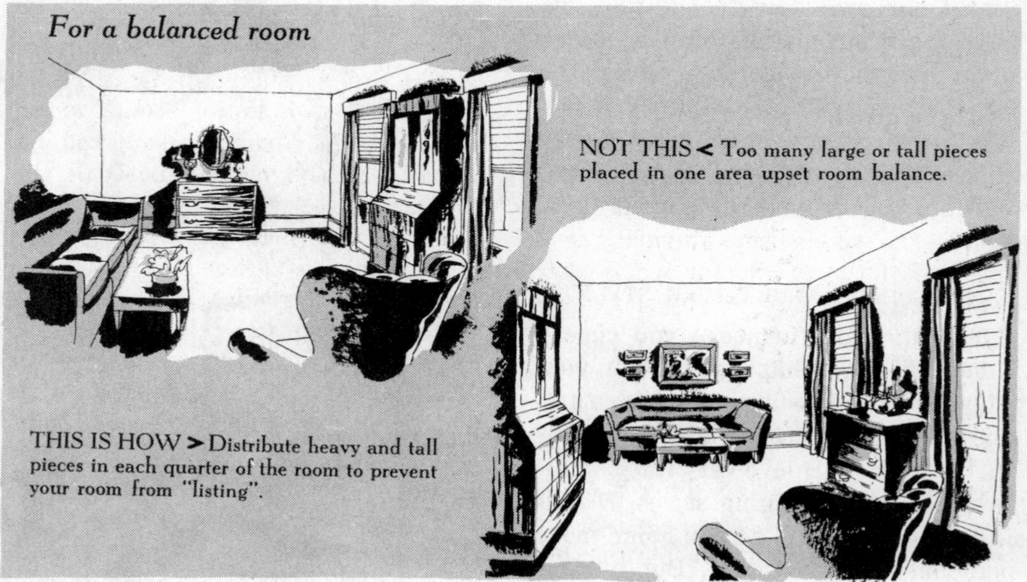

For a balanced room

NOT THIS < Too many large or tall pieces placed in one area upset room balance.

THIS IS HOW > Distribute heavy and tall pieces in each quarter of the room to prevent your room from "listing".

Selecting a piano for the small room

NOT THIS < A large piano is grand—but not in a small room.

THIS IS HOW > A console piano is scaled to the small room and helps produce the effect of spaciousness.

contribute to producing the same general effect. Woods and finishes need only express the same feeling—either formality or informality, richness and elegance or simplicity and rusticity. You will discover that furniture legs are often an indication of which styles may be mixed.

There is a romance to styles that is especially enjoyable. Styles are bound up with history and with peoples. Styles tell of the hopes and ideals of these peoples and of the conditions of the times. Styles reflect the spirit of the historical period during which they arose. Period styles, types of pieces, the woods used, all varied with the life of the people for whom they were designed. This is why styles differ in what they express.

The Elizabethan age was robust, rowdy and rough. It was an age of development and expansion. The times were coarse and forthright. The furniture style of that day was in keeping with this spirit. It was massive and crude, imposing but uncomfortable. Furniture at that time had only begun to acquire mobility. And all these characteristics may be applied to the age itself.

The spirit of the 18th century Georgian period was captured faithfully by the great designers of that time—Chippendale, Hepplewhite and Sheraton. The times had mellowed and grown refined. Its horizon was much broader than that of the 16th century. Richness was sought in beauty and in exquisite detail rather than in overwhelming size. Comfort was stressed. Variety had entered into the life of the people. And all this shows in Georgian furniture.

The preferences that lead you to select one style rather than any other may also take into account other factors. If you especially like the luxurious texture of silk, tapestry and damask, you would then select a style that goes well with these fabrics. Mahogany, satinwood and rosewood all would go well. And Georgian furniture uses such woods. You may, instead, prefer homespuns, hooked rugs, pewter and rough textures. These are

Lamps adapted to informal period styles

NOT THIS ▲ Classic urn bases with silk or parchment shades are formal traditional.

THIS IS HOW ▼ Pewter lamps with homespun shades are distinctly informal and adapted to provincial styled homes.

the accompaniments of Colonial New England style. Your choice will be guided accordingly.

You may prefer solid woods to veneers. Or you may prefer deep rich brown or bleached woods. The style you select should use the wood you like. Your budget may play a role. You may not be able to afford expensive inlays or veneers. But you may like the less costly solid wood of some maple pieces.

The type of house in which you live may help you to decide upon a style. If you have a Georgian house, you may want to furnish your home in that style. A Colonial cottage may lead you to select Colonial styles. A cottage or bungalow usually suggests an informal style. A small apartment may require the use of modern combination or double-purpose pieces.

A FEW DON'TS

There are a few don'ts you should consider in choosing your style. Don't permit your judgment to be swayed by what you may consider "all the rage." A vogue for a certain style—it might be any style—may suit a large number of persons. But it may not suit you.

If you like informality, don't succumb to one of the strictly formal styles. English Regency won't do for you. If you prefer formality, certain Provincial pieces will not accord with your decorative plan. Certain styles lend themselves only to formal treatment, other styles are labelled definitely informal.

Every style has its own way of achieving beauty. It achieves beauty through expressing the spirit that is native to it. You can't produce grace and delicacy with French Empire style. If you were to try to foist such an effect upon this style, you would not accomplish your purpose. You can't attain beauty by falsifying the spirit of your style.

What you want your home to express is an essential ingredient of your decorative purpose. Your purpose can be realized only if it is embodied in the *spirit* of the style you choose. There must be an organic relationship between your purpose and your style. They must be in accord with each other.

For the very modern fireplace

NOT THIS ∧ Accessories in formal balance are out of spirit with the asymmetric fireplace.

THIS IS HOW ∨ Place accessories in informal balance to accent the over-all asymmetry.

In decorating your home, you may begin your planning from either your purpose or your style. If you have a clear idea of the purpose you aim to achieve, then your choice of style should fit in with this purpose. If, instead, you begin your planning with a clear preference for one particular style, then you must be sure that your purpose jibes with your style selection. Your purpose and your style must be keyed to each other.

Both your purpose and your style selection should arise from the same set of preferences. Otherwise, you would be swopping preferences in the middle of the stream. Once you assure yourself that your decorative goal is one that can be attained with the style you want, then the rest of your decorative problems are simplified. The color scheme you choose will be one that harmonizes with both these factors. Your choice of accessories will also conform to them. You need then only concern yourself with grouping your furniture so as to secure convenience, comfort and the effect you plan.

DISTINGUISHING STYLES

Before you decide upon your style and purpose, you should find out what distinguishes one style from another. These distinctions will tell you what each style expresses. They will tell you which styles mix well together. With this knowledge you will be able to make a wise and satisfying selection.

WILLIAM AND MARY (1688-1702)

The reign of Mary Stuart and her Dutch consort lasted until 1702. They are therefore the first of the 18th century English monarchs. Though only a few of their pieces are reproduced today, William and Mary's reign exerted a profound influence upon subsequent development of furniture styles. They brought to England the Dutch notion of *comfort* and *hominess.*

With the emigration of Dutch craftsmen, furniture became more readily available. It also became lighter in weight, upholstery became common, walnut replaced the traditional English oak and curves softened the earlier rectilinear lines. The *highboy* and the *cabriole leg* made their appearance.

The Hugenot weavers who emigrated to England after Louis XIV's revocation of the Edict of Nantes, introduced and popularized new fabrics. Printed chintz and linen, as well as silk, velvet, damask, brocade and tapestry, added color and pattern to the furniture of this period. With the rise of commerce, lacquered furniture was imported from China, along with wallpaper and accessories.

The influence of William and Mary accompanied the early English settlers to the American colonies. Colonial Early American furniture grew out of this amalgam of Dutch and English ideas.

QUEEN ANNE (1702-1715)

During the Queen Anne period, the innovations in furniture design of William and Mary's reign were further developed. Under Queen Anne, furniture began to be constructed to meet the needs of the home rather than the castle. Comfort—so familiar a nation to us today—led to the introduction of new pieces and the modification of former pieces. Furniture was designed to conform to the human figure. Upholstery was overstuffed for additional comfort. The *settee* or *loveseat* was originated at this time, consisting of two chairs joined together, with a squab cushion and continuous curvilinear arms.

The *fiddle-back* chair, named after the shape of the center splat spooned to fit the body, is a typical Queen Anne piece. It is illustrated in the charts, *Calvacade of Furniture Styles* on the inside of the front cover. The front legs of this chair feature the cabriole curve, with a scallop shell carving at the knee and a ball and claw foot. The rear legs, though occasionally cabriole, usually were plain and splayed. Stretchers, if used at all, often took the shape of the letter H.

Small tables came into prominence. The round pedestal table, with tilt top, was supported by a turned shaft

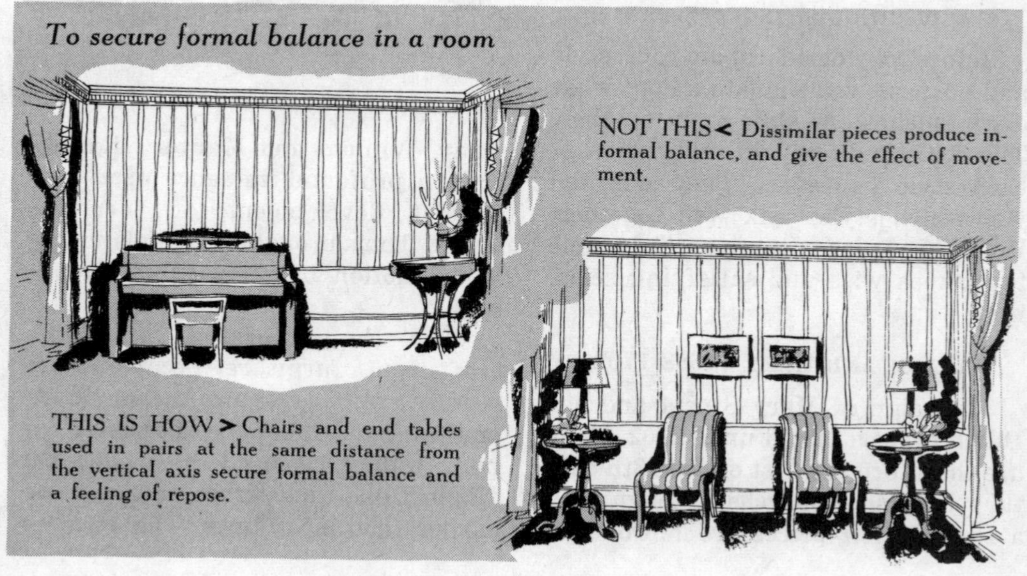

To secure formal balance in a room

NOT THIS < Dissimilar pieces produce informal balance, and give the effect of movement.

THIS IS HOW > Chairs and end tables used in pairs at the same distance from the vertical axis secure formal balance and a feeling of repose.

Faithful to the spirit of Queen Anne is this restful and dignified bedroom. The large canopied bed, with its graceful tester and simply turned wood posts, is an attractive example of the period style, as is the bench with its cabriole legs. The wing chairs are modernized Queen Anne pieces. The rambler rose wallpaper with vertical stripes and the formal window treatment contribute to the over-all effect.

on a tripod base. The three legs of the base were cabriole. The design of this table influenced both Chippendale and Duncan Phyfe. Gate-leg and drop leaf tables also mark this period.

The chests and cabinets of Queen Anne no longer used the hooded arch of William and Mary, but substituted the *broken pediment* or bonnet top. Many of the cabinets, finished in lacquer or gilt, were used for bric-a-brac. The broken pediment was also used to decorate the highboys of this period. Low chests, which consisted of the lower portion of the cabinets, found widespread favor. Closely allied decoratively to the lowboys were the flat-topped kneehole desks. The Queen Anne mirror, adopted by the American colonists, was tall, slender and well proportioned. Some were capped with a hood bearing the distinctive shell motif.

Walnut continued as the most popular wood, though oak persisted and mahogany made its debut. The Queen's own interest in needlework led to the use of crewelwork, printed linens, figured chintzes and petit point, while tapestries, velvets and damasks continued in use. Colors were pure and brilliant along with soft blues and greens.

Queen Anne furniture is readily distinguishable by its *simplicity* and its use of *curves*. Compared to earlier styles, pieces are lighter in weight, smaller in scale, more pleasing in line. Design was keynoted to comfort. Beauty resulted, not from lavish embellishment, but from attractive proportions and symmetry. The Dutch cabriole leg, the scallop shell, the broken pediment with its occasional urn finial, all serve to characterize Queen Anne pieces.

The Queen Anne style was a transitional one. It modified the styles of earlier periods and led to the designs of the master craftsmen of the later 18th century. This style fits well into our homes today. The simpler of the Queen Anne pieces are informal, mixing well with Colonial New England and early Chippendale. The more decorative Queen Anne pieces go well in the formal Georgian home.

CHIPPENDALE (1718-1779)

Queen Anne was succeeded on the throne by a succession of three Georges who ruled from 1715 until 1810, the Georgian period. It was an age famous for its Samuel Johnson, Boswell, Garrick, Sir Joshua Reynolds as well as the American Revolution. In the main, early Georgian furniture followed the Queen Anne design, but carvings became more elaborate and ornate. Furniture was gilded. Casters were used for chairs and tables. The cabriole leg was ornamented with satyrs, lions' heads and leaf designs at the knee and with a paw foot.

In 1749, Thomas Chippendale opened his shop in London. He was the first of the master craftsmen who lent their names to styles they devised. The designs Chippendale originated are still widely reproduced. Original Chippendale items bring large prices today.

During different periods of his career, Chippendale drew his inspiration from different sources. His work, therefore, may be classified according to the influence that guided him at the time. The first Chippendale pieces were derived from the English styles of the Queen Anne and Early Georgian periods. The style of the French Regency and Louis XV next influenced him. Later, Chippendale's work expressed the Chinese influence. The fourth influence, in the last days of his career, was the Gothic.

Chippendale is pre-eminent for the chairs he designed, both with and without arms. His chairs are sturdy and broad, with a masculine spirit. Incidentally, Chippendale is respon-

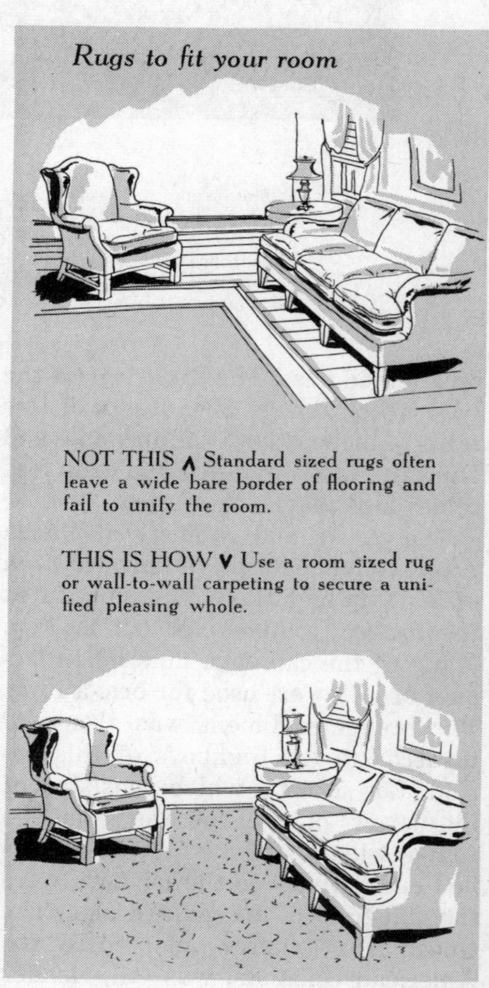

Rugs to fit your room

NOT THIS ^ Standard sized rugs often leave a wide bare border of flooring and fail to unify the room.

THIS IS HOW v Use a room sized rug or wall-to-wall carpeting to secure a unified pleasing whole.

CASUAL AND HOMEY COMFORT

A whitewashed brick fireplace forms the attractive background of this casual living-dining room with its air of homey comfort. The wooden chairs—one with a ladder back and the other with bannister spindles—are typically Colonial. So is the trestle dining table standing against a wood plank wall. The upholstered wood bench presents a readily adaptable idea, now becoming increasingly popular. An apothecary's jar serves as the base of the table lamp. The wall-to-wall contemporary carpeting, in a delightful avocado green, continues up the stairs. This carpeting is woven in a looped pile of varying heights to create a textured tree-bark effect.

BLONDE BEAUTY IN THE BEDROOM

Modern furniture, in blonde birch, lends a cheerful note to an attractive bedroom. The bedspreads are simple and tailored, with patterned shams to match the pattern in the stunning cornice. The draperies repeat the avocado green of the bedspread. The upholstery of the easy chair is cocoa beige, with round toss pillows in dark chocolate brown. The around-the-corner picture grouping is eye-catching. The twin beds are matched by a pair of night stands as well as by an eight-drawer dual dresser. Walls and carpeting are greige.

MODERN IN A FESTIVE MOOD

A red brick wallpaper—contrasted in color by two green philodendron plants—highlights one wall of this Modern dining room. A scalloped cornice, in soft blue to match the remaining walls and the chair seats, frames the sides and top of the window which is covered with a woven wood blind. Glass-chimneyed Modern hurricane lamps add a festive note to the dining table setting while the china sets off the blue-green dinnerware attractively.

sible for standardizing the height of the seat from the floor. If you refer to the *Cavalcade of Furniture Styles,* you will see illustrations of several typical Chippendale chairs.

The *ribband-back* chair illustrates how Chippendale blended diverse influences in his designs. The center splat, which is open, is derived from the Queen Anne fiddle-back chair. The interlacing bands that form the broad top rail with its graceful bow-shaped curves are derived from the French Louis XV. The front legs are cabriole —again Queen Anne—but feature the classical acanthus motif.

The *ladder-back* armchair with its pierced horizontal rails and plain straight legs, is a pleasing fusion of French and Chinese influence. The upholstery entirely covers the seat frame and is attached to the apron with a double row of decorative brass-headed tacks. The *Chinese styled* chair catches the spirit of the Orient in its pattern. The straight legs and Chinese decorative details enjoy widespread popularity today. Other Chinese Chippendale chairs feature pagoda tops, a center splat of fretwork and bamboo legs. Chippendale used lacquer and japanning. He also used gilt to set off his intricate carving. The wing chair is another typical Chippendale piece. It is characterized by its straight legs and very fine proportions.

Chippendale settees had arched backs, the arms were rolled outward, the legs were straight or cabriole. The upholstery that Chippendale used was varied—toile, needlework and tooled leather as well as silk, brocade and damask.

Chippendale's pieces owe much of their beauty to his extraordinary ability as a wood carver. Because mahogany lent itself very readily to his beautifully detailed carving, Chippendale used this wood extensively. For the succeeding Georgian designers, mahogany became the favorite wood, and both Elizabethan oak and Queen Anne walnut were supplanted by it. The Georgian period is often called the Age of Mahogany.

Also famed are Chippendale's cabinets, secretaries and highboys. The broken pediment, which Chippendale adopted, was usually carved with *facing C's* that served as Chippendale's trademark. The bookcases and cabinets have well designed paneled wood or glass doors. His French-type chest of drawers bears the bombe front. The French rococo gilt mirror is one of Chippendale's most sought after pieces.

Chippendale also produced large numbers of tables of various types. The center shaft of these tables is sometimes elaborate in detail. He used the Queen Anne tripod base in his tilt top tables. The borders of these tables were intricately carved in *pie-crust* form.

Though he borrowed many of his decorative designs, Chippendale blended them into subtle proportions with beautiful over-all effect. It is a mark of his genius that he usually improved upon his sources. The characteristics that distinguish Chippendale's pieces are their superb artistry, the rich texture of their mahogany and the exquisite detail of their carving. Chippendale was the foremost wood carver of his age. His decorations are not mere ornamental additions but are unified with the structural elements of his design.

Perhaps no other name is so glamorous as his in the history of furniture styles. Chinese Chippendale and the smaller pieces of his early designs

Italian provincial furniture in rich fruitwood here adorns a delightful bedroom with many a decorative touch. The white chintz quilted bedspreads and bolsters are trimmed with gold braid. The cornices also consist of quilted white chintz and gold trimming, while gold braid again is found in the floor-length curtains. A chaise with clean, simple lines provides seating comfort. The wrought iron table which serves as a vanity is a novel touch. Besides white, the color scheme includes tones of beige and deep gray, with the wallpaper supplying pattern interest.

Ever-lovely French Provincial provides the furniture in this spacious formal bed-sitting room. The headboard of the full-sized bed is outlined with ball fringe, as is the top of the two-piece bedspread. Glass lusters add a period touch to the lamps which stand on night tables finished in antique white and gilt. The exposed wood of the chaise repeats this finish, a favorite with the French Provincial style of furniture. Simple soft sheer curtains cover the window. Mahogany tables and side-chair offer contrast both in woods and style.

A contemporary sectional sofa here combines with more-popular-than-ever French Provincial tables to form a lovely around-the-corner conversation grouping. The corner table, with its cut-away upper tier, not only keeps the table lamp clear of elbows but allows access to the broad lower shelf. The corner lamp, too, repeats the black and white of the upholstery fabric in its shade. And though the two lamps differ, they do go well together, being the same in scale and height and having carved wood bases.

Provincial furniture with Old World charm against today's suave background highlights this attractive dining room setting. The walls are fashionably dark in tone, with white trim and dining appointments. The lower section of the windows bears a brise bise curtain — a provincial French treatment now popular — flanked by sill length draperies. A pair of scales serve as fruit bowls on the oval cabriole-legged table. Note the attractive carving on the provincial hutch. A sculptured floral carpet, with a ground of hard twist yarn, introduces a pleasant pattern into the room.

A curved sectional sofa—its seat cushions and back upholstered in a bold pattern—here stands against a dark wall for contrast. For such a sofa, a round or oval cocktail table is especially appropriate. Curved sofas—one-piece or sectional—may capitalize to the full on a corner, a broad window or a fireplace. To tie the pieces in this picture together, the club chair is upholstered in the solid fabric found on the sofa. Behind the sofa, too, is an accordion-type door, much used as room dividers.

A pair of Modern sectional pieces, upholstered in a nubby fabric, here capitalize on a corner to form an attractive conversation center. Accessories, in the form of matching prints on the walls, table lamps, round cocktail table and porcelain bibelots, introduce a restrained Chinese note. Flowers and plants also provide a pleasing touch of color to this setting. The club chair in the left foreground is upholstered in a damask with a diamond motif. The wall-to-wall carpeting is a hard twist broadloom—a type ranking high in popularity.

An unusual cocktail table—its design inspired by an airplane view of the Mesa lands of the American Southwest—provides the focus of a stunning conversation center in a Modern combination living-dining room. The dramatic quality of the furniture is enhanced by the simple and uncluttered functional arrangement of the pieces. The sofa and matching bench both consist of foam rubber on a webbed frame. Along with the chairs, these pieces are upholstered in a beige and white textured fabric. The white is picked up in the walls, sheer curtains, accent rug and in the Italian Creme marble floor. Toss pillows on the sofa of pink and chartreuse introduce color.

One-room bachelor quarters is the theme of this handsome setting which, though compact, gives a feeling of roominess. The around-the-corner bookcases, their recesses painted a warm red, form an attractive background for the desk center. The striking window shade of natural linen with charcoal adds a note of elegance. The charcoal is picked up by the chair and ottoman whose blonde wood frames contrast with the mahogany butler table. A light wood paper in a checkerboard pattern covers the walls and repeats the pattern of the oak flooring.

are today's favorite selections from his work.

ROBERT ADAM (1728-1792)

In discussing the selection of furniture, it was pointed out that the architecture of your house may influence your choice of furniture style. The importance of this point is emphasized by the career of Robert Adam.

Adam himself was not a furniture craftsman, but an architect. He became interested in classical architecture, traveled to Italy and visited Rome and the newly uncovered ruins of Pompeii. Upon his return, Adam led a movement that was instrumental in reviving English interest in forms and decorative motifs patterned after the ancient Roman ideals. This *neo-classic* movement, however, ran into difficulty. The furniture style of the period was not suited to Adam's neo-classic architecture. He found it necessary to design furniture that would harmonize with his concepts.

Robert Adam and his three brothers established on architectural and interior decoration business in 1760 under the tradename Adelphi, meaning "brothers." The Adelphi met with immediate acclaim and Robert Adam was appointed architect to the king. They themselves did not manufacture furniture but drew up designs that were executed by other craftsmen, including Chippendale and Hepplewhite.

In keeping with the classical spirit, the furniture designed by Adam was varied in design, refined in line and geometric in proportion. Straight lines and curves were both employed. The style is delicate and graceful. Adam chairs dropped the cabriole leg for the straight tapering leg, either square or round, plain or fluted. The chair backs similarly vary from oblong to shield shape. The chair backs and rear legs were curved. Cane was sometimes used for the center panel of chair backs. Seats, arm rests and occasionally chair backs were upholstered. Stretchers were seldom used.

Robert Adam is best known for the sideboard, which he popularized for

For roomy, orderly arrangement

NOT THIS < Avoid a diagonal or cater-cornered placement for large pieces of furniture.

THIS IS HOW > Be sure the furniture is parallel to the wall for a roomier, more orderly arrangement.

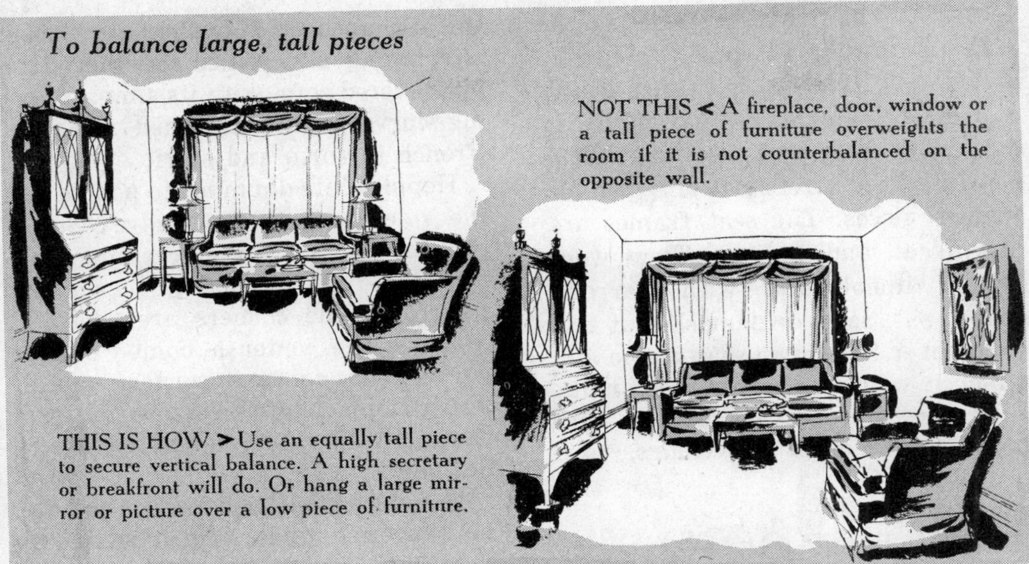

dining room use, the console table, the cabinet and the settee. Adam sideboards were semi-oval or rectangular in contour, often with a marble top. The decoration consisted of carving in low relief of classical motifs. Some pieces used human and animal figures for ornamentation. The woods were mahogany and the lighter satinwood, often painted, inlaid or gilded. The fabrics were brocades, damasks and striped satins. Adam green was a favorite color.

The Adam pieces were principally intended for the dining room. Originally creating for the homes of the very wealthy, the Adam brothers did, however, greatly influence furniture styles of their period. The *Classic Modern* style of today owes its simplicity of line to the style of the Adam brothers.

HEPPLEWHITE (?—1786)

The two main influences in the designs of George Hepplewhite are the neo-classicism of Adam and the French style of Louis XVI. As with Chippendale, however, these influences were modified by the individuality of the designer. Hepplewhite's furniture, though slender and delicate in appearance, is actually sturdy. In scale, his furniture is smaller than that of his predecessors, with emphasis on *curved lines* and *lightness.* As a result, it is feminine and refined in spirit, graceful in appearance. His furniture was constructed of mahogany and satinwood, with inlays of rare imported woods.

The *Cavalcade of Furniture Styles* illustrates three typical Hepplewhite chairs. He confined ornamentation almost wholly to the chair backs. His *shield-shaped* back is pierced, not solid as it was in the original Adam design. Unlike the practice in earlier styles, the chair back is low, freed from the seat frame and supported only by two posts—a design that may suggest extreme delicacy. The front legs are straight, very often with a *spade foot,* while the back legs are raked.

The *oval-back* chair uses as its

decoration the Prince of Wales feathers, a motif that Hepplewhite originated. The *interlocking heart* chair, with its St. Valentine's day motif, is especially lovely and beguiling. Hepplewhite used stretchers only for his heavier pieces. The seat frames are curvilinear and various. They were usually upholstered with narrow-striped silk, satin or damask that was pulled over the entire seat frame and attached with decorative brass nails.

Hepplewhite settees usually followed the lines of his chairs, with shield-shaped and oval chair backs alternating and joined together. His upholstered sofa, with its simple flowing curves and out-turned arms, is French in form and spirit.

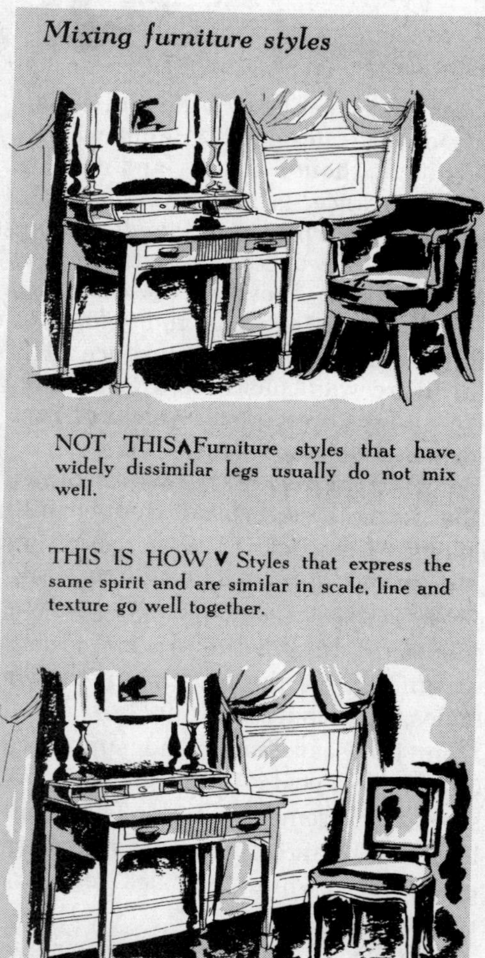

Mixing furniture styles

NOT THIS ^ Furniture styles that have widely dissimilar legs usually do not mix well.

THIS IS HOW v Styles that express the same spirit and are similar in scale, line and texture go well together.

Hepplewhite did much to popularize the sideboard. He not only reduced the size of the Adam creation, but introduced the *serpentine curve* for its front. The corners are typically *concave,* the center a bombe convex curve. The concave corners distinguish Hepplewhite's sideboards from those of Sheraton, a contemporary designer.

Hepplewhite is well known, too, for his Pembroke table, a form devised by Sheraton. This type of table is delicate and graceful, with a pair of circular drop leaves. The design is classic in its restraint and simplicity and marked by pleasing proportions. The double pedestal table, for dining room use, is similarly simple in its line. Many fine mahogany reproductions of these pieces are used in our homes today.

The furniture that Hepplewhite built was intended, in the main, for homes designed by Robert Adam. This furniture embodies the dual purpose that Hepplewhite set for his design, "To unite elegance and utility, and blend the useful with the agreeable." This aim has a modern overtone and, in fact, much in Classic Modern is derived from this master craftman.

SHERATON (1751—1806)

It is sometimes difficult to distinguish between the styles of Hepplewhite and Thomas Sheraton, the fourth of the great 18th century English furniture designers. The reason perhaps lies in the fact that both these men drew inspiration from the same sources, the neo-classic movement and Louis XVI. In addition, Sheraton and Hepplewhite influenced each other. Sheraton's later designs were influenced by the style of the French Empire.

The difference between the designs of Hepplewhite and Sheraton is often one of detail. Thus Sheraton sideboards are characterized by *convex* corner construction in contrast to Hepplewhite's concave corners. Sheraton sideboards are, as a result, somewhat more capacious than those of Hepplewhite.

Like Robert Adam, Thomas Sheraton was not himself a manufacturer, but a designer of furniture. His designs are exquisite and ingenious, his contributions original and important. His life was a constant struggle against poverty. His varied ability permitted him to act as a drawing master, lay preacher, writer and publisher. The designs he created are contained in several books that he wrote.

Sheraton's designs are *small in scale, delicate* and *simple* yet structurally sound and sturdy. If anything, Sheraton's furniture is even narrower and more slender than that of Hepplewhite. Unlike Hepplewhite, Sheraton stressed the *straight line,* though he did use some curves. Sheraton employed more underbracing than did Hepplewhite and seldom covered the entire seat frame of his chairs with upholstery.

Sheraton chairs illustrate his preference for the straight line. The chair back is rectangular or occasionally square. The rear legs and posts of the chair back are continuous. The chair seat is forthright in its lines, sometimes caned. The legs taper and are square or round, often reeded.

Sheraton used the classic urn, lattice work and rectilinear bars to form the panel of the chair back. He also used the lyre back, derived from Adam and made famous by Duncan Phyfe. The use of horizontal bars, as in the third chair illustrated in the *Cavalcade of Furniture Styles,* shows French Empire influence. The bar connecting the back braces and paralleling the chair seat is a distinct Sheraton contribution.

Sheraton is renowned for his tables. He devised the *Pembroke table.* One of his dining room tables is the precursor of present-day *double-duty* pieces, an idea Sheraton gave to the world. It consists of a drop leaf table to which may be fitted two half-round end tables. The two end tables can be used together or separately, depending upon the combination desired. Sheraton's delicate five-legged card table is, as its extra leg indicates, an extension table.

Sheraton desks, famous for their secret compartments, are often double-duty as well. He designed the first roll-top desk and the first twin beds. He also popularized the kidney-shaped table from the French style of Louis XV. His kidney-shaped tables serve both as dressing table and desk, as the upper drawer and mirror section is removable. Sheraton mirrors, in gilt frames, embody both his rectilinear lines and restrained classic urn finial. His breakfront exhibits very fine proportions and pleasing glass paneled doors. Sheraton breakfronts and tables find ready reception in today's homes done in the traditional style.

Sheraton used mahogany and satinwood, the latter mainly for his living room pieces. He introduced the use of harewood. Sheraton is noted for

the delicacy of his inlays, his distinctive form of decoration. He also used veneers and restrained carving as decoration, while some of his chairs are painted with a soft green background color. Plain and striped silks with dainty floral design as well as gold and silver brocades were his favorite upholstery materials. Especially fond of cool blue, he used this color combined with white, black or yellow, in his upholstery.

The last of the great 18th century designers, Sheraton is perhaps the greatest of them all. His originality and contributions are unsurpassed, even though his predecessors had developed the art of furniture design to new heights.

MIXING GEORGIAN STYLES

Sheraton furniture mixes so very well with Hepplewhite pieces that one authority has referred to the Hepplewhite-Sheraton style. Both these styles blend wtih Adam, Duncan Phyfe, Classic Modern, and certain of the Louis XV and Louis XVI pieces. In addition, certain of Sheraton's pieces that employ Directoire and French Empire characteristics, will blend with these early 19th century French styles.

The smaller-sized Chippendale pieces, as well as Chinese Chippendale, are readily usable with the late 18th century Georgian styles of Adam, Hepplewhite and Sheraton. These styles mix well, not only because they are similar in scale and in woods, but they all embody the 18th century English tradition and spirit, modified by classic and French influences. More, each style reflects the personality of the creative spirit that designed it. As a result, mixing secures a rich yet subtle variety.

The Georgian Age was the golden age of English furniture design. If you wish to achieve dignity, richness and graciousness in your home, you can do no better than choose these styles.

LOUIS XIV (*Quatorze*—1643-1715)

With Louis XIV, the great Renaissance movement began to ebb in France. A new influence arose—the baroque style. This style replaced the straight lines of Renaissance furniture with *short, stopped curves* and reduced the size of the pieces. The baroque style, in time, developed into the flowing serpentine curves of the rococo style, a style that influenced the work of English designers from Chippendale onwards. At its extreme, all lines were curved.

Louis XIV loved splendor and pomp. At his famous court in Versailles, he indulged his love with an extravagance that has never been surpassed. The construction of this famous palace stimulated art work throughout France. Cabinet makers, including Andre Charles Boulle who devised the decorative Boulle work process, were set up at the newly established Louvre. Tapestry and silk factories received royal patronage and support.

French furniture of this period was movable though bulky. As the baroque tendency developed, the later Louis XIV chairs became feminine in appearance. Size was further reduced, upholstery no longer covered the arms and seat frames. Curves softened the straight lines and the arms acquired a graceful sloping curve while the legs became cabriole in front, ornately carved at the knee and terminated in scroll or hoof feet. The rear legs were gracefully curved. Even the X-shaped stretcher took on a sinuous serpentine curve. Carving in low relief appeared on the apron of the seat frame.

Because of the enormous hoop skirts in vogue at the time, ladies had to sit on stools or taborets. Benches were also used. The sedan chair made its debut. The sofa and chaise longue also provided seating facilities.

LOUIS XV (*Quinze*—1715-1774)

Louis XIV outlived his son and grandson. Upon the monarch's death, the succession fell to his great-grandson, then five years of age. A regent, Philippe of Orleans, governed for the first eight years of Louis XV's reign.

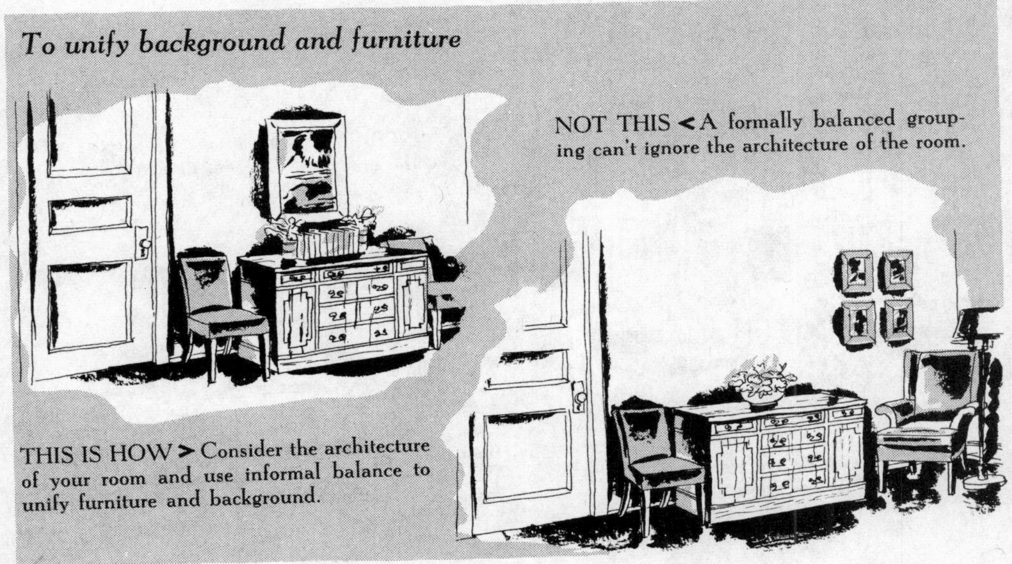

The restraining influence of Louis XIV's imperious will was ended. Under the regent, frivolity and gayety reached new heights.

The French Regency furniture of this period reflected this subtle change. Although the baroque tendency still ruled, rococo ornamentation appeared. The tendency toward daintiness and femininity of size, line, color and decoration, which evidenced itself during the late years of Louis XIV, received new impetus. This style is, accordingly, a transitional one.

As Louis XV's reign continued, the baroque influence waned. *Femininity* in line, size and spirit grew more pronounced. Frivolity and gayety expressed themselves in the feeling of the style. Tapestry mirrored the feminine trend, portraying romantic and pastoral scenes. Never were *curves* so freely employed. Restraint was swept aside, under the siren call of the rococo. Ornamentation became elaborate and luxurious, an end in itself.

Under the guidance of Madame Pompadour, the Chinese influence became marked. This influence spread into a vogue for *chinoiserie,* a French interpretation of Chinese decorative motifs. *Asymmetric balance* appeared in the design and ornamentation of chair aprons, so deftly executed that the onlooker had to look closely to detect it.

The strong deep colors of the early Renaissance period gave way to soft, dainty feminine pastels and silvery grays. Chinese lacquer acquired wide popularity. New woods came into use, along with walnut, mahogany and oak which still retained favor. Wood was painted and gilded and marquetry was extensively used. This style is responsible in large measure for the French Provincial style of furniture in vogue today.

LOUIS XVI (*Seize*—1774-1793)

There was much that was beautiful in the rococo style of Louis XV. It did, however, lose its sense of moderation. Reaction set in. The time was

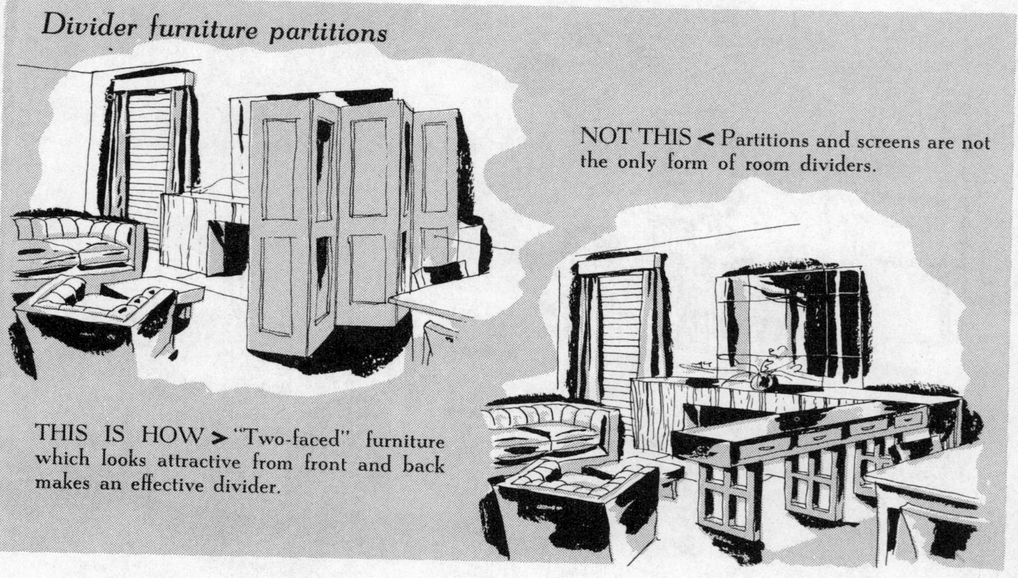

Divider furniture partitions

NOT THIS < Partitions and screens are not the only form of room dividers.

THIS IS HOW > "Two-faced" furniture which looks attractive from front and back makes an effective divider.

ripe for a new style. The new style that arose was, like that of the Adam brothers in England, a classic style, influenced by the archaeological discoveries at Pompeii. After Louis XVI and Marie Antoinette ascended the throne, neo-classicism was encouraged. Emphasis was upon the simple life, a romantic Rousseauistic return to nature.

The neo-classicism of Louis XVI was refined and delicate, simple in its lines, exquisite in its craftsmanship. The classical was blended with the utilitarian. *Straight lines* and *rectangular forms* largely replaced the curves and ovals of the earlier style. Decoration was subordinated to line, producing a dainty, graceful effect. Love knots, bows and arrows, cherubs, doves and honeysuckle were used in decoration to accent the feminine note.

Mahogany, satinwood and rosewood were employed, usually enameled or gilded. Damasks, taffetas, and brocades were usually striped. Toiles de Jouy, bearing pastoral scenes, appeared for informal rooms.

The furniture was reduced in size. Curves appeared only in oval chair backs and in arms. The cabriole leg was replaced with a tapering, straight leg, reeded or fluted. The low *ottoman* came into use. The small powder tables—poudreuses—grew in favor. Beds were placed in curtained alcoves. Their head and footboards were upholstered.

The style of Louis XVI influenced the French Provincial styles so popular today. The Louis XVI style, despite its increasing simplicity, breathed an air of elegance, formality and aristocracy.

FRENCH PROVINCIAL

The French styles that we have so far considered were all court styles. These court styles, however, influenced the furniture style throughout France. The styles that we shall refer to as French Provincial were the styles that developed in the provinces. The influence of the court styles was uneven in its effect. Local differences in custom and tradition, climate, and native craftsmanship contributed to these differences. The ease of communication also played a role. The provincial style that developed is, nevertheless, classifiable into two general types—*city* and *country* style. The *Cavalcade of Furniture Styles* makes this distinction clear.

The country folk, peasants in the main, were traditionally conservative. Their resources, furthermore, were limited. The furniture that they built for themselves, or that local cabinet makers constructed, was simpler in design than that of the city resident. Furniture styles changed far less swiftly among the country people and were less influenced by the vogue of the court. What was built was expected to last. In the construction, they used the woods that were at hand. They interpreted the fashion so as to meet their particular needs and fit their surroundings. *Utility* and *comfort* were of greater moment than ostentation and luxury.

The city Provincial style is far closer to the spirit of the court styles. It did simplify the rococo curves and embellishment of the Louis XV manner. It similarly softened the straight lines and rectangular shapes of the Louis XVI style. The city style copied the court in making the upholstery a part of the chair. *Subdued curves* were used, with pleasing effect, in the chair backs, arms, apron and legs. *Restrained carving* was used for decoration.

Fashionable is the word for this formal living room done in the graceful manner of the French Provincial style. The soft curves of the furniture are in pleasant contrast to the rectilinear lines of the panelled wall. Decorative marble, popular once again, forms the top of the square coffee table, with its slender cabriole legs and distinctively carved apron.

Much of the furniture sold today as Louis XV is actually the modified Provincial furniture in the city style. This style retained the femininity of the court. The beds in the city style usually have upholstered headboards with delicately curved wood frames. This type of bedroom furniture is very popular today.

As a rule, city style furniture is *formal* in spirit as well as *feminine*. It uses—not the rough weaves and cottons of the informal country style — but silks, damasks, satins and smooth textures. It combines well with Aubusson rugs and tapestries. Walnut, chestnut and fruitwoods are employed. It is, very often, a restrained, simplified, beautiful rendering of the style of Louis XV.

One of the chief differences between the country and the city style is evident in the chairs and settees. The country style uses a *ladder-back* type, fitted with a removable squab cushion, a cane or straw seat. The legs frequently combine the straight rounded leg of Louis XVI with the cabriole leg of earlier styles. The lines are straight, the shape rectangular. Curves, if used, are gentle. Decoration is unpretentious, consisting of a simple urn finial, bun feet and turning. The over-all effect is simple, sturdy, *informal* and "countrified."

The city style chair, however, not only would have unremovable upholstery, but it would conform more closely in line to either Louis XV or XVI. It would have less of the country and more of the city in it. The back would be slanted, the arms upholstered, the apron would bear a serpentine curve, and the legs would be cabriole. The effect would be dignified and graceful, not rustic, sturdy and quaint as was the country style.

The country style used handmade weaves and toiles de Jouy. The furniture was finished in wax without staining or painted in bright colors. Little attempt was made to attain intricate detail. Some of the larger pieces—tables, armoires and cabinets—were common to both styles. Armoires added open shelves to become cupboards for bric-a-brac.

The country style blends well with early New England Colonial, informal Queen Anne and cottage and farmhouse types of furniture. The city style goes well with the more formal Queen Anne pieces, with the simpler Georgian and Chippendale pieces, Louis XV and Louis XVI, Duncan Phyfe and Classic Modern.

DIRECTOIRE (1795-1799)
FRENCH EMPIRE (1799-1815)

The French Revolution, which began in 1789, introduced a spirit of republicanism into France. The spirit was a revulsion against everything that smacked of aristocracy and the ancien regime. Liberte, egalite, fraternite was the slogan. With the execution of Robespierre, a Directory of five men was established to rule France.

Under the five-man Directory, a Jury of Arts and Manufacturers controlled the design of furniture. Royal and aristocratic tendencies were purged. The Directoire style, the style that replaced the designs of Louis XVI, was a transitional one. It retained the classic elements, the influence of Greece and the Roman Empire, but simplified ornamentation. Decoration was classic or bore such republican motifs as the eagle and tricolor cockade. The furniture of this period is unpretentious yet graceful in its classicism, pure in line and slender in proportion. Striped brocades, damasks and velvets were used, along with yellow, black and gold.

Directoire furniture finds use in almost every room of the modern

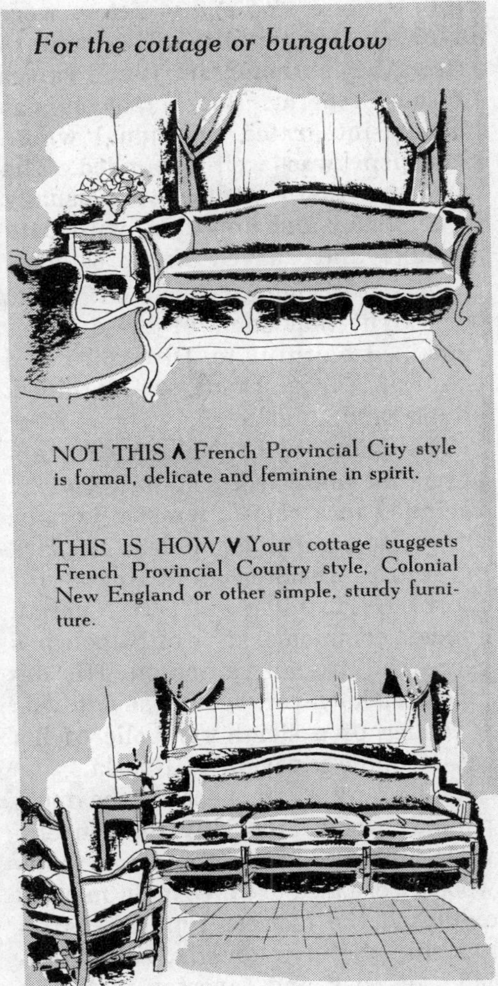

NOT THIS ∧ French Provincial City style is formal, delicate and feminine in spirit.

THIS IS HOW ∨ Your cottage suggests French Provincial Country style, Colonial New England or other simple, sturdy furniture.

home. It is formal, yet unaffected. Directoire chairs and bedroom furniture are appealingly graceful in line.

With the rise of Napoleon and the initial success of his army, the Directoire style developed into the French Empire style. This style reflected the dominating personality of the military leader who inspired it. Napoleon's love of pomp and splendor, his military prowess, his admiration for ancient Italy, Greece and Egypt, his dynastic ambitions, all contributed to the formation of the style.

The style was not a homogeneous, clean-cut one. Too many factors were involved. The stylists attempted to reflect the character, spirit and values of the Emperor. But Napoleon was not an integrated individual whose classicism was well grounded. The furniture that resulted was usually large, heavy and imposing, with both straight and curved lines, ostentatious and grandiose in effect. Yet to the extent that some of these pieces remained faithful to Directoire and classical forms, they were dignified, simple and unaffected.

The influence of Napoleon is apparent in many ways. His initial N, encircled in a classic wreath, became a favorite decorative emblem. His lack of stature resulted in a vogue for short beds, fashioned after a Venetian gondola commemorative of Napoleon's successful Italian campaign. His detractors, however, would say it was a replica of a sleigh symbolic of his catastrophic invasion of Russia.

Mahogany again became the most popular wood, especially for veneers, with rosewood. Ebony and the fruitwoods were also used. Ormolu mounts exhibited the highest type of craftsmanship. Solid color silk, satin, brocade, damask and tapestry were the fabrics. The colors were ruby red, bright yellow, royal blue and purple, emerald green and gold.

Today's French Empire reproductions, usually of bedroom and dining room furniture, are smaller in scale. They nevertheless retain the classical line as well as French Empire decoration and color. Both the Directoire and French Empire styles influenced Duncan Phyfe in the creation of the Federal American style.

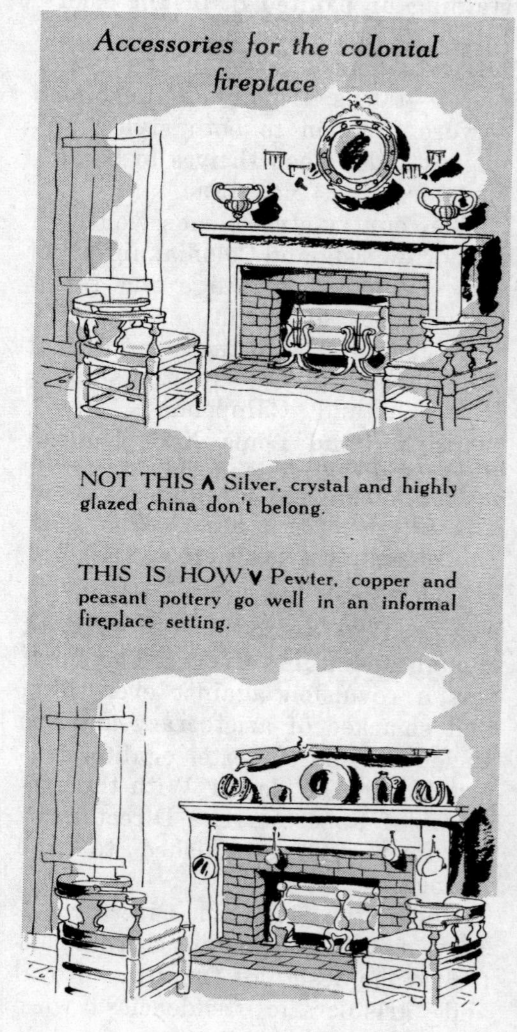

This authentic New England Colonial dining room eloquently testifies to the skill of early American cabinet makers. The spooned curves of the fiddleback chairs, with their rush seats and turned legs, are especially attractive. The massive court cupboard is sturdy and well proportioned. Note also the hanging corner cabinet, the wainscotted wall, the pewter and china accessories, and the wide plank floor.

BIEDERMEIER (1800-1830)

The influence of the French Empire style led the people of Germany and Austria to create a variation that has been named Biedermeier, after a character who appeared in cartoons of the day. "Papa Biedermeier" was supposed to typify the views of the populace.

This style simplified the decorative excesses of the French Empire pieces. The classic decorative motifs were augmented with figures of common flowers, animals and humans. This addition very often introduced a simple playful note and gives this furniture a spirit of liveliness, gayety, humor and informality.

Light woods were used, with contrasting dark woods as insets. Stencilled borders contributed to the appeal of these pieces. Lines were simplified, sturdiness was stressed, ornateness and elaboration were eliminated. Biedermeier furniture is used today for bedrooms and dining rooms, though occasional pieces produced for the living room introduce a quality all their own.

COLONIAL NEW ENGLAND (1720-1800)

The American colonists who left England in the 17th century brought little in material goods with them. Instead, they brought courage, determination and ambition. Their first aim was to achieve a foothold in the New World, to obtain the necessities for survival. They hewed the forests, tilled the soil and built rough shelters within stockades. Their flintlocks were their ever-present companions. Only after they had conquered the immediate demands of existence were they able to indulge their austere artistic impulses. Then they sought comfort and a humble beauty consistent with their deep religious spirit.

The craftsmanship of the colonists was of a high order. They recalled the styles that they and their forebears had used in 16th and 17th century England, and patterned their pieces after them. In doing so, however, they were not content simply to copy. They varied the originals, added new features to them and gave them a final form and spirit that are distinctively American. From these modest beginnings, a style arose—Colonial New England.

The colonists took the English Windsor chair of the Restoration period and produced it in several varieties. One variety added an additional set of spindles to the top of the chair back that served as a head-rest. This quaint innovation received the name *combback Windsor*. Other variations were known as the fanback and the loopback. The seats were saddle shaped. The spindles, legs and stretchers were turned. Native woods replaced the yew wood of the English original. *Rockers* were a Colonial invention.

If you refer to the *Cavalcade of Furniture Styles* appearing on the inside of the back cover, you will see illustrations of early American furniture. The ladder-back and splat-back chairs are also typical New England pieces. The rear legs and back posts of these chairs consisted of one continuous straight shaft with decorative turnings. These chairs all appeared in a variety of forms. Some had arms, others omitted them. Seats were rush, cane or wooden. Few chairs were provided with cushions.

The bannister-back chair was also produced. The fiddle-back chair was adopted from the Queen Anne model.

For a cheerful dinette

NOT THIS ʌ Entire pieces of furniture painted in solid bright colors are hard to live with.

THIS IS HOW v Paint the furniture in soft, muted colors and stencil gay tulips and hearts on chairs and around the windows in Pennsylvania Dutch fashion.

Stencilled "him" and "her" chairs capture the gay flavor of the Pennsylvania Dutch style. The triangular cupboard in the corner with its characteristic tulip design is both attractive and useful. Informal furniture of this style goes well in the small dinette.

The Queen Anne cabriole leg was given a club foot. Its curves were reduced, the shell carving on its knee was made less prominent. This variation of the cabriole leg was given the picturesque name—*bandy* leg.

Tables appeared in a wide variety of pleasing forms. The trestle table was an early form. The gate-leg table of the rural England of William and Mary's time, with its drop leaves, was a favorite Colonial piece. This table led to the delightful *butterfly* table, a Colonial invention that gained its name from the shape of the support for its drop leaves. A curious early Colonial double-purpose piece is the *chairtable.*

Many pieces combined different woods. Maple and pine were widely used woods, along with birch, walnut, fruitwoods, hickory and oak. Decoration was restrained and simple, appearing in wood turning and flat carving. Handwrought hardware took decorative forms. Brass, pewter and silver were popular accessories, as andirons, sconces, candle-holders and teapots. Bevelled mirrors of the Queen Anne type, in broad frames, also were popular.

Crewelwork, cretonnes, homespuns and calicoes, with small all-over patterns, were the distinctive Colonial fabrics. Candlewick bedspreads and patchwork quilts are also typically Colonial. The New Englander used *quaint* mixtures of colors—mustard yellow, cranberry red, blue and olive green. Tan, brown and beige were also used, while white was a favorite color.

Today, Colonial New England furniture may be used with bright clear colors that express informality. The Colonial style is charming in its quaintness. It is *picturesque, simple* and *sincere,* with an individuality of its own, offering vast possibilities to one on a limited budget. Its sturdiness and character make it a wise choice for children's rooms.

This style mixes well with Queen Anne. It blends exceptionally well with Pennsylvania Dutch, French Provincial country style and early Chippendale pieces form pleasing combinations with it. This style is often combined today with upholstered pieces, unknown in early times, but which capture the same gay, informal spirit.

PENNSYLVANIA DUTCH

The German settlers, who began to arrive in Pennsylvania in the late 17th century, produced a gay and charming Pennsylvania Dutch style that is popular today. These settlers, like the early Puritans, were religious refugees. Their religious convictions were strong. Unlike the Puritans, however, they felt that life should be joyful and pleasant. This attitude permeated their homes and furniture.

Pennsylvania Dutch is simple, varied and utilitarian, and expresses a *lightness* and *friendliness* that are a pleasure to behold. One type of chair consists of four tapering round legs, straight in line but attached at a pleasant angle, with a plain wood seat and an attractively carved solid wood back. The armchairs resemble the New England ladder-back chair and fiddle-back chair. If anything, the wood turning is somewhat plainer, the seat square.

Tables similarly bear a family resemblance to the New England style. The *sawbuck table* resembled the trestle table. While in the New England style the trestles usually consisted of two straight, crossed diagonals, the Pennsylvania Dutch trestles are decorated with curves. The drop leaf table was also used by the Pennsylvania Dutch, with butterfly supports for the leaves, heavy, low stretchers and term legs. Dressers, cupboards, chests, wall cabinets, beds and settees likewise were constructed in many different, gay forms.

The lighthearted, informal quaintness of Pennsylvania Dutch is a spirit that holds wide attraction today. Many a room has been done in this style at very little cost. The recipe merely calls for unpainted furniture, a few stencils and some paint. Paint the furniture any color you wish. Stencil the picturesque hearts, tulips and fourleaf clovers, which were the symbolic decorations of these people, in bright, vivid colors on your furniture. Blue, red, yellow and lavender are favorites. Add rag rugs and colorful cotton fabrics. Use a wallpaper with the same motifs. Your room will be cozy and pleasant.

Pennsylvania Dutch is a simple, sturdy *country* style. It mixes well with other informal, spontaneous styles, like Colonial New England and French country Provincial. If you turn back to illustrated color scheme number six in the last chapter, you will see another illustration of this carefree, delightful style.

DUNCAN PHYFE (1768-1854)
FEDERAL AMERICAN

As the American Colonies prospered, many pieces of Georgian furniture were imported from England. The finer homes of Philadelphia, New York and Virginia created a demand for the fashionable English styles. Craftsmen sprang up in the Colonies who adapted the Georgian styles to American tastes. The less lavish Queen Anne style was superseded by a vogue for Chippendale. Especially did Chinese Chippendale catch on. Mahogany became the preferred wood. While all this did not serve to create a distinctive new style, it did pave the way for Duncan Phyfe, one of the greatest designers of the 19th century.

Phyfe's work falls into three periods, his ealiest period being between 1795 and 1820. During this period, Phyfe felt the influence of Adam, Hepplewhite and Sheraton. Phyfe took Adam's lyre back and gave it a new beauty. He adopted the pedestal base for his tables and endowed the flared legs with a graceful outward sweep. The cornucopia leg was a favorite for his sofas, as you may see by referring to the inside back cover.

Phyfe's use of the *curve* is consummate. His tables are perhaps his outstanding work, while his sofas attained a beauty never reached before. The furniture that Phyfe produced during this first period of his career is considered his finest. *Elegant* and *formal,* it mixes especially well with the styles of the Georgian designers who influenced him.

As a result of the War of 1812, British styles lost favor in America. Meantime, the styles of the Directoire and the French Empire had spread across the ocean. Phyfe trimmed his work to conform to this new taste. The style that arose is the Federal American.

Under the sway of this style, furniture became massive and elaborate, with much embellishment. The restraint of the Georgian designs was abandoned. Phyfe was forced to cater to the popular taste. He adopted the Roman curule with paw feet for his chairs. Veneering was extensively used. *Patriotic motifs*—gilded eagles, stars and stripes—took the place of the Napoleonic N. The acanthus leaf carvings, sheaves of wheat, laurel and pineapples were similarly featured.

Phyfe used a wide range of colors. Marine blue was a favorite. Deep, bright reds, grass green, yellow and champagne were also used. For upholstery, Phyfe used horsehair and mohair in addition to silk, satin, brocade and damask.

Federal American, in today's reproductions, has shed a large share

Arranging furniture in the formal room

NOT THIS < Asymmetry in furniture arrangement is full of life and movement and makes for informality.

THIS IS HOW > Dignity, reserve and formality come with bisymmetric balance. It's also restful and soothing.

of its superfluities while the intrinsic merit of its lines and forms has been enhanced. Genuine Federal American pieces go well with their modernized version. Federal American mixes well with Directoire and French Empire, as well as with English Regency.

ENGLISH REGENCY (1810-1820)

George III was declared mentally incompetent in 1810. The Prince of Wales was appointed regent and served in that capacity until he ascended the throne as George IV in 1820. The furniture style that crystallized in England at that time takes the name English Regency. It should not be confused with the French Regency style that developed under Philippe of Orleans a hundred years earlier.

The English Regency style drew its inspiration from the later Sheraton and from the classical. As a result, the English Regency style, with its *classic form,* bears a similarity to French Empire and Federal American. This likeness seems paradoxical, for both France and America were seeking a style that would have little or nothing to do with English design.

Mahogany, satinwood and rosewood were the chief woods of English Regency. Black lacquer and gilt were used with the fruitwoods. Ormolu, metal and ebony inlays ornamented the designs. Stars and lions' and griffins' heads appeared in decoration, as

English Regency furniture in a faithful period setting is an ever popular style for the present-day home in the traditional manner. The plumed pedestal table and the gilt mirror are typical Regency pieces while the dark walls with contrasting white wood trim are distinctive of the decoration of this period. The swags and jabots of the draperies and the bisymmetrically balanced arrangement of the furniture are in keeping with the restrained, dignified atmosphere of the room.

A Victorian tufted satin chair blends with the curved lines of drapery and flower stand, and contrasts with the vertical stripes of the wallpaper. A patterned glass curtain is used for the window.

did lions' and dogs' paws. Bamboo trim, metal and grille work were popular. Hardware was an important element of decoration.

The facades of classic Roman buildings, complete with pilasters, inspired the designs of secretaries, credenzas, bookcases and highboys. Tall fluted columns were used as flower stands. Metal grille work supplanted the earlier paneled glass doors. Upholstered stools, reminiscent of the Roman curule, desks and pedestal tables with columnar shafts, similarly evidenced classic influence. Striped fabrics of damask, silk and brocade were used as upholstery. The most popular color was Regency green, which was combined with browns and reds. Gold, black and white usually served as accents.

This style is now reproduced in *sophisticated* modernized form. English Regency mixes well with both French Empire and Federal American. Sheraton, Duncan Phyfe and Chinese Chippendale also blend well with it. It produces an effect of *richness, elegance* and *formality.*

VICTORIAN (1837-1901)

The furniture style that arose during the gaslight era of Queen Victoria in England spread to America. It was a period of propriety and sentimentality, of prosperity and a deep-seated affection for the home. The Victorian style contains elements of Greek classicism and Louis XV. To Napoleonic French Empire it owes its addition of Venetian and Egyptian influence, while the building of the Suez canal inspired the use of Turkish motifs. Diverse as were its sources, many pieces of Victorian furniture are quaint, homey and delightful.

The furniture was substantially constructed. Pieces varied in size from the small-scaled table to the oversized sofas and gigantic dressers. While straight lines appear, voluminous curves were used. *Black walnut* became the popular wood. Other woods were stained to match this dark tone. Papier mache was used for chairs and tables. Mirror frames were ornate and gilt. Mother of pearl found use as inlay. Tables had thick columnar pedestals and marble tops formed many a flat surface.

Upholstery was overstuffed, tufted and fringed. Dark colored brocades, velvets, satins and brocatelles were used, along with horsehair and mohair. Heavy drapes that excluded the light covered the windows, lambrequins shrouded mantels, doors and table legs. Tasselled cord was hung

A dramatic fireplace keynotes an unusual Modern room. The comfortable sitting-reclining pieces, upholstered in foam rubber and suggestive of Japanese pieces, are long, low and practical. A bamboo shade carries out the Oriental motif, as does the color scheme of yellow, beige and hot orange. In keeping with the contemporary spirit, the furniture arrangement gives a feeling of spaciousness unmarred by a clutter of accessories.

in loops on the wall. Mauve, lilac, lavender, with browns and tans, composed the color schemes. The cutglass chandeliers were elaborately adorned with bunches of glass grapes and gilt bronze leaves. Black-lacquered cast-iron surrounded the fireplaces.

Bric-a-brac held so important a place in the decor of the typical Victorian home that *whatnots* were especially designed for them. Whatnots served as repositories for a widely assorted collection of items, from shells and star-fish to porcelain figurines. These cabinets often had open shelves covered with a fringed draw curtain. Wooden draw pulls replaced metal on chests and bureaus, while stuffed birds and flowers under glass bells were favorite embellishments.

The Victorian style mixes well with all the 19th century styles. The modern rendition of Victorian has definitely improved upon the original. Based upon the better designed pieces, the modernized Victorian reproductions are smaller and more pleasing in scale. Comfort has been introduced through the use of softer fabrics. The voluminous curves have been modified. Ornamentation has been simplified, while brilliant colors have supplanted the original dark, muted shades. Quaintness and hominess—the outstanding characteristics of this period—have, however, been retained.

CLASSIC MODERN

Just as Victorian and English Regency styles have been presented in a modernized form, so other period styles have been adapted to the needs

Modern in feeling, this combination bedroom-sitting room is furnished with pieces authentically Chinese in design. A textured rug underlies an extension game table, armchairs and a lacquered coffee table. The walls are off-white, the curtains an off-white damask with metallic thread, the bedspread and upholstery are of yellow chenille, while the furniture finish is an almond tone. Abstract paintings carry out the Modern feeling.

and wants of contemporary living. These up-to-date adaptations of the styles of the past are known as Classic Modern. The best in Classic Modern is patterned after the best forms and designs of yesteryear. To these are added modern materials, modern fabrics and precision methods of manufacture. Comfort and utility are stressed, lines and decoration simplified, size is reduced to meet present-day requirements, ornamentation is pared away.

One of the typical changes that Classic Modern has made is the *simplification* of furniture legs. Gone are the term legs, bulbous melons, intricately carved, turned, fluted or reeded legs. In their stead are clean-cut legs, splayed, straight or tapering. The cabriole leg has been stripped of its shell carving, its slender ankle and its ornamental foot. The modernized cabriole leg reproduces the essential line—the element that is the essence of its beauty. As a result, Classic Modern makes its appeal on the basis of the essential art elements that it incorporates into its designs, not through extraneous ornamentation.

The variety of woods at the disposal of Classic Modern is greater than ever before. Since carving and other forms of embellishment are eliminated, Classic Modern emphasizes the beauty and grain of natural woods. Modern technique has brought the art of furniture finish to a new peak. *Bleached* and *pickled* woods find widespread use, while a wide gradation of colors is available. Veneers in modern versions are especially attractive, while contrast is often secured through the use of different woods.

Classic Modern may faithfully reproduce the form of a Duncan Phyfe lyre-back chair. In doing so, however, not only does it use modern attractive fabrics, but it uses woods other than the dark mahogany that Phyfe originally used. If it uses a wood in a bleached finish, the Phyfe chairs may be combined with other light colored woods or used to contrast with dark woods. A table, patterned after Louis XVI, might be combined with the Phyfe chairs. Accordingly, Classic Modern may use any period style that suits its wants as its point of departure.

In spirit, Classic Modern is many-faceted. It can be formal or informal, though it tends more to the formal. In setting the mood, upholstery textures and colors play important roles, as does the finish of the wood. One informal type is known as Swedish Modern. This type combines simpli-

Functionalism is evident in this delightful Modern styled home. The two-faced divider supports a free flowing table and offers a novel magazine rack beside the desk. The webbed construction of the chairs, the continuous linoleum, the shaggy scatter rug, the wallpaper panel and the asymmetric mat of the water color are but a few of the many points of interest that arouse wide enthusiasm for Modern interiors.

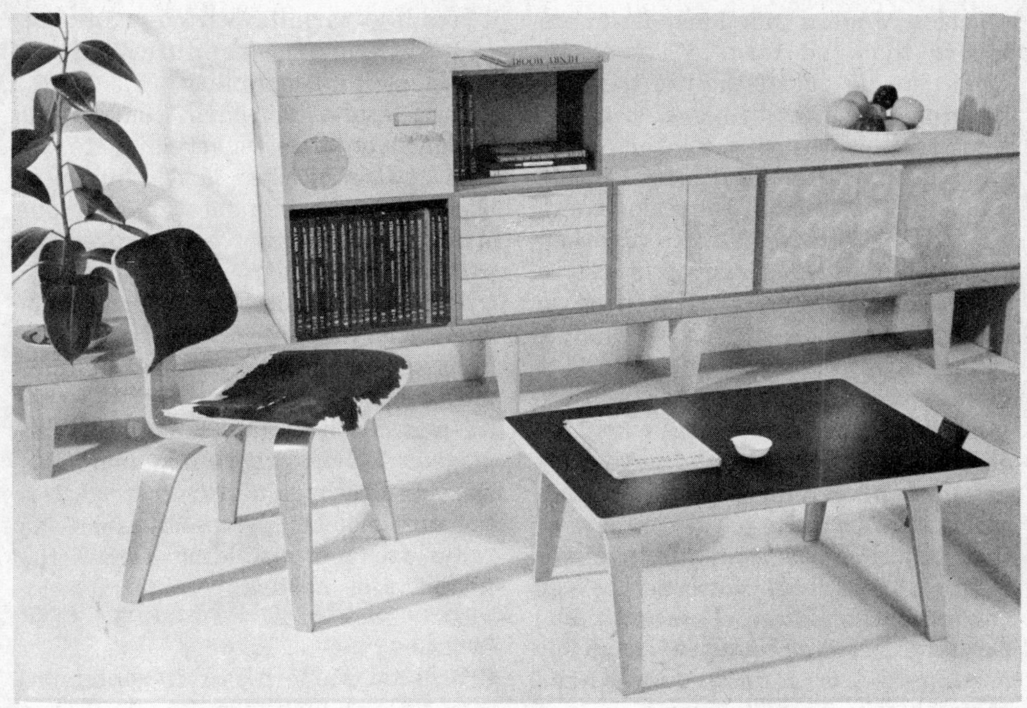

Ultramodern lightweight molded plywood furniture here previsions the home of tomorrow. New materials and processes modify traditional designs. The radio, unit cabinets and bookcases are of uniform size and may be grouped variously on separate benches. Evans Products of Detroit produces, for manufacturers, molded plywood furniture components and radio cabinets by an exclusive process. The designer is Eames.

city with the beauty of the traditional.

Functionalism is an important consideration to Modern. *Unit* and *sectional* pieces offer far greater flexibility than is possible with the older forms. Built-in furniture saves space. Not only do such pieces offer increased convenience, but they permit better and more beautiful furniture groupings.

Accessories also appear in many new fabrics and forms. Mirrors and glass are employed for furniture, walls, doors and floors, as well as for room partitions. Colors are more varied than ever. Combining the beauty of the traditional with the convenience and comfort of the new, Classic Modern is particularly well adapted to modern homes.

ORGANIC MODERN

Unlike Classic Modern, Organic Modern creates its own designs, sophisticated new ones that have not heretofore appeared. It is, in consequence, boldly experimental. But the challenge that this experimental approach offers has attracted men whose names, in time, will rank with the foremost designers of the past. Aalto, Eames, Saarinen are just a few of the names we associate with this movement.

Organic Modern dates to the architectural work of Louis Sullivan in

America. Modern functional designers believe that the form of furniture should spring out of the use that the furniture is meant to serve. Comfort is primary. In securing comfort, however, beauty of line and form results.

One of the criteria these designers apply, therefore, is fitness to function. The designers also consider fitness to the material that they use, as well as fitness to manufacturing technique. These three standards have guided them in creating furniture designs.

The chairs of Organic Modern design are lightweight and molded by new manufacturing techniques into shapes that conform to the contours of the body. Seats are broad and fitted with rubber shock absorbers. Well formed backs give to allow additional comfort. *Molded plywood* is widely used, as well as *tubular metal.* Armchairs may feature legs and arms in one continuous piece. Tables are low, many of them assuming the shape of free flowing curves. Tables and chairs are often fitted with detachable molded wood legs. The designs of individual pieces are as varied as the ingenuity of their designers.

One of the outstanding contributions of Organic Modern is *unit* and *sectional* furniture. Units are demountable for shipping and may be arranged in a wide variety of forms on low unit benches. Unit furniture is ideally suited to space saving, while it readily permits varied grouping and use. Sectional furniture similarly possesses this flexibility.

New materials have contributed enormously to the variety and sturdiness of Organic design. Aluminum is used for both ornamentation and construction. Finishes are waterproofed, permitting outdoor use. *Plastics* are widely employed, as is laminated plywood. Tubular metals contribute to lightness, while new fabrics contribute to beauty and durability. Lucite, leather, rubber and latex are employed. Allied to these new materials are new methods of furniture manufacture. These processes—such as radio frequency welding—allow the introduction of features that the designers of the past could not even imagine.

Organic Modern is our contemporary style of furniture. Its low shapes and horizontal lines make for informality and restfulness, while its unit pieces offer new possibilities of convenience.

In creating designs through a careful study of function, modern designers are preparing the way for entirely new concepts of living. Our streamlined age is revealing new vistas. We may yet usher in an era in which the technological skills of man will yield new values, and beauty will enter intimately into the lives of each one of us.

CHAPTER SIX

Expressive Backgrounds

Walls, ceilings, woodwork, doors, windows and floors serve as the backdrop against which the drama of your furnishings act out their role. Properly treated, this background can enhance your entire room. It can play up the good points and subdue the bad points of your room. It can attract attention to itself or direct attention to the foreground. The background may, therefore, play an active or passive part in the decoration of your home.

How you treat the background depends upon the effect you wish to create. For relaxation and quiet, the background will be subdued. For gayety and laughter, it will add its voice to the over-all effect. A formal room will treat its background differently from an informal room. Dramatic treatment of the background will suit a room keyed to sophistication, modernity or novelty. The background of Junior's room will vary from Sister's, while that of a rumpus room will contrast with a study. The room expressing dignity and reserve, mellowness and the charm of a historical period, will want a treatment that conforms to this spirit.

The background is an integral part

For the combination room

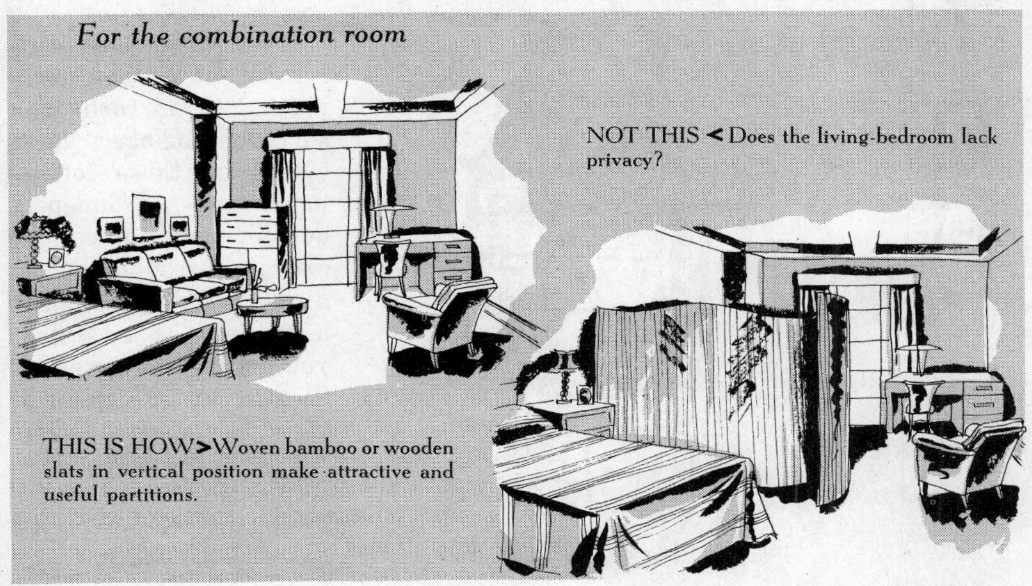

NOT THIS < Does the living-bedroom lack privacy?

THIS IS HOW > Woven bamboo or wooden slats in vertical position make attractive and useful partitions.

of the decoration of your room. It can blend so quietly and inconspicuously with your furniture and accessories that one is scarcely aware of its presence. It can contribute the decorative adornment of your room through introducing color, pattern and interesting texture. It can set the very mood and spirit of your room. Or it can become the focus of attention.

In decorating your room, you must decide which of these roles the background will play. The role you assign it must, however, be in keeping with the over-all effect you intend for the entire room. You must accordingly key the treatment of the background with that of the foreground.

You will be assisted in your decorating if you plan the steps on paper in advance. Decide upon the effect you wish to create. Or, if you prefer, decide upon the style of your furniture. Your next step is to choose your color scheme. The effect you intend will indicate what type of line will predominate in your room as well as what type of texture. If these basic elements go well together and express your purpose, you have successfully blocked out your decorative plan.

In planning the treatment of the background, remember too, that adjoining rooms should be keyed together. The background of these rooms need not be identical. Their treatment should, however, express a similar spirit. This is easily achieved by repeating at least one color in each of the rooms, whether the rooms are to be papered or painted. Reversing color schemes is another effective means of unifying adjacent rooms.

We shall consider each component of the background in its turn. You should remember, however, that these components are not independent of one another, nor are they separate and distinct from the room as a whole. The treatment you choose for each of them is but one phase of a single underlying plan. All these components together must contribute to producing the type of room you want for your home.

Recognizing Chippendale highboys

NOT THIS<Are you baffled by the complexity of spotting different styles?

THIS IS HOW> Remember that Chippendale usually carved facing C's in the pediment of his highboy as his trademark.

WALL TREATMENT

The walls of your room present you with a splendid opportunity for expression in home decoration. Walls comprise the largest area of your room. Handled well, walls can enhance your room and its furnishings. In fact, a well-chosen wall treatment is a must. The best in furniture and accessories can hardly overcome the handicap of poorly done walls. Well-treated walls can beautify your room and help to produce the effect you desire.

To attain distinctive results with your walls need involve no greater expenditure of money than to succumb to the drab, the listless and the non-committal. It does require planning. It means foregoing neutral, "safe" finishes that are without distinction. Even if the walls are to serve merely as a foil for your furnishings, you must integrate them with your room. Walls should add to the over-all effect. Your room will profit thereby.

The many variations of treatment that walls permit is the secret of their great potentialities. Their texture may range from the smoothness of glass to the roughness of craftex or the three-dimensional effects of sculptured wallpaper. In hue, they may vary from the uncolored finish of natural plaster or wood to any color or combination of colors you desire. They may pick up or contrast with the colors of the foreground. They may be absolutely plain, depending for decoration upon hangings, pictures and mirrors, or they may be highly patterned and decorative in themselves. The patterns you select may possess any type of motif, from stripes to scenic representations.

You may alter the size, shape and appearance of walls by your treatment of line, color and pattern. You may attain dramatic effects through treating one or two walls differently from the others. Do the possibilities sound bewildering? They need not be. Just let your preferences and your decorative purpose guide you, tempered by your good taste, a knowledge

This textured wallpaper is so realistic in effect that one wants to touch it to re-assure one's eyes! Textured paper goes well in the Modern room. The lamp is fitted with an attractive gold paper lamp shade.

of what is possible and by your means.

PAINTED WALLS

In almost every home, the walls are constructed of plaster, wood or wallboard. These materials are most often treated with paint or covered with wallpaper, wood, fabrics, mirrors or plastics. Occasionally the plaster is left in its natural color, especially if a colored plaster was used originally in the construction. The walls may be painted with oil paint or with water paint such as calcimine or casein paint. Many paints contain DDT, which provides protection against insects. If painted, the walls may be given a flat, glossy or semi-gloss finish.

Flat paints yield a dull mat finish, while glossy paints are true to their name. Glossy finishes produce glare and for this reason, glossy enamel finishes are usually restricted to kitchens, bathrooms and laundries where the qualities of enamel—washability and resistance to soiling—are especially desirable. Enamels, however, may be mixed with oil paints to produce any degree of gloss that is desired. Mat finishes have the advantage of subtlety of light and shadow, with a resultant softness and tingeing of colors that are pleasing and blend well with the entire room.

The texture of the finished painted wall may be smooth or rough and finished in any color of your color scheme. A sand float finish, fashioned with the palm of the hand, a trowel or a brush, can produce textured interiors that correspond to period styles of decoration. Craftex is another type of rough plaster finish. These finishes may further be glazed to introduce varying effects of light and shadow.

Various other effects are possible with painted walls. They may be stippled to produce an irregular, slightly pebbled surface that gives a soft muted effect. Mottling produces a variegated color effect while glazing may yield a rich harmony of tonal effects. A spatter finish may be attained by spraying bright accents of color on a gray or neutral finish. Misting resembles spattering and is produced with a spray gun. Even luminous fluorescent and phosphorescent paints may be used to decorate novel patterns on a wall. These patterns glow softly in the dark or when ultraviolet light activates them. Marbleized effects are also possible with paints.

A LIVING-DINING GROUPING

A pair of easy chairs, upholstered in a swirl textured pattern containing coral, brown and white, serve as dividers in this Modern living-dining room. Cotton carpeting in brown and rich draperies in chocolate brown contrast with the blonde wood furniture. The table lamp consists of a base of naturally textured driftwood, while a pair of Modern metal candelabra stand on the dining area buffet.

A COLOR SCHEME FOR PLEASANT DINING

Solid birch furniture here conveys a note of quiet modernity. The curved legs of the dropleaf dining table match those of the chairs. This motif is picked up in the finger pulls of the china buffet as well. A bit of driftwood calls attention to the plants in the built-in flower box. An easy-to-live-with color scheme of rose, turquoise and café-beige sets off the blonde wood and, with accents of green, sets the mood for pleasant dining.

FEMININE AND PROVINCIAL

French Provincial furniture—one of the popular traditional styles of today—here strikes a feminine note. The quilted cornices match the top of the bedspread, the draperies match the dust ruffle. The built-in triangular cabinet allows the bed to stand obliquely in the room —a space-saving device for close quarters.

In painting walls, a priming coat is first applied to prevent absorption of the covering coats of paint. The wall is next treated with an undercoat of paint, usually in the color of the desired finish. A final coat is then added.

If you intend to match wall color and fabrics in your room, it is easier to match the color of the paint to that of the fabrics than to try to match the color of fabrics to that of the paint. You will find it wise to have a large sample of the fabric available for the painter when he mixes paints, since it is difficult to match paint colors to small samples of material. Another safety measure is to be present when the painter actually mixes the paint. Have the painter try out his color mixture on a small area of the wall so that you can compare the color when the paint is dry. This will often avoid unhappy results if you satisfy yourself that these colors are right.

Wallpaper that simulates the coarse textured grain of wood and possesses all the beauty of a genuine wood finish makes a pleasing wall treatment for the informal home of today.

WALLPAPER

Wallpaper is a favorite means of decorative wall treatment, more popular today than it has been for a number of years. Any wall may be wallpapered, even rough textured ones, though these first must be smoothed down. Present-day wallpapers offer a wide selection of colors, textures and patterns adaptable to every room, in every mood and designed for every taste. Besides being washable (scrubbable in some instances) and sunproof, modern wallpaper may be procured that simulates sculptured and architectural effects such as wood paneling, wainscoting, pilasters and cornices. Marbleized effects are also obtainable with wallpaper.

The choice of color in wallpaper is no different from the choice of color in wall paint. Your color scheme determines what color to use on your walls. In fact, you can adopt your color scheme from a wallpaper that you especially like just as readily as from a piece of fabric, a painting or a natural scene. The wallpaper you select can repeat the diverse colors that appear in your room and thus tie the room together. Or at the other extreme, the wallpaper may introduce a note of contrast.

A hand painted Chinese scenic insert in light tints against a dark cocoa marbleized wallpaper distinguishes the treatment of one wall of this foyer. A panel mirror on the oposite wall heightens the rich effect.

Strong contrast in color, you may recall, should be limited to relatively small areas. A large room can stand a greater degree of contrast than can a small room. As with paint, contrasting wall treatment is possible. A simple method is merely varying the wallpaper in pattern or color for one or two of the four walls, or using a decorative wallpaper panel on one wall.

Patterned paper may be used around the headboard of a bed with novel effect, while the other walls are papered with a plain paper or even painted. Wallpapered borders and ceilings are frequently used with painted walls. Other interesting effects may be achieved by using wallpaper on window valances and around mirrors. Wallpaper curtains that resemble fabrics may be used as wall drapes. Wallpaper may also be used in closets for cleanliness, attractiveness and as an inducement to orderliness. Cedarized DDT wallpaper is available for this purpose.

While some wallpapers are plain, most of them offer patterns, either as background or as decoration. Floral motifs, geometric patterns such as squares and diamonds, stripes, plaids, diagonals, chinoiserie, marbleized effects, pictorials, impression-

For the room with a dado

NOT THIS ∧ Dado painted to match solid colored wall loses decorative value.

THIS IS HOW ∨ Paint or paper dado in a dark shade and use a pale tint for the upper wall. Let the ceiling match the dado for added interest.

Glass curtains surrounded by a stencilled floral border introduce a pleasant note into this child's bedroom. A shaggy rug permits bare feet to romp on the floor. Shelves and chest for toys indicate the thoughtful planning of this room. The youth bed is especially well adapted to the active, growing child. Even the dark baseboard is calculated to conceal scuffing and kicking.

A free-hand painted plaid wallpaper in beige and light blue acts as a mediator and secures pleasing all-round harmony in this modern combination living-bedroom. The wallpaper harmonizes the pronounced vertical lines of the full hanging red curtains with the equally pronounced horizontal lines of the sofa and the coffee table. Such a wall treatment plays an active role in home decoration.

istic studies — all these and many other patterns are available today in wallpaper. Pattern in wallpaper is produced through screen, aquatint, block and machine printing, with the first two processes becoming of increasing importance. Aquatint papers may be used to cover large areas or as individual wall panels. These papers reproduce authentic water color paintings with all the beauty of coloring found in the originals.

In selecting paper, consider the amount of pattern in the rest of the room. If rugs, upholstery or draperies stress pattern, a plain wallpaper is usually advisable. A child's bedroom should have a simple, regular pattern, not a restless one that is full of movement. As a rule, a busy pattern disrupts harmony within a room. In papering walls, the pattern should be one that permits interruption by architectural features, such as doors and windows, and irregular heights and lines of furniture. Scenic wallpaper usually requires a large unbroken area.

Patterned and plain surfaces should be balanced throughout a room. The choice of a patterned paper naturally brings in the factor of scale. A safe guide to follow with regard to scale is to use small sized patterns in small rooms, medium sized patterns in medium rooms and large sized patterns in large rooms. If the wallpaper pattern contributes to the over-all effect you desire to create, this rule may successfully be disregarded. Wallpaper pattern and color should be selected with thought to the fabrics you use in the room. Wallpaper and fabrics may match, blend or contrast, in texture as well as in pattern and color. The effect you intend is again your guide.

To hang tie-back curtains

NOT THIS < Curtains tied back at the middle look prim and precise.

THIS IS HOW > Tie the curtains either high or low for more pleasing lines and proportions.

The texture of wallpaper may be smooth or rough. Wallpaper embossed to imitate rough plaster is available, as is paper with a sculptured effect. Sculptured wallpapers, which produce a three-dimensional effect and simulate wood grain or matting, are a recent innovation. These papers, made of plastic, achieve pattern through the interplay of light and shadow. Flock paper, which simulates the nap of fabrics, is also obtainable, as is mica paper with its rich satiny texture.

With fine-grained woods, such as mahogany, walnut and the rare woods, a smooth paper and wall are desirable. An open-grained wood, such as oak, may take a coarse-grained paper or wall finish, as can large rooms and large pieces of furniture. A masculine room may use rougher textures than a feminine room.

Wallpapers date back, in popular use, to the 18th century. In consequence, they are now designed to harmonize with furniture styles of different periods. Toile de Jouy scenics, floral and classic motifs and tapestry papers are suitable for the 18th century English or French room. Chinoiserie and pictorial wallpapers go especially well in Chippendale rooms. The 19th century styles used panoramic scenes very widely. Simple floral and geometric designs, as well as wood paneling papers, fit the Colonial room. Provincial styles use gay and colorful papers. Pennsylvania Dutch may repeat its characteristic designs in the pattern of the wallpaper. The Modern room can select an impressionistic design. Though wallpapers are associated with historical periods, freedom of choice is entirely permissible. The goal is not museum-like authenticity so much as a livable quality that appeals to us.

In selecting a paper, remember that there is a difference between the sample and its appearance on the wall. The pattern on the wall will look *smaller* while the color will look *darker* than they do in the samples. It is advisable to pin up two strips of wallpaper on the wall and try them out for a few days. Observe them in natural daylight and under bright and subdued illumination. You may then decide you should choose a different paper. If your walls are in poor condition, a wallpaper can conceal the blemishes, provided the paper has an all-over pattern, since plain paper might accentuate the underlying blemishes. For the novice who wants to paper a wall, wallpaper

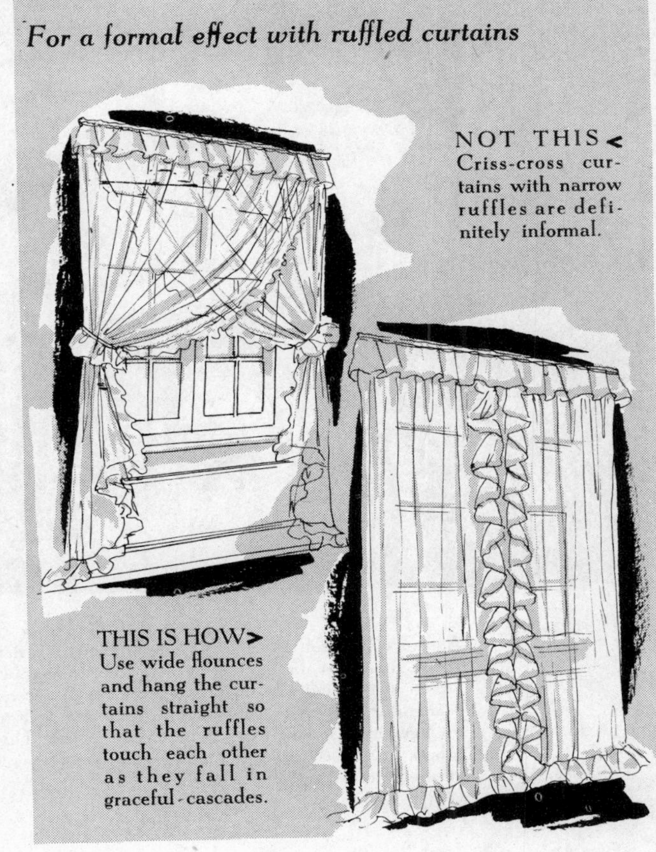

ready-pasted for hanging is available. This paper need only be moistened and applied to the surface.

To calculate the number of rolls of wallpaper required for the walls of a room is a simple matter of arithmetic. Add the widths of the walls to be papered—all four widths if you intend to paper each wall, three widths if you intend to paper only three. Then multiply this sum by the height to which you intend to paper the walls, either to the molding or the ceiling. This product equals the area of the surface to be papered. Next, subtract the area of the architectural openings of your room, the doors, windows and fireplace. This gives you the net area to be papered.

A roll of wallpaper is *ordinarily* 18 inches wide by 24 feet long, a total of 36 square feet, though dimensions do vary. It is advisable to allow for waste in matching patterns. Therefore, divide the net area to be papered by 30 and carry the fraction to the next higher number. This will give you the number of ordinary

A wall of natural wood, in which variations of grain provide added interest, forms the background of this room. The figured veneer of the buffet is especially marked and indicates a recent trend in Swedish Modern styling. The lightweight chairs are equipped with handgrips for mobility — a hint for your television center. The furniture legs contribute to the feeling of lightness, while the conventionalized bird motif of the print is gay and cheerful.

sized rolls you will require. For the ceiling, divide its area, found my multiplying its length and width in feet, again by 30, and carry to the next higher figure. It is well to remember that the smaller the pattern, the less waste in matching adjacent strips.

A glass brick window lights up the beauty of this graceful stairway. The metal railing is very attractive and modern. Especially does the curved wall recess for accessories add an interesting decorative touch.

OTHER WALL FINISHES

Both painted and papered walls may be stencilled or decorated with decalcomanias. These designs may be applied in regular or irregular repeats. A wide variety of patterns is available in both. Or you may cut stencils out yourself. Simple patterns are especially appropriate for children's rooms. The gay tulips and hearts of the Pennsylvania Dutch style are very popular. For novelty, these decorations may be used around a window, a headboard of a bed, a dining alcove or a recessed area. They will brighten up a kitchen as well as a game room. They can introduce a bright splash of color into your living room in an attractive pattern and thus draw attention to a dominant center of interest.

Fabrics may be applied as wall coverings in much the same way as wallpaper or they may be sewn together and fastened to the wall with battens. Patterned chintz, printed linen and grass cloth all find decorative use as wall coverings. Even rough textured canvas and hand-dyed burlap have been used with fine effect, while more delicate fabrics may lend a feminine touch to a room. Tapestry still finds use in connection with period rooms, while linoleum, leather and fabrikoid have proved their worth as wall coverings.

Wood walls have enjoyed popularity since the days of Queen Elizabeth. Walls wainscotted with solid or veneer panels may be formal or informally rustic. The formal treatment lends a feeling of dignity and grandeur to a room, while the simplicity of the rustic finish gives a feeling of cozy hominess and charm. Oak, pine, maple, mahogany, walnut as well as rare woods may be left in their natural grain finish or may be stained or painted. Squares of highly figured woods set with their grains running in different directions produce a modern touch. Plywood is also widely used as wall covering and as furring to produce structural changes.

Wood walls may be simulated. Wallpaper with a wood grain surface is available for this purpose. Modern insulating wallboard panels and

planks may also be used as wall facing either in their natural form or painted. Wallboards are obtainable in a variety of colors. They are well suited for attic or game room and lend themselves very readily for use in living room and bedroom. Soundproof fiberboard acoustic tiles are meeting with wide acceptance.

A novel effect may be achieved through using Venetian blinds, not only as window curtains, but as wall covering. Woven bamboo and wood slats may also be used for these purposes. For an interesting modern effect, the slats may be used in a vertical position. These forms of wall covering are equally well adapted to use as room partitions or screens, and find especial usefulness in double-duty rooms. Venetian blinds made of plastic are now obtainable in varied colors to carry out your color scheme. These blinds are lighter in weight and easier to clean than those with which we are familiar.

Mirrors, too, have long been popular as wall coverings. They are particularly well adapted to producing a feeling of modernity in a room, while they impart a distinctly feminine feeling to a bedroom. Mirrors may be clear or colored and are well fitted for brightening up a room, reflecting the treatment of the opposite wall, and producing a feeling of spaciousness in a room. Gunmetal mirrors may also be used.

Glass bricks are a recent development in building material. They are translucent and diffuse light throughout the entire room. Such bricks are suitable for interior as well as exterior walls. Heat resistant bricks or tiles may be used for fireplaces. Picture glass windows have also recently come into favor both as exterior and interior walls and as sliding doors. An exterior wall consisting of picture glass windows literally brings the splendor of the outdoors into the room. This treatment is superb for the home distinguished by the beauty of its outdoor view.

Plastics are used in the home as wall sheathings. One such plastic—Di-Noc—can be decorated by a photographic process to resemble wood, stone or marble. Photomurals, too, may be prepared by photographers as wall covering. They may be made up from photographs, maps, scenic wallpaper, drapery material, prints or etchings. Usually they are finished in black and white or sepia, though they can be painted with pastels or oils. The choice of subject matter for photomurals is limitless.

WOODWORK

The trim in a room may be left in its natural color, painted or stained. Woodwork may match, blend or contrast with the colors in your room. The modern treatment is to match walls and woodwork. Beautifully grained wood is, however, left its natural color. Wood trim, stained dark, tends to overshadow a light wall. The trim may take the background color of the wallpaper, or it may be painted a white or off-white color. In a small room, the wood trim should match the walls or be painted a slightly darker color than the walls. A contrasting color may be used in a large room.

CEILINGS

Ceilings present large areas. Until recently, however, ceilings seldom received much attention. They most often were painted a calcimine or enamel white, so as best to reflect light. Today ceilings are often wallpapered, even when the walls are treated in a different manner. In selecting a wallpaper for a ceiling, remember that it will be viewed from all angles. Hang your sample on the ceiling when you try it out, for a paper suitable for a wall may not be suitable for a ceiling.

If painted, the ceiling color, like the woodwork, may be neutral, or it may blend, match or contrast with the walls. Mirrors have also been used for ceilings, as well as sturdy wood timber, wood panels and stencils. In a small room, or one with sloping walls and ceiling, walls and ceiling are best painted or papered as a unit. A too-high ceiling may be lowered in appearance by an advancing color, while a receding color will have the opposite effect.

The treatment of windows and floors will be considered in the next two chapters.

A traditional wall treatment here sets the stage for lovely Modern mahogany furniture. The traditional wallpaper has a chintz pattern and border against a white background. The chintz pattern is repeated on the corner cupboard with pleasing effect. Pink, green and blue are woven into the striped tweed of the host chairs which incorporate the colors of the side chairs. Swirl cut veneer, in an amber finish, is used for the table top and, in random cut figures, for the doors of the sideboard. The sideboard is fitted with places for glasses on the center pull out and each of the two doors. The rug is a deep brown monotone. The lighted candles on the dining table also serve to introduce a suggestion of the old into a delightful setting of the new.

CHAPTER SEVEN

WINDOW TREATMENT

WINDOWS play a more significant role in decoration today than ever before. The modern trend in window treatment seems to be—the more the better. No longer do we follow set rules about hanging the material from the window frame or using specific widths of material for each window. Emphasis is on fullness, graceful folds, long unbroken lines.

We may consider our curtains and draperies part of the background or an important decorative factor in the foreground. We can use them to call attention to particularly attractive views or structural arrangements, to alter the size of windows, to lower or heighten ceilings, to make walls or windows appear wide or narrow, or even to make our walls seem to be entirely made of windows.

For quiet, spacious effects curtains and draperies are treated as part of the background. Their colors are close or identical while plain fabrics or unobtrusive patterns are preferred. As part of the foreground, contrasting colors and bolder patterns that pick up colors in the foreground of the room are used. We usually favor gayly colored curtains in kitchens and breakfast rooms, but they may

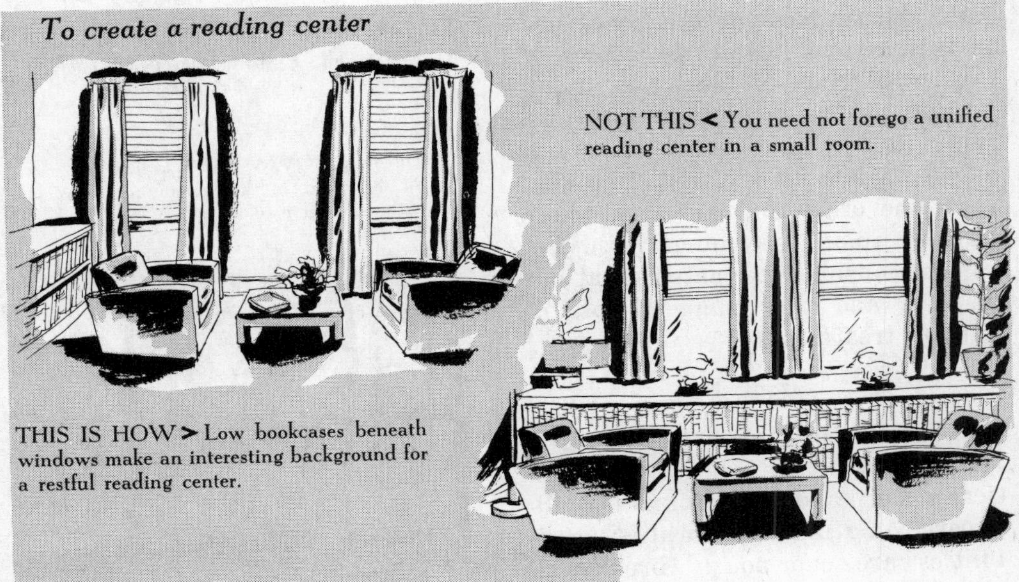

To create a reading center

NOT THIS < You need not forego a unified reading center in a small room.

THIS IS HOW > Low bookcases beneath windows make an interesting background for a restful reading center.

Straight draperies under a simple cornice with Venetian blinds mark the treatment of the broad window in this Modern room. This type of cornice is well adapted to cove lighting.

be used to perk up any dull room in our home.

Window treatment should be consistent with the spirit of your room. Rooms done in traditional styles demand different treatment from those that are strictly modern. Formal rooms take different treatment from the informal. Yet straight draperies from the top of the window frame to the floor may be appropriate to both. Where does the difference lie? In this case it lies in the choice of fabrics. Texture of fabrics is as important as are their color and line. Both fabrics and arrangement of draperies are interrelated. One suggests the other and the atmosphere of your room determines both. Let us first consider the materials at our disposal and then suggest possible window treatments.

FABRICS

Today it is possible to buy material for curtains or draperies in the identical pattern and colors found in wallpapers. As a result, decorative possibilities are enormously broadened. Many effective combinations suggest themselves. The curtain or drapery fabric may be repeated in chair or headboard upholstery, in bedspreads or accessories. It may be used as trimming or as the main fabric. Repetition of design in wallpaper and drapery is being adopted with novel effect in bedrooms.

Materials are available to us today in great variety. We may choose not only the traditional fabrics, but new ones made of glass fiber, plastics

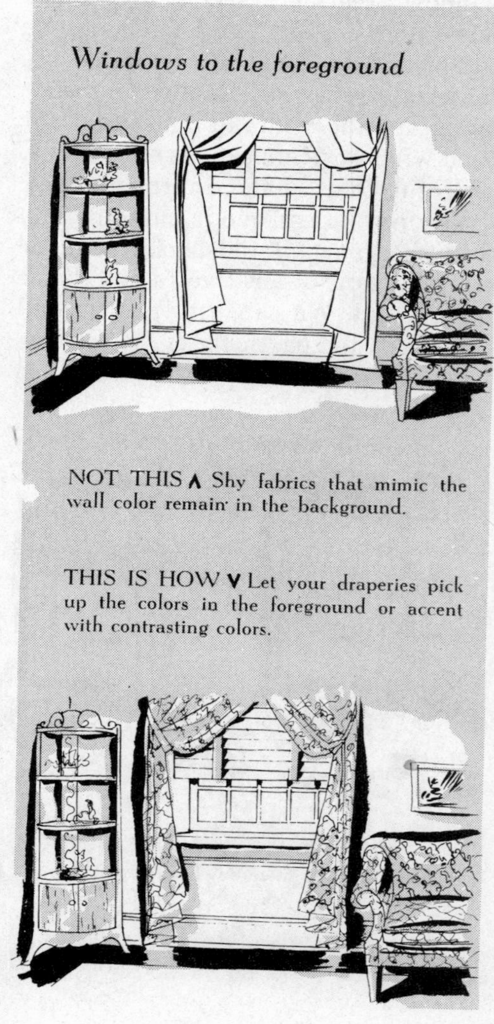

Windows to the foreground

NOT THIS ∧ Shy fabrics that mimic the wall color remain in the background.

THIS IS HOW ∨ Let your draperies pick up the colors in the foreground or accent with contrasting colors.

and other synthetics, as well as blends of old and new fibers. Blends of cotton, rayon, wool and other fibers form some of our most attractive modern drapery fabrics. Metallic threads that will not tarnish are also employed for decorative effects. Even paper is used for draperies today.

In the past, fabrics were made of animal or vegetable fibers. The animal fibers were mainly silk, wool and mohair, while the vegetable fibers were mainly flax and cotton plus some minor fibers like jute, hemp and kapok. Synthetics first appeared in the form of rayons—nitrocellulose, viscose, Bemberg and cellulose acetate. But today the synthetic field is so vast that rarely a day goes by without some innovation.

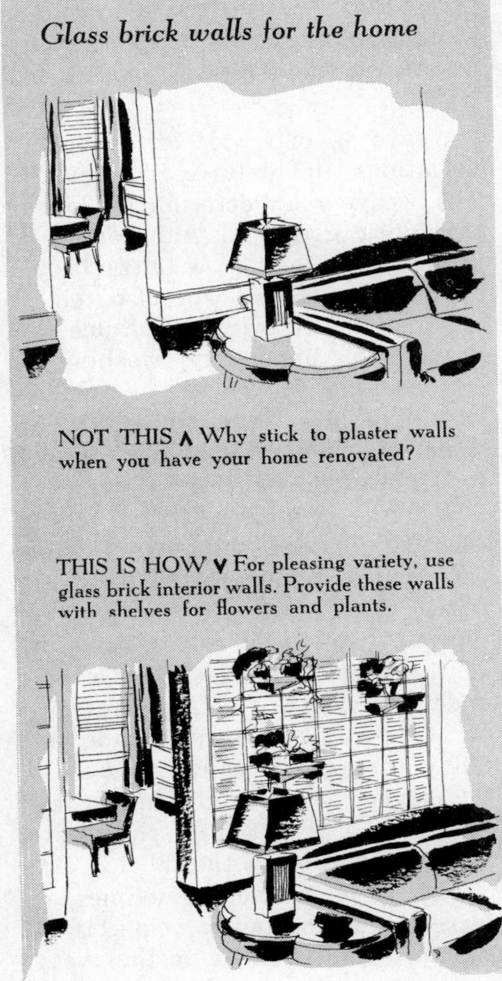

New synthetics are being produced constantly through chemically changing spinning solutions, mixing materials during spinning, varying after-treatment and coatings. While aralac, produced from milk, is the only protein synthetic widely used at this time, soybeans, corn and peanuts offer additional possibilities. Laminations of aluminum and plastics have decorative possibilities, too.

New techniques have enabled fabrics to attain new properties of great advantage to the homemaker. Many new fabrics are resistant to sunlight and fading. They shun dust and dirt. Merely wiping them with a damp cloth is sufficient to keep them clean and fresh. Some of the new fabrics are waterproof and fireproof. They are not affected by temperature, are impervious to oils and acids, resistant to ink and iodine, to moths and mildew. Ease of upkeep and safety are important factors. Good looking labor-saving plastics that are waterproof, mildewproof and translucent are of especial value in bathroom and kitchen.

It is well to remember that these properties vary from yarn to yarn. As synthetics attain more widespread use, it is wise to acquaint yourself with their special properties. You can then select them according to your needs and care for them in such a way as to assure satisfaction. Know what to expect when you make your purchase. For example, nylon is wholly resistant to mildew but material on nylon may be attacked. Synthetics,

Livable and charming is this pleasant living room furnished in maple and pine. The hand-hooked scatter rugs are attractive, as are the period prints over the sofa. The pair of lamps employ carved wood ducks as bases, while the base of the lamp on the dropleaf table next to the slipcovered easy chair consists of an old coffee grinder. The wallpaper, with flowers of pale green and ground in newly popular cocoa brown, goes well with the solid green carpeting.

other than those of protein, are resistant to moths. Fiberglas is attacked by hot solutions of weak alkali while vinylidene fibers such as Velon and Saran have limited resistance to ammonia. Therefore, avoid using ammonia for cleaning these particular fabrics.

WEAVES

Most commonly, weaving is our way of procuring fabrics from the basic fibers. Weaving—the interlacing of threads—is done by hand or machine on simple or complex looms. Most of our fabrics are woven by machine but many have the feel and look of lovely coarse homespuns.

Interesting textures are achieved through endless variation of fibers, twists, weaves and finishes. As a result, texture assumes additional importance in our decorative scheme. In fact, variations in texture are often used as the sole means of introducing pattern into our rooms.

Weave is one way of producing variations in texture and pattern. The weave may determine whether the fabric goes well with formal or informal furnishings, with traditional or modern. Weave can also tell us whether the fabric is suitable for drapery or upholstery, washing or dry cleaning, hard wear or not. We should be able to recognize the few basic weaves and know what to look for in selecting fabrics.

Weaving is done with two sets of threads. One set, the *warp* threads, extends throughout the length of the fabric. The other set, the *weft* or *filling* threads, goes across the width of the fabric, interlacing over and under the warp threads. In the strongest fabrics, the warp threads and filling threads are approximately of the same tension and number per square inch. The tighter the weave, the more durable is the fabric.

The *plain* weave, sometimes referred to as the tabby weave, is the simplest of all weaves. In this weave

DIAGRAM 6
Plain Weave

one set of filling threads passes regularly at right angles over and under the warp threads, as in *diagram* 6. Many of the fabrics most familiar to us are made of this weave. Linen, taffeta, cretonne, voile, ninon, scrim, calico, chintz and most printed materials are plain weave fabrics suitable for curtains or draperies in widely varied rooms. Some of the new plastic coated fabrics are actually coated plain weave cottons. Beutanol, a vinyl-resin coated cotton, looks and feels like the glazed chintz we have long known.

The plain weave is varied through using yarns of unequal weight and size to produce many novelty fabrics. The *basket* weave is a variation of the plain weave. In this variation, two or more filling threads pass over and under an equal number of warp threads as in *diagram* 7. This weave is not so strong as the plain weave.

DIAGRAM 7
Basket Weave

Fabrics made of it may be satisfactory for draperies but they should not be selected for upholstery where tougher wear is the rule. Monk's cloth is a familiar basket weave fabric.

Another plain weave variation is the *rep* or *ribbed* weave, where heavier warp or heavier filler threads produce varied ribbed effects as in dimity, poplin, faille and corduroy. Incidentally, corduroy is enjoying tremendous popularity as both upholstery and drapery fabric. In selecting upholstery fabrics, remember that raised ribs show wear more quickly than even weaves.

The *twill* weave in which the filling threads cross the warp on a diagonal, is one of the most durable weaves. Denim, widely used in informal rooms, children's rooms and country homes, is a twill weave fabric. Herringbone is also an example of twill

DIAGRAM 8
Twill Weave

weave. In herringbone, the slant of the diagonal is changed at regular intervals.

Satin weave fabrics are ever-popular for upholstery and draperies in rooms done in the traditional manner. The satin weave may be considered a variation of the twill weave. Warp threads are left on the surface as *floats,* thus producing a smooth shiny surface that reflects the light and is associated with satin fabrics. The filling thread skips, leaving irregular numbers of warp threads on the surface, before interlacing. This is just the opposite of the *sateen* weave where the filling threads float over the warp threads in the same irregular manner.. Sateen is widely used for lining draperies, valances and swags.

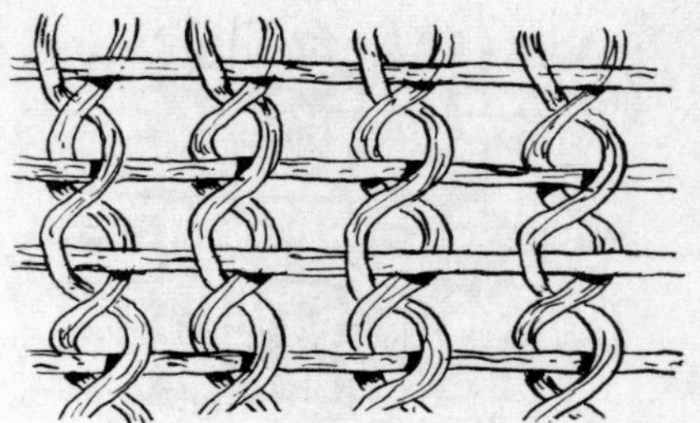

DIAGRAM 10
Gauze Weave

DIAGRAM 9
Satin Weave

Pile weave fabrics are more popular as floor covering and upholstery than as drapery material. In the pile weave there are two sets of warp threads. One set is used to form loops on the surface. These loops may be left uncut as in terry cloth, Brussels rugs or frieze upholstery material. Or the loops may be cut as in Wilton rugs, mohair, velvet, corduroy and velveteen. The pile may be long as in plush or short as in corduroy. Pile weave fabrics add interest, luxury and richness through their variation in light reflection.

Elaborately patterned weaves such as we find in damasks and brocades are produced with a *Jacquard* loom. This loom is also used for Wilton rugs. The figure weaves combine plain, satin or twill weaves so as to form woven patterns. The designs appear embossed. In damasks, the pattern is reversible but brocades are woven with the pattern only on the face side.

The term *gauze* weave is very misleading since the fabric we know as gauze is made with a plain weave. The gauze weave is an interesting one in which alternate warp threads are twisted round their neighbors and the filler passes through the loops. Marquisette is an example of a lightweight lacy curtain material employing this weave. Combination of gauze weave with plain weave is called *leno* weave. Lightweight curtains are often made with a leno or gauze weave. Other novelty weaves, like the lappet and swivel, are used for lightweight figured curtain materials. Dotted Swiss uses the lappet weave.

Double cloth weaves use two sets of warp and two sets of filler threads which interlace occasionally. When the fabric is woven, it can be separated into two distinct pieces of cloth. This weave is used for heavier materials with varied surfaces. Those suitable for upholstery or drapery fabrics are usually woven of silk or rayon.

PATTERN

Pattern may be achieved through other means than weaving. Embroidery has been used through the ages as a means of introducing variety in color, pattern and texture. Petit

Sheer curtains draped with a dark swag prove a well chosen accompaniment for this living-dining room decorated in the traditional manner. The sparkling crystal chandelier with its crimson satin shades and colored bulbs creates an aura of elegance. The antique plant stand lights up the statue upon it and supplements the candlelight of the dining table. Altogether, the effect is sumptuous and dignified.

point is a type of embroidery. Crewelwork, so popular in the time of Queen Anne, is widely used today for drapery and upholstery materials in traditional and modern rooms.

Dyeing and printing are other means of introducing pattern in fabrics. Hand blocked prints have long been known. Lovely hand blocked prints belong equally well in Colonial New England rooms or ultra-modern ones. Roller printing brought patterns in greater variety and quantity. Screen printing embodies the softness of hand blocked fabrics with the speed of quantity production that entered with roller printing. Some of our loveliest wallpapers, curtain and drapery fabrics are screen printed.

Pattern has also been introduced through tie-dyeing, batik, painting, photography and the use of stencils. The last mentioned is being widely used not only in kitchens and children's rooms but in every room of the house. Stencils are being used on walls, fabrics and furniture in many interesting and novel ways. They attain provincial effects when used in Pennsylvania Dutch fashion. Sophisticated effects result when they are used as one bold daring splash on a bedroom wall or as a window border supporting Venetian blinds and completely substituting for curtains or drapery.

Patterns have reached new heights. Never were colors so varied or so beautiful. The technician has enor-

NOT THIS ∧ Large pieces of furniture in front of a window obstruct the view and cut off light.

THIS IS HOW ∨ Use low pieces for window groupings or space the pieces so as not to block the view. Picture windows bring the splendor of the outdoors into the home.

mously increased the gradations of color available to us. Designers have used tremendous ingenuity in creating patterns in wide variety. Screen printing has come into its own. Patterns often achieve three-dimensional forms with light and shadow while hand decorating is used to achieve interesting, subtle and dramatic effects.

CURTAINS

In decorating our windows we may use curtains of various types. The term *curtain* actually covers all types—from the sheerest of glass curtains to the most elaborate overcurtains or draperies. We shall use the term curtains to apply to those of sheer material used as glass curtains, whether long or short, hung within or outside the window frame, and whether used alone or with other hangings. The term *draperies* will refer to hangings made of other than sheer materials, whether long or short, hung within the window frame or extending beyond the windows even to the point of covering entire walls. The possible arrangements are as varied as the homes we live in.

Whatever the treatment, your curtains should be full, allowing the material to fall in copious soft folds.

Striped fiber glass window and wall curtains surmount the problem of the corner window and produce a restful modern bedroom. Bedskirts of striped blue, red and yellow repeat the upholstery of the side chair.

Your choice of fabrics should be consistent with the style of window treatment and the character of your room. The chart on *Harmonizing Furniture and Backgrounds* in chapter 9 will assist you in selecting fabrics that blend with different period styles. The illustrations included in this chapter suggest possible window treatments for rooms done in different period styles. The suggestions, of course, are not exhaustive; they do, however, offer suitable and attractive possibilities.

You have to decide what purposes your window treatment is to serve. In some rooms, sheer curtains are used for their soft, delicate femininity or for their simplicity and lightness. If the room needs sunshine, the material selected might cast a sunny glow of its own. When glass curtains are used alone, they are usually hung outside the window frame to soften the lines of the window. Sheer curtains are often hung on traverse rods so you can pull them apart to let every bit of natural light in or close them to soften the light. Sufficient material is needed so that they look full and soft in any position.

You may want to use sheer curtains alone in your room. Should they be long or short? Plain or ruffled? Should they hang straight or be tied back? If your room is formal in spirit, then ruffles are usually out of place. You would be wiser to use tailored, full curtains that hang in straight lines from their pinch-pleated heading to the floor. Remember, too, that white curtains against dark walls or dark curtains against very light walls are formal in their effect.

Informal ruffled sheers are delightful in bedrooms or provincial type living rooms. They may be used with especial effect in Colonial New England type rooms without any additional window treatment. You can make these curtains very easily or you can purchase them ready made.

Oftentimes, ready made curtains are not full enough to give the desired effect. This can be overcome very readily by purchasing two pairs of ruffled curtains for each window. This is also desirable if the window is extra wide. The ruffle on inside and outside edges looks much softer than the usual inner ruffled edge with

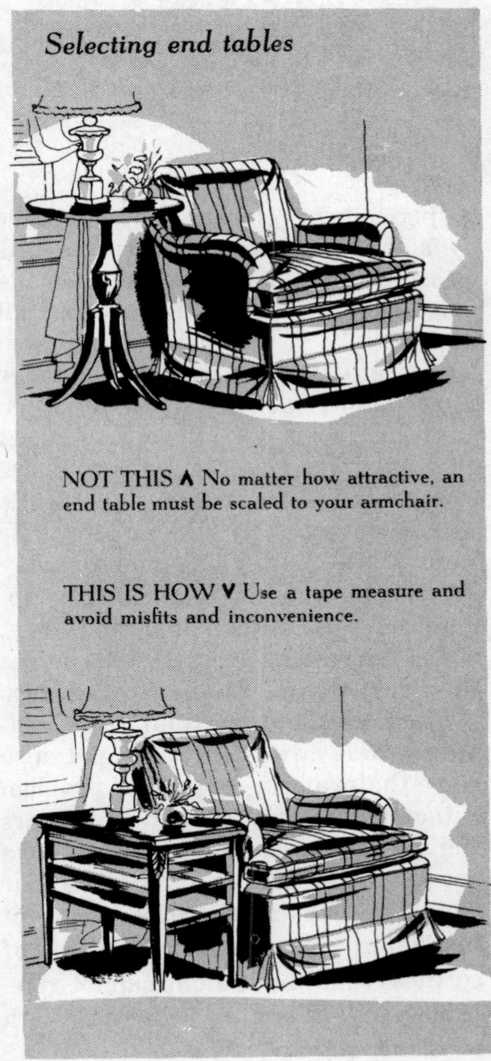
Selecting end tables

NOT THIS ^ No matter how attractive, an end table must be scaled to your armchair.

THIS IS HOW v Use a tape measure and avoid misfits and inconvenience.

a plain hem on the outside. The *This is How* illustration makes this clear. Usually too, only custom-made curtains have the full ruffle all around.

If there is some projection under the window, such as a radiator, you might use short curtains or you might eliminate the glass curtains and use side drapes, looped back high to avoid contact with the radiator. As a matter of fact, many homes today let Venetian blinds completely supplant the glass curtains and new, novel treatments suggest themselves in place of the familiar draperies.

Stencilled borders around the window frame are attractive and also solve the projecting radiator problem rather ingeniously. Stencilled borders suggest themselves for children's rooms, bedrooms, rooms done for summer—in fact, wherever you want maximum air or light with a bit of softness that blinds alone cannot give. Linoleum borders are being used in a similar manner.

DRAPERIES

In selecting drapery materials, decide on the weight and type of material, the color that fits into your color scheme and consider your walls and foreground. Do you want the windows to be part of the background or foreground? If background, you might match the color of the walls or even cover an entire wall with the drapery material. If foreground, you might use the drapery material to pick up the color of the upholstery, accessories or rug, or to tie them all together. As an alternative, you might use a patterned drapery fabric to set the color scheme for your room.

Although patterns are beautiful, be sure to take certain precautions. Too much pattern creates a restless effect. Patterns should be in scale with the room and the rest of your furnishings. Color, pattern and texture of walls, floor, furniture and draperies should speak with one voice. That doesn't mean they need be identical or monotonous, but it does mean they should express the same feeling-tone and contribute to the over-all effect.

Coarse homespuns and rough textures generally are informal and masculine. The same may be said of straight lines, plaids and stripes. They go together with clear, warm colors, with short curtains or draperies and simple window treatments. Cornices and valances, if used at all, are simple and straight in informal rooms.

Satins, damasks and brocades belong in the formal room, along with swags and jabots, draped valances and more elaborate cornices. Metallic threads, fringes and tassels also belong in the formal room. Textures and patterns, as well as style, will express formality through the use of smooth fabrics and classic patterns. Stripes, florals and geometrics also hold a place in formalized treatment, along with subdued cool colors and rich fullbodied colors. As with curtains, remember that very light draperies against very dark walls, or very dark draperies against very light walls are formal in their effect.

Whatever the pattern, whether formal or informal, it is important to realize that curtains and draperies hang in folds. What looks lovely on a flat surface or in a small area, may look very different when hung in folds from ceiling to floor or window apron. Always crush the material together as it will be in the finished drapery treatment and examine it in full length to get the over-all effect. If possible, get the effect on your own walls with your own furniture and accessories. Since it is not always possible to obtain a full length of the material before actual purchase, try to visualize the material as it will be used in your room.

The drapery style you adopt must consider the spirit of your room. Formality and informality have the greatest effect in determining just how you will style your windows. Informal treatment usually means straight tailored draperies or ruffled tie-backs — no swags or elaborate valances. A simple straight cornice or valance is appropriate, as well as a ruffled valance, especially if you want to accentuate the horizontal line or make the ceiling appear lower. The draperies may be long or short. Though short ones will stress the informal atmosphere, many of the larger patterns are more attractive when used in full length to the floor Short draperies just touch the window sill or reach the bottom of the window apron. The latter length is usually preferred. They should never be an indefinite length between floor and sill.

For formal treatment, you would, of course, use full length draperies with swags, draping, pleated headings, and simple or elaborate cornices and valances. Deep cornices and valances placed above the window frame may be used to add apparent height to the room. Long, straight draperies with simple pleated headings are appropriate for both the formal or informal room.

HANGING CURTAINS AND DRAPERIES

In hanging curtains and draperies, it is important to select the proper curtain rods. Rods may be decorative or purely utilitarian. The latter are frequently entirely covered or painted to match the wood trim to make them less obvious. The rods you select should be strong enough so they will

SUGGESTED WINDOW TREATMENTS

QUEEN ANNE AND EARLY CHIPPENDALE

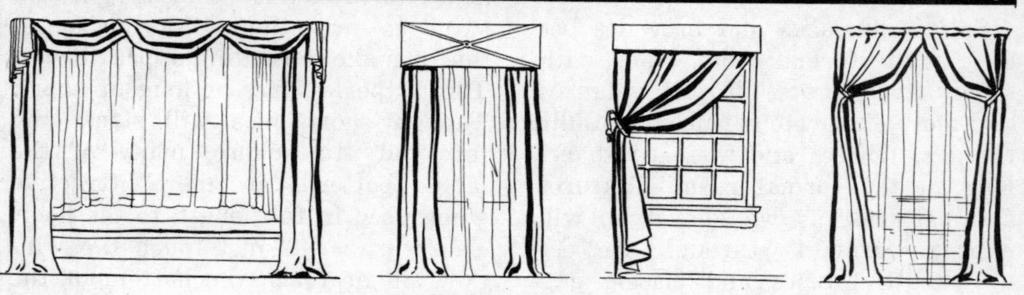

LATER GEORGIAN

ENGLISH REGENCY

VICTORIAN

SUGGESTED WINDOW TREATMENTS

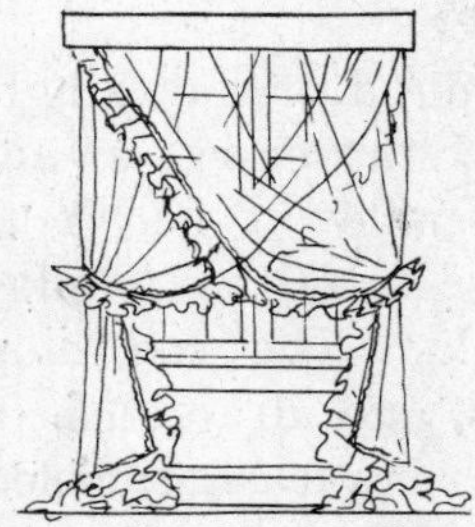
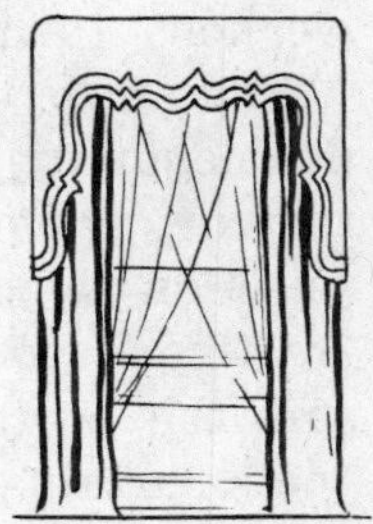

FRENCH PROVINCIAL (CITY STYLE)

FRENCH PROVINCIAL (COUNTRY STYLE)

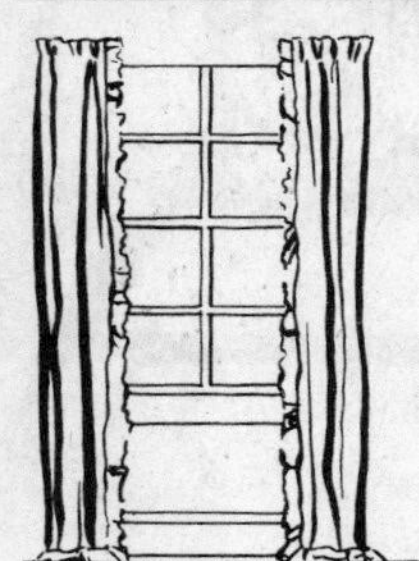

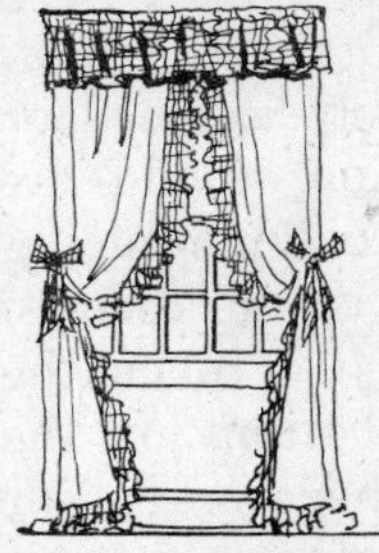

COLONIAL NEW ENGLAND

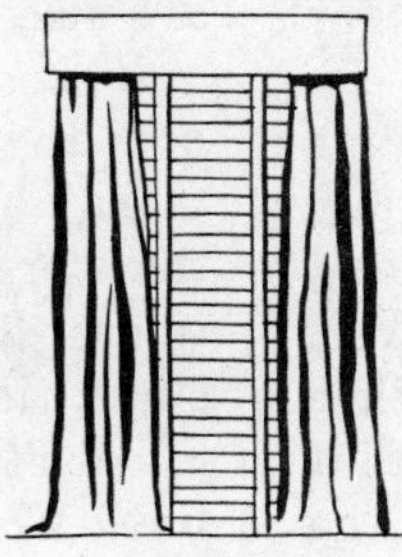

MODERN

not sag. Proper length is also a sag preventive. Overextending rods weakens them.

Rods may be round or flat, single, double or triple, stationary, swinging or traverse-pulley type. Your selection depends upon the window treatment you plan. The rod must suit the curtains and draperies. If your curtains have a casing, select rods that will slide easily through the casing slot. For glass curtains and draperies, for crossed curtains or for curtains with ruffled valance, a double or triple rod is needed.

When the valance is used to extend short curtains or draperies, a single rod is sufficient. A single rod may also be used when a valance board is used with draperies or curtains but it is not suitable for both. Usually a valance board is used for straight or draped valances that are tacked to the board after curtains and draperies are hung.

Place your rods so that the window frame is completely exposed or completely covered. You should determine placement before measuring lengths for curtains or draperies. Your curtains should just touch the sill or reach to the bottom of the window apron or the floor. For luxurious effect in very formal rooms, your drapery may extend for twelve inches on the floor. Always be sure to allow extra curtain length for draping with tie-backs.

You can hang your curtains straight or tie them back. In strictly formal rooms, they usually hang straight. Wide flounces, however, may be used in formal rooms, either tied back or hung straight so that the ruffles touch each other in the center as they fall in graceful cascades. If used in formal rooms, usually the tie-back slips through a slit behind the ruffle so that the ruffles hang free. Straight, tailored curtains are also looped back for formal effect.

It is important that tie-backs do not divide the window into the obvious quarters, thirds and halves that are the least pleasing proportions. To avoid these obvious divisions, tie back the curtains or draperies well above or below the center line. The material should hang in loose graceful folds even though tied back securely.

Rugs for the long, narrow room

NOT THIS ∧ Rug patterns that run the length of a room emphasize length and narrowness.

THIS IS HOW ∨ Select patterns that run the width of the room. Or use two or more broad rugs separated by narrow widths of bare floor.

In mounting draperies, you may use decorative wooden or metal rings that you can allow to show. In this case, sew the rings to the top edge of the curtain or drapery. Attach hidden rings or hooks three to four inches below the top edge so that they are not visible from the right side or above. Sew or pin the hooks behind each pleat of the heading, then insert each hook in a separate ring on your drapery rod.

Try to hang your draperies so as to let every bit of natural light into the room and have the window space at its maximum width. This means hanging the draperies outside the window frame so that no part of the glass is covered. It means treating groups of windows as one window. It may also mean extending the material as far beyond the window as you wish, to get the effect of spaciousness and breadth. Of course, this requires many more yards of material. For this reason, many homemakers are looking for the less expensive materials so that they can use them in greater quantity. Or they are making their own curtains and draperies. Chapter 16 will tell you how you can make your own curtains and draperies.

Full, formal, feminine and frilly describe the delicate green curtains of this French traditional bedroom. The sheer curtain material, with broad ruffled all-round flounces and low, uneven tie-backs, extends on the floor. The mirrored window valances conceal fluorescent lamps that cast a soft, diffuse glow. The attractive French Provincial chest and the pastel accessories enrich the dainty feminine feeling.

Modern rough textured wall-to-wall carpeting is here combined with furniture in the traditional Regency style to produce a pleasing room. Contrast between plain and figured upholstery enlivens the room, while once again contrasting dark walls set off the white of the wood work. Accessories are formal — of silver, porcelain and crystal, with a rich oval oil painting accenting the main center of interest in the room.

Linoleum highlights the Georgian type furniture of this formal dining room. Gray acanthus leaf wallpaper on a white background and luxurious drapery carry out the period decor.

CHAPTER EIGHT

FLOOR COVERINGS

IN CREATING present-day homes, floor coverings are essential to complete the decoration of a room. They endow a room with the warmth that is inseparable from comfort and livability. Floor coverings contribute a spirit of formality or informality, gayety or reserve, masculinity or femininity. In fact, an interesting rug — hooked, braided, Aubusson, Savonnerie, Oriental or domestic machine made—can serve as a center of interest in a room. Linoleum can similarly attract attention.

Like walls, floor coverings present a large area and serve to tie a room together. They thus contribute to the unity of a room and help to integrate adjoining rooms. In common with the other background components—walls, windows, ceiling, wood trim—rugs or carpets may play an active or a passive role in the decoration of a room. Even in a passive role, floor coverings add color, texture and often pattern to a room. Rugs and carpets may also alter the apparent size of a room.

The factors that guide your selection of a floor covering are decorative and practical. Color, pattern and texture should contribute toward fulfilling the decorative over-all effect

Partitioning the small dining-living room

NOT THIS < Divider partitions cut up a combination room obstructing light and traffic.

THIS IS HOW > Suggest the division by using two rugs or carpets separated by a few inches of bare floor.

you wish to create. The practical considerations that influence your choice are quality, price, size, shape and suitability to function.

COLOR

As with other fabrics, you may adopt your color scheme from the color of a rug or carpet that you like. Formerly it used to be suggested that the floor covering be the darkest color in the room, the ceiling the lightest, with walls, drapes and furniture between these two extremes. While this is still a safe practice, it does not of itself insure pleasing results. And it has been violated so often and so successfully that today it offers little more than one suggestion for room treatment.

The color of the rug or carpet you select is governed by your color scheme. It may be a neutral gray, brown, tan, beige or taupe or it may repeat, blend or contrast with the dominating color in the room. By repeating the color of your floor covering in your drapes, upholstery and wall, you insure unity.

Floor coverings may be monochromatic or multicolored. The monochromatic rugs and carpets may, further, consist of one solid color or contain varying tinges of one color, as in the tone on tone rugs. The number of colors available in rugs and carpets in the lower priced brackets is relatively limited. Before finally deciding upon your color scheme, it is advisable to see what colors are available in floor coverings within your price range. This is also true if you intend to select an Oriental or patterned rug. After you assure yourself that the colors you want for your floor covering are obtainable, then you can apply your color scheme to your decoration.

Remember, too, that rug colors tend to fade. You will, therefore, be well advised to select a darker colored rug that will be less affected by fading. The darker colored rugs do, however, show dust and lint more readily than do gray or blonde rugs. Solid

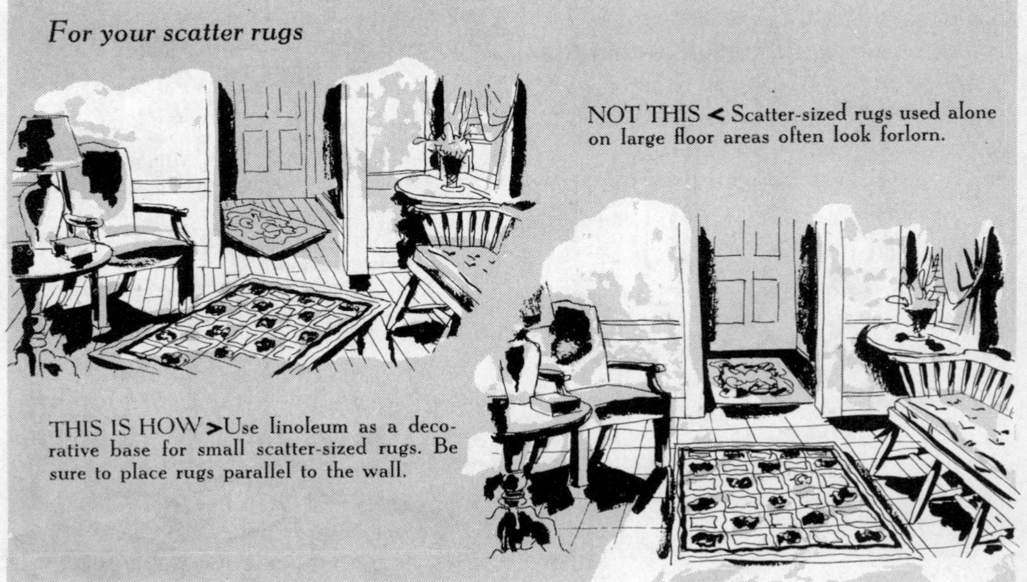

For your scatter rugs

NOT THIS < Scatter-sized rugs used alone on large floor areas often look forlorn.

THIS IS HOW > Use linoleum as a decorative base for small scatter-sized rugs. Be sure to place rugs parallel to the wall.

colored and tone on tone rugs also show footprints more readily than do patterned floor coverings. Patterned floor coverings also are suitable in the dining room as they are less likely to show stains.

PATTERN

The entire world has contributed designs for present-day rugs. In pattern, floor coverings range from the unfigured to the exotic motifs of the Orient. Flower, tree, leaf and fern patterns are favorites in rugs and carpets, while birds, shell and scroll designs afford interesting possibilities. There are geometric figures, hooks, crosses, stripes, plaids, tweeds, blocks, checkerboard designs — the list may be continued indefinitely.

Whether you select a figured or an unfigured rug or carpet depends upon the decoration of your entire room. You will want to achieve balance and moderation in the patterns you use in your room. If your floor covering is plain or two-toned, you can select a patterned or plain wallpaper, and patterned curtains, upholstery and slipcovers.

With patterned floor covering, plain walls are in good taste. You can introduce additional pattern through the other fabrics of your room. You may also use a wallpaper with a restrained pattern in this instance, depending upon the amount of pattern in the floor covering, curtains, drapes and upholstery.

The rule that no more than two of the three components—floor covering, fabrics and wallpaper — be patterned will prevent your room from becoming too busy. You can secure balance by repeating patterns and spacing them in moderation throughout the room, or you can repeat the individual colors of the pattern. The size of the patterns you use should be in keeping with the scale of your room and its furnishings. It is advisable to be restrained in the use of pattern in your room.

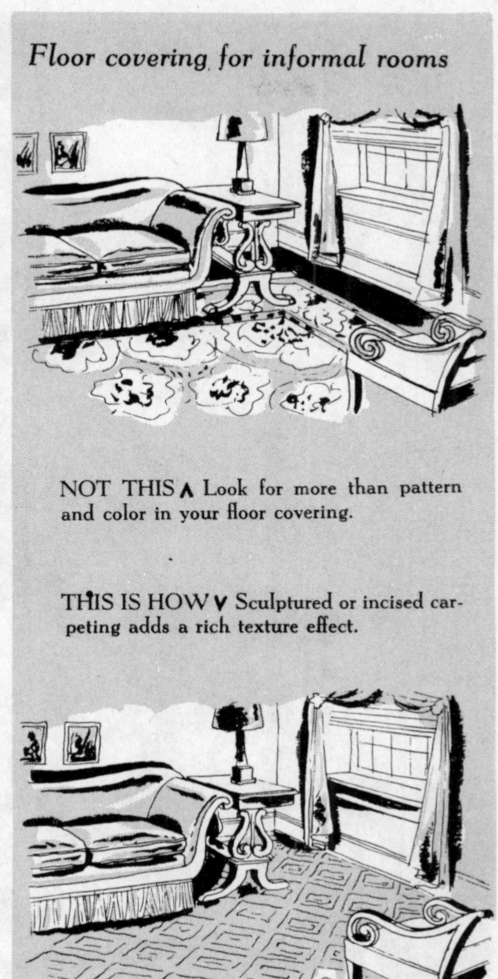

Floor covering for informal rooms

NOT THIS ∧ Look for more than pattern and color in your floor covering.

THIS IS HOW ∨ Sculptured or incised carpeting adds a rich texture effect.

TEXTURE

The texture of rugs and carpets is assuming increasing importance. Especially in monochromatic floor covering, so popular in modern decoration, is texture a major decorative element. Textured floor covering has

Oriental in style though actually hand woven in Europe, the rug has a beige pattern on a green ground and serves to point out the original terra cotta sculpture, which is surrounded by a light chartreuse frame, on the wall. The broadloom carpeting is in a deeper tone of green. To complete the monochromatic scheme, the chair and sofa are upholstered in a light green antique satin, while the walls are white.

the advantage of not showing soil and footprints so readily as plain colored carpets. It also can reproduce the textural effects of upholstery and drapery.

Textural effects are produced by the pile—the upright tufts of yarn in a carpet or rug. The pile is made of loops that may be cut or uncut. The cut or uncut pile may consist of soft twist or hard twist yarn. Yarns of several colors may be twisted together. Through varying the height and thickness of the pile, combining uncut loops and cut pile, and combining soft twist with hard twist yarns, the many different textural effects are produced.

Long uncut loops of twisted boucle yarn, varied in height, produce a three-dimensional textural effect resembling scragly cotton rugs that are very popular today. Uniform piled carpets are sometimes incised with a pattern, while looped Tapestry carpets alternate the sizes of uncut piles in different rows. Frieze carpets result from permanently twisted yarn with cut or uncut loops.

A pattern may consist of high-cut pile with the uncut loops serving as the ground. Brocade attains an embossed effect through combining soft, straight yarn for the ground and hard twisted, crinkled yarn for the design. In sculptured carpets, a cut pile is used to form a pattern or to give the effect of light and shadow. Other effects are obtainable through hand-tufting.

RUGS AND CARPETS

Rugs differ from carpets in that rugs are units, woven ordinarily in a number of standard sizes. Carpets are produced in standard widths, but may be obtained in any length desired for ordinary use and usually are plain or have an all-over design that may be cut at any point. Broadloom refers to carpeting, usually of Velvet weave, woven on a broad loom, which obviates the need of seams. In width, carpeting varies from 27 inches — the so-called ¾ width, used mainly for halls and stairways—to 18 feet.

Domestic rugs vary in size from the small scatter rug to the outsized rug and are available in over forty sizes. In fact, Chenille rugs are obtainable in widths up to 30 feet and, woven to order, are obtainable in practically any size and shape. The most common rug sizes are:

27 inches x 54 inches
36 inches x 63 inches
4 feet 6 inches x 6 feet 6 inches
6 feet x 9 feet
7 feet 6 inches x 9 feet
9 feet x 12 feet
9 feet x 15 feet
11 feet 3 inches x 12 feet
11 feet 3 inches x 15 feet
12 feet x 21 feet

With this large variety of sizes, it is often possible to secure a standard sized rug that will satisfy the requirements of your room size.

Broadloom makes it possible to lay carpeting from wall to wall, even if the room is irregularly shaped. Allowances can be made for jogs, alcoves and other irregular architectural features. Wall-to-wall carpeting not only gives a luxurious and spacious effect but helps in arranging furniture. Rugs that leave a border of bare floor no wider than 6 to 12 inches also produce a rich effect.

The price of rugs varies with the weave and the material. Jacquard weave rugs are more costly than Axminster and Velvet weave rugs, worsted yarn more expensive than woolen yarn. Worsted yarn is made of long staple wool yarn. It is hard, smooth, lustrous and combed to lie straight

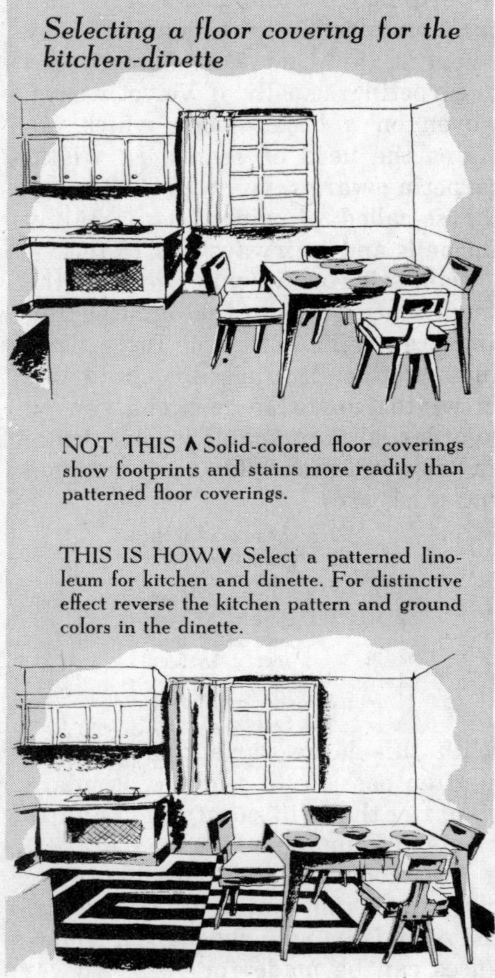

Selecting a floor covering for the kitchen-dinette

NOT THIS ∧ Solid-colored floor coverings show footprints and stains more readily than patterned floor coverings.

THIS IS HOW ∨ Select a patterned linoleum for kitchen and dinette. For distinctive effect reverse the kitchen pattern and ground colors in the dinette.

and parallel. Woolen yarn is soft, loosely twisted, with short fibers that lie in all directions to produce a felt-like texture. Rayon is often blended with wool, as is cotton, in carpet making.

The weave of a piled rug refers to the way in which the pile tufts are fastened to the backing. Of the machine weaves, Chenille is the most expensive, followed in order by Saxony, Lustre, Wilton, Axminster, Velvet and Tapestry. In order of popularity, Axminster accounts for the most yardage, followed by Velvet and Wilton.

High, medium and low quality rugs are obtainable in each of these weaves. From the standpoint of durability, it is better to purchase a high quality rug of a less expensive weave than a low quality rug of a more expensive weave. The quality of a rug or carpet depends upon the density (compactness) of the pile per square inch, the height of the pile, the amount and quality of the wool or worsted in the rug and the construction of the carpet. The greater the density of the pile, the United States Bureau of Standards reports, the better wearability in a rug, other factors being equal. A dense, low pile rug, accordingly, is preferable to a loosely woven high pile rug.

In constructing the under surface of a rug, jute or a blend of jute and cotton is used for backing, as is wood-pulp yarn. Jute is most satisfactory. A firm back, which can be detected by fingering, comes from a tightly woven filling. Occasionally, sizing is used to offset loosely woven construction. If you detect a lack of firmness, a thin, loosely woven construction or a sleazy feeling from sizing, the rug is of low quality.

As a rule, price reflects quality. Long-term economy, however, may make it advisable to spend a trifle more for your carpet or rug. Very often, a few dollars more will result in years of longer wear. In fact, many of the better-grade rugs improve with age.

RUG WEAVES

Rugs are divided into hand made and machine made. In both these types, rugs may be woven flat or with a pile. In the machine made pile

A SUMMER SETTING

A fireplace wall in a Modern room here finds employment as a backdrop for summery plants. With attractive results, too, for plants do make colorful accessories, as do the contrasting pillows on the attractive loveseat.

DRAMA IN WINDOW TREATMENT

Here a formal window treatment, which turns a corner to cover parts of two walls, forms the background for informal bedroom furniture. The ruffled draperies, consisting of an allover print in gold, are framed by a correlated gold wallpaper and extend from a plain cornice to the floor. Metal tiebacks hold the draperies up. The drapery fabric is repeated in the dust ruffle and in the channel back armchair. The pink chintz of the draw curtains is also repeated in the top of the bedspread. The cotton rug is a pink beige.

WARM, INVITING COLONIAL CHARM

Mellow planking forms the background of the fireplace wall of this casual room. The remaining walls are dark green, the carpet is also of green though lighter than the wall. The pair of fireside barrel chairs are upholstered in a green and white check, the ruffled gingham curtains are in the same tone. The pewter accessories carry out the Colonial motif of this warm, charming room.

weave, the loops may be cut or uncut.

Axminster, a cut pile rug, resembles Oriental hand woven rugs in its construction. In the Axminster, however, the pile tufts are inserted mechanically and held in place by the weft threads without knotting. Axminster rugs may, like Orientals, use an unlimited number of colors. Very often, Oriental patterns are reproduced in Axminster rugs. Like Velvet rugs, Axminsters contain less wool per square inch than do Wilton or Brussels rugs. All the wool in Axminster and Velvet rugs appears on the surface as pile tufts, except for the small amount of wool yarn used in attaching the tufts to the carpet back.

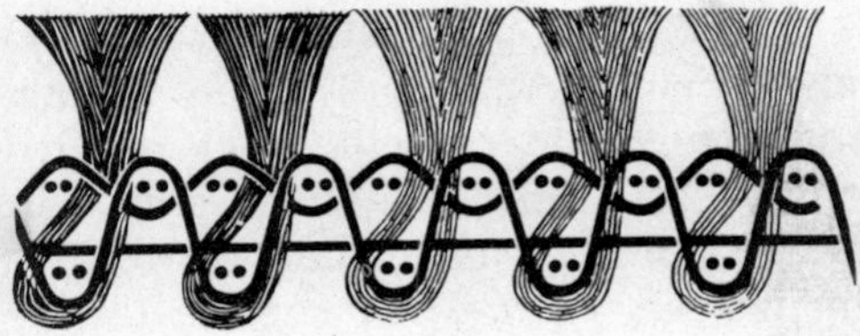

DIAGRAM 11
Axminster Weave

Axminster is recognizable by the ridges on its back. These ridges consist of stiff jute weft and allow the rug to be rolled lengthwise, but not crosswise. Four ridges to the inch mean fair quality in the lower-priced range. Seven or more ridges per inch are considered standard and are likely to wear more than twice as long as the four ridge rug.

In *Velvet* rugs, the wool pile is woven over wires and cut. Cotton furnishes the weft, wool and cotton the warp. Additional firmness and body are supplied by a stuffer of jute warp yarns heavily sized. *Tapestry* rugs are similarly woven, except that the pile loops are left uncut. Pattern is produced in these two weaves either by direct printing on the woven rug or by drum printing of the warp yarn before it is loomed. Both methods produce an indistinct design.

DIAGRAM 12
Velvet Weave

Most plain-colored rugs are of Velvet weave. The better quality Velvets are durable and resemble Wiltons. As all the wool in both Velvet and Tapestry rugs is in the pile, these rugs lack the resilience of Wilton rugs. The best quality Velvet and Tapestry rugs use ten wires to the inch, with a pile 15/16 inch in height. Unless the pile is long and compact, these rugs may *grin*—i.e., the body of the carpet shows between the rows of pile tufts. Looming with three weft yarns to each wire of pile tufts gives better results than two shots to the wire. The terms, Wilton Velvet and Tapestry Brussels, are both misnomers, attempting to capitalize on the superior Jacquard weave carpets.

Wilton and *Brussels* carpets are both woven on the Jacquard loom. They differ in that the Wilton has a cut pile, the Brussels—a Victorian favorite—an uncut loop. The Jacquard loom limits the number of colors to five, though planting may increase the number of colors to as many as twenty-six. The system of pattern cards used in the Jacquard loom produces clear-cut designs. The pattern cards are perforated, directing the strands of colored yarn that will appear in the surface pile. All the other five yarns, in a six frame weave, are buried in the body of the rug. The loops of pile are formed over wires and woven into the base of the rug for body and firmness.

Wilton rugs are made of both woolen and worsted. The woolen yarn produces a softer pile, with less resilience and compactness. A longer tuft in the woolen Wilton also results in a less clear design than the worsted. One grade of highly twisted woolen Wilton is known as the *Saxony.* The finest quality in these Jacquard weaves is made of six frames, with thirteen rows to the inch and three shots to each wire. Jacquard weaves often show the color of the yarn in the back of the carpet, a fact that distinguishes this weave from Velvet and Tapestry.

DIAGRAM 13
Wilton Weave

Chenille rugs are the luxury fabrics of the machine made weaves and usually are made only on order. This weave employs two looms. One weaves the weft blanket, colored to produce the desired design, on widely spaced lengthwise cotton yarn. This blanket is cut into long strips between the lengthwise yarn. The fringe ends are then steamed and pressed together into the shape of a V, with a resultant furry caterpillar appearance. Chenille, in fact, is the French term for caterpillar. Chenille differs from other rugs in that it uses strips rather than yarn. In the second loom, the strips are carried through the warp or catcher threads. The strips are combed and tufted by hand. The backing of this rug is of wool.

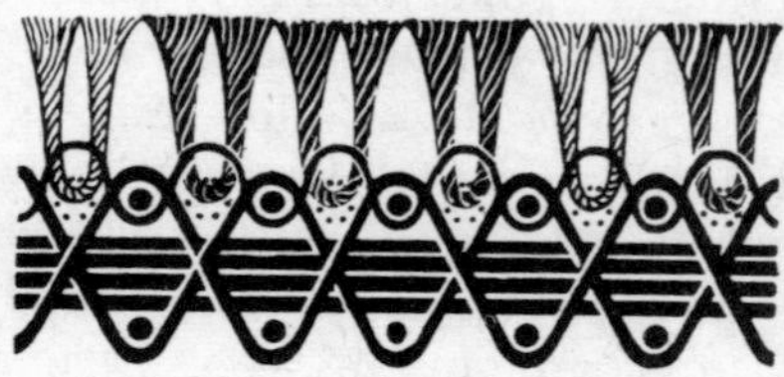

DIAGRAM 14
Chenille Weave

Lustre-type or sheen-type rugs, formerly called American Orientals, are machine made reproductions of Oriental rugs. These rugs are Wilton or Axminster in weave and of worsted or woolen yarn, with soft cotton as the warp and weft. These rugs are soft and pliable, without sizing, and can be folded exactly like Orientals. The lustre is produced by crushing or bending parts of the pile surface to give the effects of light and shadow. Lustre is still further increased by removing the scales of the wool fiber, a process known as mercerization. In addition, chemical washes heighten the lustre.

Fiber rugs are usually plain flat woven. They are made of wood pulp, sisal, hemp and other material. Wool is often woven in combination with these fibers. They frequently have stencilled patterns. Especially adapted for summer use, fiber rugs, however, cannot withstand hard wear. Grass rugs are waterproof and usable out of doors. They are reversible,

A rich Oriental rug keynotes a spirit of richness and good living in this 18th century styled dining room. The bull's eye mirror over the black marble fireplace draws attention to the novel wallpaper that repeats the design of the window treatment. The crystal chandelier and the fine tableware add the final touches of opulence to this room.

usually plain on one side and patterned on the other. The Japanese grass rug uses a rice straw. Linen rugs are also produced in plain weave. The popular Indian Drugget is another flat weave rug suitable for summer use.

ORIENTAL RUGS

Through the years Oriental rugs have set the standard for excellence in floor covering. As a result of growing demand, these rugs have begun to reflect Occidental influence in design and color. In 1860, aniline dyes were introduced into the Orient and replaced the native vegetable and insect dyes, many of which had been unfathomed family secrets for generations. Chemical washing, to reduce their brilliant coloring, is necessary before Oriental rugs may be used in present-day homes.

The pile surface of Oriental rugs is most often of wool, though silk and camel's hair are used. Wool also comprises the warp and weft, though cotton is sometimes used. Three weaves are used in Oriental rugs—the Kilim, Soumak and pile surface. The first two are flat weaves. Kilim resembles tapestry, the weft yarn alternately going over and under the warp. Design is introduced by varying the colors of the weft yarns and is reversible. Soumak rugs are also flat woven, with a herringbone design produced by the use of diagonal colored weft yarns.

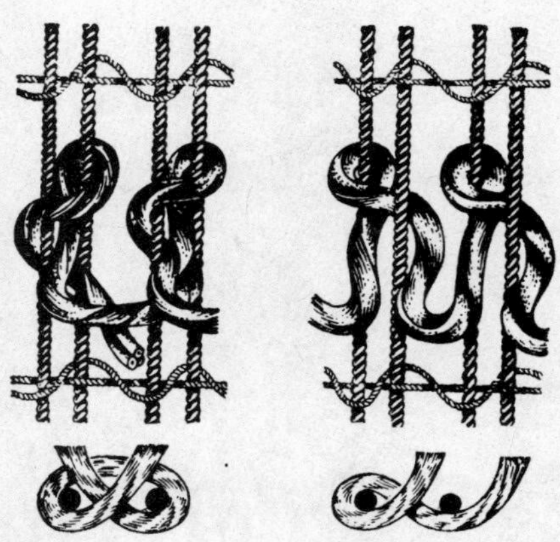

DIAGRAM 15
Ghiordes Knot Senna Knot

The pile surface rugs use either the Turkish Ghiordes knot or the Persian Senna knot. The latter knot permits a greater density of pile tufts as well as greater uniformity. The number of knots per square inch determines the quality of Oriental rugs. Modern Orientals of good grade have 100 to 200 knots per square inch, while the highly prized early Oriental rugs may have as many as 400 or 500 knots per square inch.

Oriental rugs may be classified on the basis of the country in which they were produced. The rugs of different countries vary in design, color, texture and craftsmanship. The *Persian* rugs, usually of wool with cotton warp and weft have floral, curved, bird and animal designs and soft colors. Kashan, Kirman and Sarouk rugs are popular Persian rugs.

The *Turkish* rug is bright in color, with both conventionalized floral and geometric figures. The Kilim, Kurdistan and Saraband are of this type. The Turkish prayer rug, characterized by its mithrab or prayer niche, is well known and is of scatter rug size. The Mozul rug uses both camel's and goat's hair, while the Anatolian is a relatively low priced favorite.

Caucasian rugs feature geometric figures, cold, clear-cut colors and include the famed Cashmere and Daghestan rugs. *Turkestan* rugs are the most familiar of the Oriental rugs. The pile is short, closely woven and lustrous, patterns are mainly geometric. The colors are red and brown, tinged with blue, rust and chocolate, and fit well into present-day color schemes. The Bokhara is a Turkestan rug.

Chinese rugs use the Senna knot, a clipped pile for design and soft blue, yellow and neutral colors. Motifs are symbolic, many being of religious significance.

Indian rugs, rather rare today, are coarsely woven and heavy in texture. The designs exhibit Persian influence, with red as the main color. The inexpensive Numdah rug, of pounded goat's hair felt, with strongly contrasting colors and highly figured embroidery, is a prominent Indian type, as is the Drugget.

OTHER HAND MADE RUGS

Both *Savonnerie* and *Aubusson* rugs are suggestive of French period furniture. The Savonnerie is a hand-tufted rug, with woolen or worsted piles and a deep velvet nap. It is more luxurious than the Aubusson, a flat-woven tapestry rug of silk and wool. The Aubusson is ornate in design, feminine in spirit and occasionally features a central medallion.

Hooked, braided and *rag* rugs are all reminiscent of early America. The hooked rugs use a backing of burlap, canvas or monk's cloth. Strips of cotton, wool or silk cloth are drawn through the backing, forming loops on the upper side that may be cut or left uncut. Braided rugs use strips of material that are braided together. Both hooked and braided rugs are frequently woven in oval shape. Rag rugs consist of narrow strips of rags as the weft, with heavy cord as the warp.

Navajo rugs are popular, as are Mexican *serapes*. Both are flat woven and reversible. The Navajo rugs use gray, black and white colors, with accents in red, and geometric patterns. geometric patterns of serapes, which Blue, white, red and brown mark the usually are fringed.

HARD FLOOR COVERINGS

A number of hard floor coverings are available, including linoleum, tile and rubber. *Linoleum,* the most popular of these durable floor coverings, is a linseed oil and cork preparation pressed onto a burlap, jute or felt base. Three types are manufactured —*plain, inlaid* and *printed*. Plain linoleum is especially adapted to severe wear. Battleship linoleum is the thickest gauge and can endure heavy duty. Marbleized and jaspe linoleum both are two-toned, with the latter giving a striated effect.

Inlaid linoleum may be used to produce pleasing and interesting patterns. This type consists of blocks,

An oval braided rug on an allover patterned carpet blends with the country style furniture of this informal room. The lightness and gayety of the wallpaper add to the pleasantness of this bungalow room, as does its asymmetrical furniture grouping. Furniture of this type is well suited to the budgeter and to the small home.

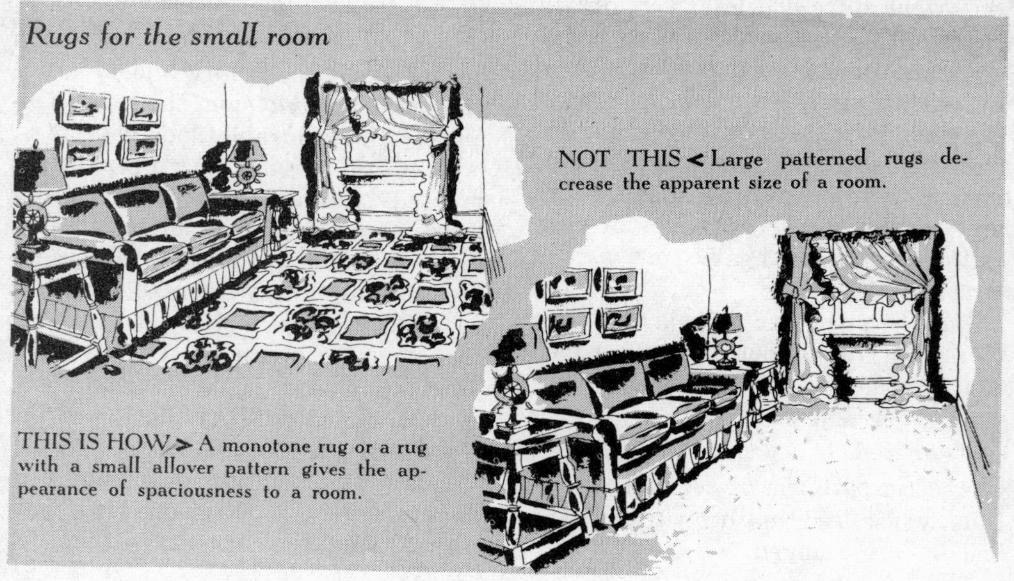

in all ranges of color, and permits the use of decorative insets. Formal as well as informal effects are obtainable with linoleum. Designs are also printed, stencilled or embossed on linoleum.

Linoleum dents and cuts and the plain colored types show dust and footprints readily. In laying, the floor must be absolutely smooth. Linoleum, further, should be cemented to the floor to avoid buckling. It may be fitted to cover irregularly shaped rooms, as well as cut out for fixed pipes, legs and other obstructions. Grade depends upon gauge and backing, the felt base being the least expensive. Linoleum is finding increased use in all the rooms of the home. Used as a base for small scatter-sized rugs, linoleum adds a highly decorative border.

Felt base coverings consist of processed felt saturated with asphalt. They resemble linoleum, are inexpensive and give moderate wear. Grade is based on weight and thickness.

Tile flooring may be asphaltic or ceramic. Both types are fire resistant, not damaged by water and laid on felt bases. Tile, however, lacks resilience, is noisy and cold. Like linoleum, it is easy to clean. It is adaptable to the American Southwest style of Spanish architecture, as well as to kitchens and bathrooms.

Rubber flooring offers resilience and quiet, though it may buckle. It is laid in sheets or blocks upon a felt base.

SPIRIT

Rugs contribute to creating the spirit that we desire for our room. A formal room calls for a different rug from an informal one. As furniture styles reflect spirit, period furniture requires a suitable type of floor covering. French Provincial court style uses a different rug from Victorian or American Federal. Machine made domestic rugs are woven in so broad a variety of pattern, color and texture, that a suitable Wilton or Axminster may be obtained for any style or spirit.

Oriental rugs belong in the formal room, where they give a feeling of richness and beauty. Small scatter-sized Orientals, however, may be used in informal rooms. Lustre-type rugs, which so closely resemble Orientals, are similarly well suited for the formal room. The Aubusson rug provides a perfect floor covering in a French styled formal room and complements the softly curving, feminine furniture. A Savonnerie rug is even richer in appearance and goes well also in an English Regency room.

The rough textures and gay colors of hooked, braided and rag rugs enhance the Colonial, provincial and cottage style rooms. Navajos and serapes make interesting wall hangings as well as informal floor coverings. The monochrome, tone on tone and sculptured rug likewise are well adapted to the modern home. In the next chapter we present a chart listing further suggested floor coverings for the period style home, as well as suggestions for the other background components.

Twist combined with cut-pile for textural interest produces a new carpeting with the effect of rippling waters. Carpeting of 27-inch width, as here, permits seaming and often minimizes waste in a wall-to-wall treatment. The rear wall in a dark color offers effective contrast. The planter coffee table with metal legs and the tall lamp are functional and attractive, as is the natural wood grain of the divider wall.

Blending traditional furniture and modern coloring, this bedroom uses blue American Beauty chintz not only for its bedskirts but also for two of its walls. The waled corduroy of the bedspreads is blue, as is the mohair damask upholstery of chair and ottoman. A pair of bedside tables and tall crystal lamps, which are ordinarily reserved for use in the living room, give the necessary scale and distinction to the bed grouping, and demonstrate the flexibility of today's furniture. Two 18th century chests complete the furnishings of the room. The two other walls are an aquamarine, the monotone rug is a green chenille.

CHAPTER NINE

HARMONIZING FURNITURE AND BACKGROUND

IF YOU hope to create a beautiful and harmonious room, you must harmonize your furniture and background. Both must express a uniform spirit. They must be related to each other in color, pattern, line and texture. In addition, they must be in scale to each other and to the room as a whole. And there must be balance among the components of your room so that everything in the room gives the effect of belonging together.

Too often in home decoration the background is treated without regard to the furniture. Especially is this true in the home that is being redecorated in part. Masculine furniture will not harmonize with a feminine background. Simple furniture looks out of place against an elaborate background or one that is highly ornamented. If the background is to serve as a foil to set off your furniture, then it must be appropriate to the foreground. Both must blend together so as to produce one over-all effect for your room.

PLANNING YOUR DECORATIVE SCHEME

Harmony is achieved in the planning stage of room decoration. You cannot achieve a harmonious result

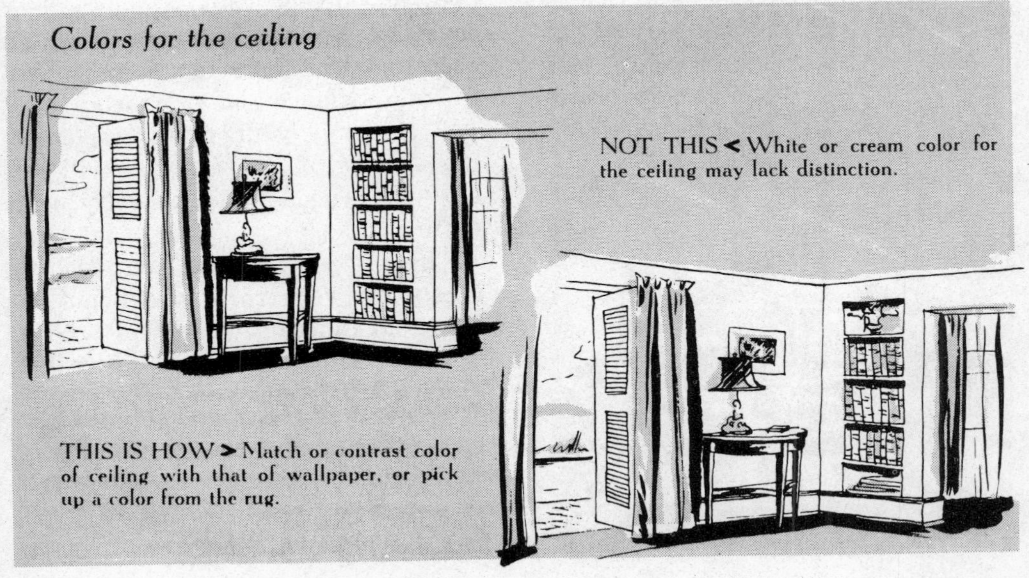

Colors for the ceiling

NOT THIS < White or cream color for the ceiling may lack distinction.

THIS IS HOW > Match or contrast color of ceiling with that of wallpaper, or pick up a color from the rug.

unless you are guided by a consistent plan. You cannot translate inconsistent plans into reality and expect to create over-all unity in your room. Somewhere in your room decoration, any discrepancy in your plan will show up. Most often the shortcoming becomes noticeable in the failure of the background to harmonize with your furniture.

Just as you plan a color scheme, so must you plan a decorative scheme that considers each phase of the room decoration. For unity, you must plan each phase from one consistent point of view. The viewpoint you apply is one that you derive from your decorative purpose, embodying as it does the effect that you wish to create and the needs that you must satisfy.

Your decorative scheme must be one that is carefully worked out. In formulating a scheme, you can assure a harmonious result if you follow a step by step process that deals successively with each phase of decoration. If you take each of the following steps in order, you can readily devise a good decorative scheme.

1. Decide upon the effect that you wish to create in your home and that fulfills your wants and needs.

2. Select a style of furniture or, if you prefer, mix styles that carry out your purpose.

3. Adopt or devise a color scheme in keeping with the effect you desire and with your style of furniture.

4. Decide upon the kind of lines, patterns and textures that you will emphasize to carry out your effect.

5. Plan the distribution of all the elements — color, line, pattern and texture — in the walls, windows, floor covering, upholstery, furniture and accessories of the room, with an eye to scale, balance and emphasis.

6. Arrange your furniture, creating centers of interest that will satisfy your needs and beautify your room.

The effect or spirit you wish to create for your room and home has a double function—it serves both as a guide in planning your entire decorative treatment and as a goal to aim at in your decoration. As a goal, the effect you adopt for your home should be in keeping with your taste, preferences and needs, and those of your family. Remember, your home

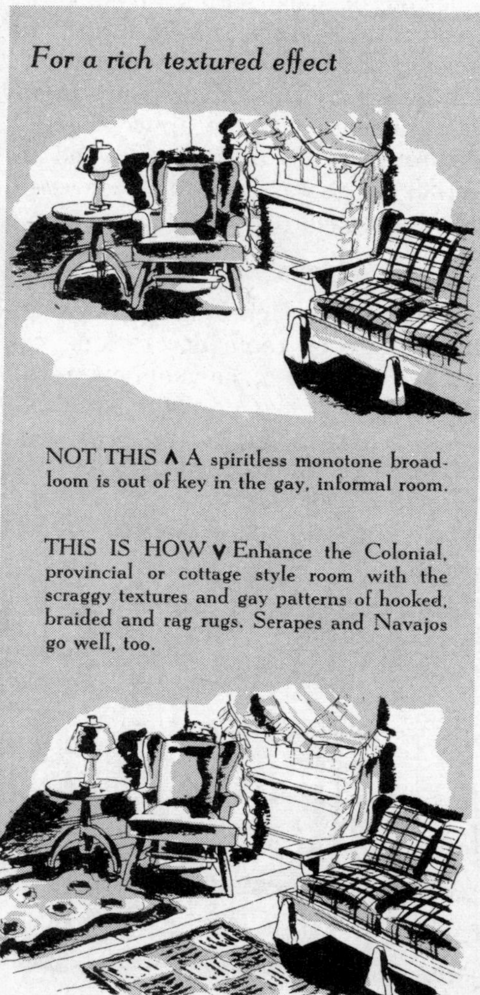

For a rich textured effect

NOT THIS ∧ A spiritless monotone broadloom is out of key in the gay, informal room.

THIS IS HOW ∨ Enhance the Colonial, provincial or cottage style room with the scraggy textures and gay patterns of hooked, braided and rag rugs. Serapes and Navajos go well, too.

will embody this effect and you will have to live with it. If your home is to satisfy you, you must adopt an over-all effect that suits you and your family.

As a guide, the effect you select delimits automatically the range of furniture styles and color schemes from which you may choose. It indicates what kind of lines, patterns and textures are appropriate to achieving your purpose. Obviously, you cannot attain a formal effect with informal styles of furniture. Nor can you attain an informal effect through the strictly formal styles. The same consideration applies to the other decorative elements.

The effect you select for your home may be any one of a large number. It may be formal or informal, restful or gay, masculine or feminine. The formal treatment may be dignified and elegant, simple and restrained, hospitable and inviting or aloof and reserved. Your home may be sophisticatedly formal or sophisticatedly informal. No matter which effect you choose, select one that you are certain you like.

The style of furniture that you select, as the second step in planning your decorative scheme, should appeal to you and your family no less than does the effect you selected. The style must be one that can carry out your decorative purpose. Each period style has, as chapter 5 explained, a rather definite character. For this reason, a knowledge of which styles accord with your decorative purpose is important. Styles that are kindred

A knotty pine fireplace wall combines with furniture and accessories in the Early American tradition to create the hospitable mood of the Americana living room. The colorful printed linen draperies, which are hung straight, and the upholstery are in keeping with the spirit of the period. The furniture arrangement emphasizes the informality of the room. The corner grouping forms a convenient bridge center.

HARMONIZING FURNITURE AND BACKGROUND

	CHIPPENDALE	HEPPLEWHITE	SHERATON	FRENCH PROVINCIAL Court Style	FRENCH PROVINCIAL Country Style
WOOD	Mahogany	Mahogany, also satinwood, sycamore, chestnut	Mahogany, satinwood also rosewood, sycamore	Fruitwoods, walnut, chestnut	Waxed or painted local woods
DECORATION	Carving, brass tacks Chinese motifs, lacquer, caning	Delicate carving, classical motifs, veneer, painting, inlay	Inlay, restrained carving, veneer, painting, caning	Carving, soft curved lines	Simple motifs or devoid of ornament. Cane seats
FABRICS	Toiles, cretonnes, printed linens, tapestry, worsted damasks, brocades, velvets, tooled leather	Striped damasks, floral and striped silks, satins, taffeta, moire	Plain, striped and delicate flowered silks, damasks, gold and silver brocades	Floral and striped silks, toiles, printed linens, needlepoint, tapestry, antique satins, chinoiserie	Toiles, plaids, homespuns, simple cotton fabrics
COLORS	Chinese yellow, orange, brown, black, reds, greens, blues	Gray, ivory, red, soft tints of blue, rose, green	Soft blue and white, cream, yellow, gold, gray, gray-green, black	Pastels, soft faded colors	Bright, gay colors and soft, faded blues
FLOOR COVERING	Oriental or lustre type. Plain, tone on tone, or period broadloom	Oriental or lustre type in small formal patterns. Plain, tone on tone, or period broadloom. Linoleum	Similar to Hepplewhite	Aubusson, Savonnerie. Plain and period broadloom	Axminsters and flat weave-hooked rug, braided
WALLS	Wood panels Dados Painted white or soft colors Papers – scenics, chinoiserie	Panels and decorative moldings Painted soft colors Papers – scenics, stripes, classical	White wood trim Painted soft colors Papers – stripes, delicate florals, classical	Natural or painted panels Painted soft tints Papers – delicate designs	Natural or painted panels Plaster Whitewash or paint

HARMONIZING FURNITURE AND BACKGROUND				
COLONIAL New England	**DUNCAN PHYFE** Federal American	**ENGLISH REGENCY**	**VICTORIAN**	**MODERN**
WOOD Maple, pine, also birch, walnut, fruitwoods, hickory, oak	**WOOD** Mahogany, rosewood	**WOOD** Mahogany, satinwood, rosewood, also black lacquer and gilt	**WOOD** Black walnut, ebony, rosewood	**WOOD** Bleached, paneled, dark woods, plywood, lacquer, plastics, glass, mirrors, metal
DECORATION Little ornament, flat carving, turnings, handwrought hardware, quaint patterns	**DECORATION** Carving, brass mounts and terminals, caning, classic and patriotic motifs	**DECORATION** Metal grill work, ormolu, carving, inlays of ebony and metal, bamboo trim	**DECORATION** Ornate carving, inlays of brass and mother-of-pearl, gilt fringe	**DECORATION** Relies on beauty of grain, contrasting woods, veneers, caning, plastics and metals
FABRICS Calico, homespun, cretonne, crewelwork, printed linen, gingham, candlewick and patchwork quilts	**FABRICS** Horsehair, silks, satins, brocades, damasks, woolens, mohair	**FABRICS** Striped silks, satins, damasks, velvets, brocades	**FABRICS** Horsehair, large-scale patterned chintzes, damasks, brocades, velvets	**FABRICS** Varied weaves, yarn combinations and textures Leather Plastics
COLORS White, tans, mustard yellow, light brown, cranberry red, black, blue, blue-greens	**COLORS** Reds, champagne, marine blue, yellow, grass green	**COLORS** Regency green, white, black, dull gold, deep reds, brown	**COLORS** Heavy, muddied colors, mauve, purple, purplish reds, brown, deep greens, rose Today — brilliant colors	**COLORS** Much beige, gray, white and strong color accent Contrasts of light and shade
FLOOR COVERING Flat weave rugs, hooked, rag, braided Linoleum with scatter rugs	**FLOOR COVERING** Oriental or lustre type Plain or period broadloom Linoleum	**FLOOR COVERING** Wiltons, Axminsters Plain or period broadloom Linoleum	**FLOOR COVERING** Brussels, patterned rugs—large florals and scrolls Plain broadloom in dark colors	**FLOOR COVERING** Monochromes, rough textured, hand woven Linoleum
WALLS Natural or painted panels, rough-hewn planks, rough plaster—plain or painted Papers — quaint small all-over patterns	**WALLS** Decorative plaster Painted walls Papers — period, scenics, classic and patriotic	**WALLS** Painted—dark colors, white trim, white pilasters Marbleized effects Classical-frieze borders Striped papers	**WALLS** Painted dark colors Scenics, large floral and scroll patterns, classic and nautical motifs	**WALLS** Painted Papered Mirrors, glass, murals, linoleum Contrasting walls

in spirit go well together and may be mixed. If you have a marked preference for a particular style, then your effect must conform to your choice of style.

To harmonize your furniture with the background, you must assure that they both express the same spirit. If you have decided upon a spirit and have analyzed it carefully, you will the more readily be able to determine how to treat the background so as to produce a harmonious whole. Your furniture, moreover, must be in scale with the background and with your room if you are to achieve unity.

Your choice of a furniture style will influence your choice of a color scheme, the third step in planning your decorative scheme. Just as your choice of an over-all effect delimited the number of styles that could carry out your purpose, so your choice of a style delimits the colors you may use and the mood your color scheme can set. Let us see how this works out in an example.

If your furniture style is formal, then your color scheme must similarly be a formal one. However, any number of color schemes may express a spirit of formality equally well, just as several different period styles are each equally formal. Does this mean that you can use the same formal color scheme for any formal period style, or use a formal style with any formal color scheme?

No, you cannot. Not only must the background be one in spirit with your furniture style but it must be decoratively appropriate to your furniture. Only in this way can you attain a measure of authenticity in re-creating a period style or can you create a completely harmonious effect in your room. The English Regency room will accordingly want to adopt a color scheme that differs from that of the French Provincial court style room, though both these styles are formal.

Jane and her husband, you may recall, both wished for beauty and comfort in their home. Like formality,

For the irregular room

NOT THIS < A room full of jogs and juts makes decoration difficult.

THIS IS HOW > Straighten out the irregularities with furring that can be papered or painted.

however, these qualities are too diverse and indefinite to serve as an effective guide in achieving a decorative purpose. You must ask yourself, therefore, what other qualities besides formality or informality you want your home to incorporate. You must define the spirit you wish to create in your home quite carefully.

The difference in treatment necessary for the Regency and the French Provincial court styles lies in the fact that, aside from formality, they each express distinctive characteristics. These distinctions define the spirit of these period styles. The chart in chapter 5, *Mixing Furniture Styles,* will help you determine precisely what spirit typifies different period styles and which period styles are suitable for carrying out your decorative purpose. If you refer to this chart, you will see that the Regency style is dignified and elegant, while the French Provincial court style is feminine and delicate.

Your room will accordingly differ in treatment as it is one style or another. The Regency room uses dark colors, with white and gold accents. The French Provincial court style uses soft pastels and light tints. The distinctive traits will also be evidenced in line, texture and pattern. Thus the Regency room may use period broadloom carpeting or linoleum, while the French Provincial room may use an Aubusson or Savonnerie rug.

We have listed suggested treatments for different period styles in a chart that accompanies this chapter. This chart will aid you in harmonizing your furniture style with the background. It will enable you to adopt an authentic color scheme for your period color harmony, as well as use appropriate textures and fabrics.

COLOR COORDINATION

In harmonizing background and foreground, the system of coordinated colors can help you. Under one such system, sponsored by the Institute of Carpet Manufacturers of America, manufacturers of fabrics, wallpaper and floor coverings have keyed the

For dining room floors

NOT THIS▲ The usual patterned linoleums are not distinctive in the formal dining room.

THIS IS HOW▼ Use linoleum with radiating patterned inlays for a handsome effect.

colors of each of their products to one another. Individual manufacturers are also keying colors of solid and printed fabrics together. Thus, when you buy draperies, you can assure yourself that they match the particular color of the floor covering or upholstery material you intend to buy. Through coordinated colors, matching the colors of one item to another is simplified.

You should remember, however, that in matching items, the presence of one color in common does not automatically insure harmony of patterned and multicolored fabrics. You may, for example, match a solid colored rug to a patterned drapery fabric with success or a solid colored fabric to a patterned rug. But the moment you try to match a patterned drapery fabric to a patterned upholstery material or multicolored rug, the need for a color plan is apparent.

Even though multicolored fabrics have one color in common, the other colors may clash and their spirit may differ. Two items that each match or blend with a third, need not necessarily go well together. If you guide your selection by your color scheme, you will find the system of coordinated colors a great advantage in obtaining just the right color values and intensities for your room. This system does not, however, obviate the need for a color scheme as is so often alleged. But used to carry out your plan, it is a tremendous advantage to the home decorator.

In harmonizing your furniture with your color scheme, remember that a color scheme takes in the entire room, background as well as foreground. You will have to distribute your colors throughout the room so as to secure balance. You will want to highlight a center of interest with a contrasting color emphasis. Remember, too, that light values go well with a light background, dark values with a dark background. The Regency room will, therefore, use shaded foreground colors to harmonize with its background, while the French Provincial court style room will use tints to harmonize with the background pastels.

Your colors should tie your room together as well as contribute to its mood. List the colors in your scheme.

Decide which one is dominant. List the parts of the room and the furnishings to which color is to be applied. Bear in mind the arrangement you intend for your furniture and accessories so that you may distribute your colors. Use your accenting colors in moderation, and then chiefly to emphasize a center of interest. Above all, remember that your color scheme is your agent. You are the one who selects it. With care it will express the effect you wish to create in your room.

If you have a marked preference for a color scheme, it may serve as the starting point of your decorative scheme. Effect, style of furniture or color scheme may, accordingly, serve as your point of departure in planning your room harmony. Regardless of which of these three you start from, be sure to coordinate the other two phases of your scheme to it. Your effect must accord with your color scheme, as must your choice of a furniture style.

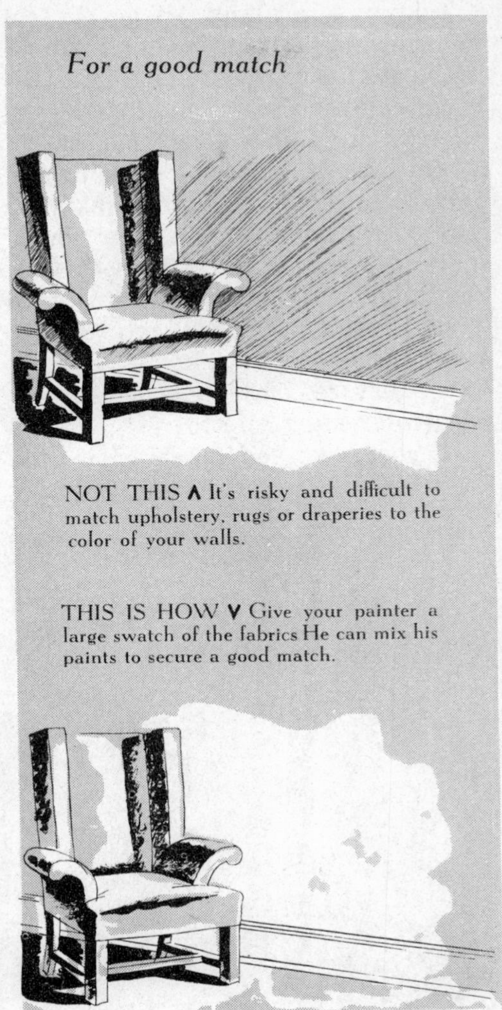

For a good match

NOT THIS ∧ It's risky and difficult to match upholstery, rugs or draperies to the color of your walls.

THIS IS HOW ∨ Give your painter a large swatch of the fabrics He can mix his paints to secure a good match.

LINE, PATTERN AND TEXTURE

While as a rule we plan our colors carefully, we do not ordinarily plan schemes for the other basic elements —line, form and texture. Yet these elements are important in harmonizing your furniture and background in creating an attractive home. They too must carry out the effect that you wish to produce in your home. The fourth step in planning your room decoration is concerned with them.

The spirit that you decide upon for your home determines your use of these basic elements. A formal room will stress vertical lines, a restful room horizontal ones, a feminine room curves. Similarly, your room will stress certain forms and textures. *Colors for Your Purpose,* in chapter 4, lists some of the ways in which the basic elements contribute to creating specific over-all effects.

The predominant kinds of basic elements are tools with which you attain your decorative purpose. Their psychologic effects must be in keeping with this purpose. The basic elements make for unity through the methods of repetition and dominance. They also introduce variety and thus produce beauty.

Texture is a highly adaptable tool in home decoration. Rough textures which have a masculine overtone, belong in a masculine room, though they may be used in moderation as an accent even in a feminine room. The texture of your upholstery material may be repeated in your floor covering, draperies and wall treatment. The kind of wood in your furniture is associated with those textures that serve to arouse a similar feeling. Other textures may serve as contrast with interesting effect.

If you have too much color, too many kinds of lines, or too diverse textures, you are bound to get a heterogeneous effect. The background, therefore, must repeat the dominating types of basic elements in the furniture. The finer you sift out the differences in these elements, the more harmonious will be the over-all result that you create. In addition, you must consider pattern in your room. From one point of view, pattern is form plus color used for decorative effect.

In related color schemes, pattern and texture assume an increased importance. A related color scheme cre-

The Americana dining room offers several suggestions for harmonizing foreground and background — choose draperies and upholstery with the same colorful floral design. As a further step toward harmony, choose a chandelier shade the color of the walls. The walls and metal shade of this room are painted a pale yellow. A mirror adds to the unity. A tier table serves as a decorative stand for the philodendron plants.

ates harmony. But it must be protected from its tendency to lapse into monotony. You may legitimately use bold patterns and contrasting textures to produce variety in such a room.

With a contrasting color scheme, however, you have assured variety. The weakness lies on the unity side of the ledger. You must, therefore, transfer your pattern and texture resources to this account and emphasize unity through them. Your patterns and textures may be gay and bold, but use them to tie together furniture and background. You can repeat patterns and textures in both furniture upholstery and draperies or, in a bedroom, repeat them in the bedspread, curtains and on the walls.

The more pattern you use, the more movement, liveliness and buoyancy your room expresses. The room with a large amount of varying pattern may lack harmony and give the effect of garishness. For this reason it is a counsel of caution to add—don't overdo pattern in your room. Much, however, depends upon the size and type of the pattern, its coloring, distribution and the effect you desire to create.

Also, be sure that the pattern you select is suitable to the members of your family. Preferably, a child's bedroom should use patterns that are meaningful and of interest to the child, not adult geometrics, stripes or abstracts. Pattern and other decoration must also be appropriate to your furniture style. The style and fabrics you select for your window treatment should harmonize with the spirit and furniture of your room. Chapter 7 illustrates suggested window treatments for different period rooms.

The spirit of the pattern will tell you whether it catches the effect you

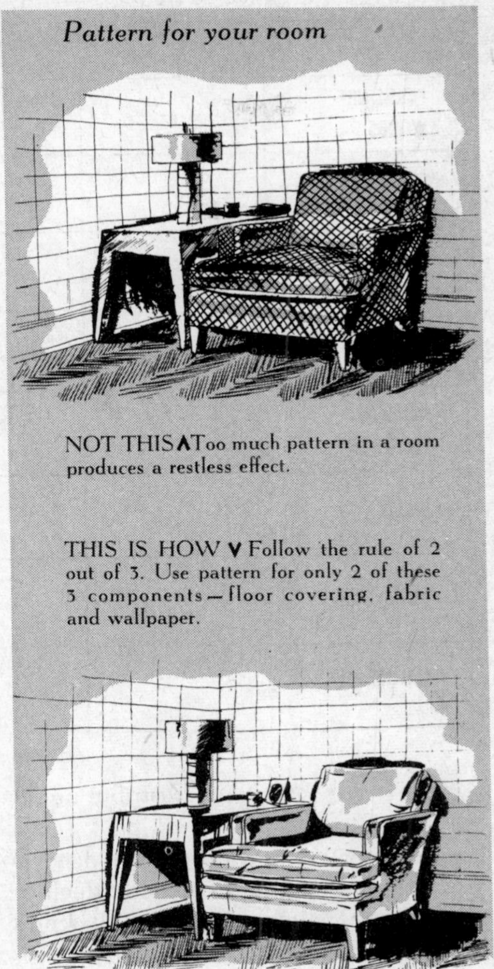

Pattern for your room

NOT THIS ▲ Too much pattern in a room produces a restless effect.

THIS IS HOW ▼ Follow the rule of 2 out of 3. Use pattern for only 2 of these 3 components—floor covering, fabric and wallpaper.

desire for your room. Country styles of furniture go best with patterns having simple motifs, while the more elaborate styles may use figured damasks and satins, carvings, veneers and inlays, as well as more intricate designs.

DISTRIBUTION

Planning the distribution of the basic elements and of pattern is the fifth step of your decorative scheme. Distribution is a practical matter, and is carried out in the light of the effect you desire to create. In our step by

	LINE	TEXTURE	PATTERN	COLOR
FURNITURE WOODS				
UPHOLSTERY				
ACCESSORIES				
FLOOR COVERING				
WINDOW TREATMENT				
WALLS				
WOOD TRIM				
CEILING				

DIAGRAM 16

Distributing Your Decorative Elements

step process of planning your decorative scheme, you have already decided upon your color scheme. You know which colors will be applied to the large areas, which subordinate and which reserved for accent. Your effect has also directed which type of line, pattern and texture will predominate in your room.

Now all that remains is to allocate these various items to specific components of your room. This can most easily be done by drawing up a chart as in *diagram* 16 and filling in the requisite information. You can then check each vertical row to assure that the elements you want to dominate actually do. Remember, the specific type of element that dominates in your room will produce a specific psychologic effect. Be sure that the effects of the dominant elements agree with one another and conform to your decorative purpose.

There are several considerations that guide the distribution of the basic elements. The dominant elements should be given the widest distribution throughout the room. Accenting elements should be limited to attracting attention and, therefore, used in moderation. Your guide to achieving pleasing proportions in the distribution of the elements is the Rule of the Golden Section. Avoid precise divisions, avoid isolating any one element in one section of the room, and avoid sharp contrasts—except for emphasis—between adjacent areas of your room.

In repeating elements and patterns throughout a room, you harmonize your furniture and background. The elements that are repeated, however, need not be identical. They may vary. Just be sure that the elements you associate together express the same spirit. Repeat these elements in furniture, accessories and floor covering, walls and window treatment.

The final step in planning your decorative scheme is furniture arrangement. The most important furniture groupings in your room will form the focal points of attraction. Furniture arrangement is, therefore, largely a matter of dominance, of creating centers of interest. These centers serve certain practical needs. In addition, they are decorative and lend distinction to a room. Through creating a center of interest, you also serve to harmonize both furniture and background. The topic of furniture arrangement is discussed in the next chapter.

This bedroom is decorated and furnished in a manner reminiscent of bygone times. The spreads and canopies of the beds match the pattern of the ceiling wallpaper. The fringed curtains and valance enhance the rich, feminine decor, as do the deep tufted velvet chair and crystal chandelier. The curule benches at the foot of each bed, as well as the pert footstool, add an interesting touch.

Distinctively Modern are the beauty and comfort that individualize this remarkable living room. The chintz upholstery of the curved sectional sofa bears pink and dark plum floral designs with green leaves set off against a brownish slate field. The monochrome carpet is Celadon green, while the leather of the table top is a slightly lighter tone of green. The lamp base is brown, with white raised polka dots and a white shade. The chair is upholstered in natural unfinished leather. All the woods consist of bleached mahogany in a light beige or amber finish. Yellow and gray complete the scheme of the room.

CHAPTER TEN

FURNITURE ARRANGEMENT

A PLEASING furniture arrangement can accomplish wonders for a home. Through grouping furniture together, the appearance of individual pieces is enhanced. An easy chair by itself appears, at best, to be little more than a well-made piece of furniture. Grouped with an end table that is within easy reach, a lamp that sheds a soft light, and an ottoman, the grouping offers an invitation to sit down, read and relax. As a unit, the group provides conveniences and comforts that are not obtainable with isolated pieces.

Even the room participates actively in an attractive furniture arrangement. The good points of the room contribute to the arrangement, while bad structural features are minimized or overcome. A pleasing arrangement gives the impression that the room and furniture are ideally suited to each other. A grouping and a room can blend so harmoniously that it is difficult to imagine that the structure of the room was not purposely planned for just the arrangement that you have. Furniture arrangement performs one of the magic transformations of home decoration.

To create pleasing arrangements of furniture requires—*planning in advance.* Rooms vary in size, shape and

For the small study-bedroom

NOT THIS < Why cramp your activities with furniture groupings that eat up space?

THIS IS HOW > Place a bookcase and chest back to back for an attractive modern arrangement.

structural features. Choice of furniture styles and pieces differ. The temperament and activities of families for which rooms and groupings must provide are individual. The over-all spirit that you wish your home to embody similarly differs. Your planning must take all these factors into consideration. Planning on paper is valuable to the refurnishing homemaker, too, for it permits her the more readily to figure new arrangements.

Because planning is essential to the creation of effective arrangements, this book includes a page of ruled paper on which you can draw your floor plan to scale. And it includes silhouette figures of living room, dining room and bedroom furniture, scaled to represent the size of average pieces of furniture. You can place tracings of these figures on your floor plan and determine, by actual experiment, which furniture arrangements will yield the most satisfactory results for you.

DIAGRAM 17
Tracing Furniture Figures

DRAWING THE FLOOR PLAN

If you are to obtain the best possible furniture arrangement for your room, it is necessary to proceed step by step. The first step is to measure the actual dimensions of your room. If your walls are straight, this is a simple process. If the walls present jogs, juts and irregularities, try to measure their length or width as though they were straight. Record these measurements on the bottom of the sheet of ruled paper.

The next step involves drawing the size and shape of your room on the ruled paper. Again, if your room is regular in shape, this step offers no difficulty. Just mark one spot on the ruled sheet where a horizontal and vertical line cross. Use this as your starting point and give yourself ample room by selecting an intersection in the lower right hand section of the ruled paper.

Next, let each quarter-inch division on the vertical line represent one foot of the length of your room. Count up a sufficient number of divisions from the starting point to represent the length of your room and mark the spot. Then count along the horizontal line from the starting point, this time letting each division represent one foot of the width of your room. All that remains is to count off the width again from the top of the vertical line and connect all four points.

With an irregularly shaped room, it will be necessary to measure the amount that the irregularities deviate

1/4 INCH = 1 FOOT

LIVING ROOM

SOFA

LOVE SEAT

LOVE SEAT

SECTIONAL PIECES

LOUNGE CHAIR

WING CHAIR

BREAKFRONT

BARREL CHAIR

PULL UP CHAIR

BOOKCASE

BOOKCASE

CONSOLE

FLIP TOP TABLE

CARD TABLE

OTTO-MAN

PLANT STAND

RADIO

FLOOR LAMP

CANDLE STANDS

BENCH

STOOL

NEST

HIGHBOY

CORNER SHELF

CORNER

FLAT TOP DESK

GOVENOR WINTHROP DESK

END TABLE

LAMP TABLE

PIE CRUST OR DRUM

ROUND COFFEE TABLE

COFFEE TABLE

COFFEE TABLE

LIVING ROOM GRAND

SPINET GRAND

SMALL UPRIGHT

DROP LEAF TABLE

LAMP TABLE

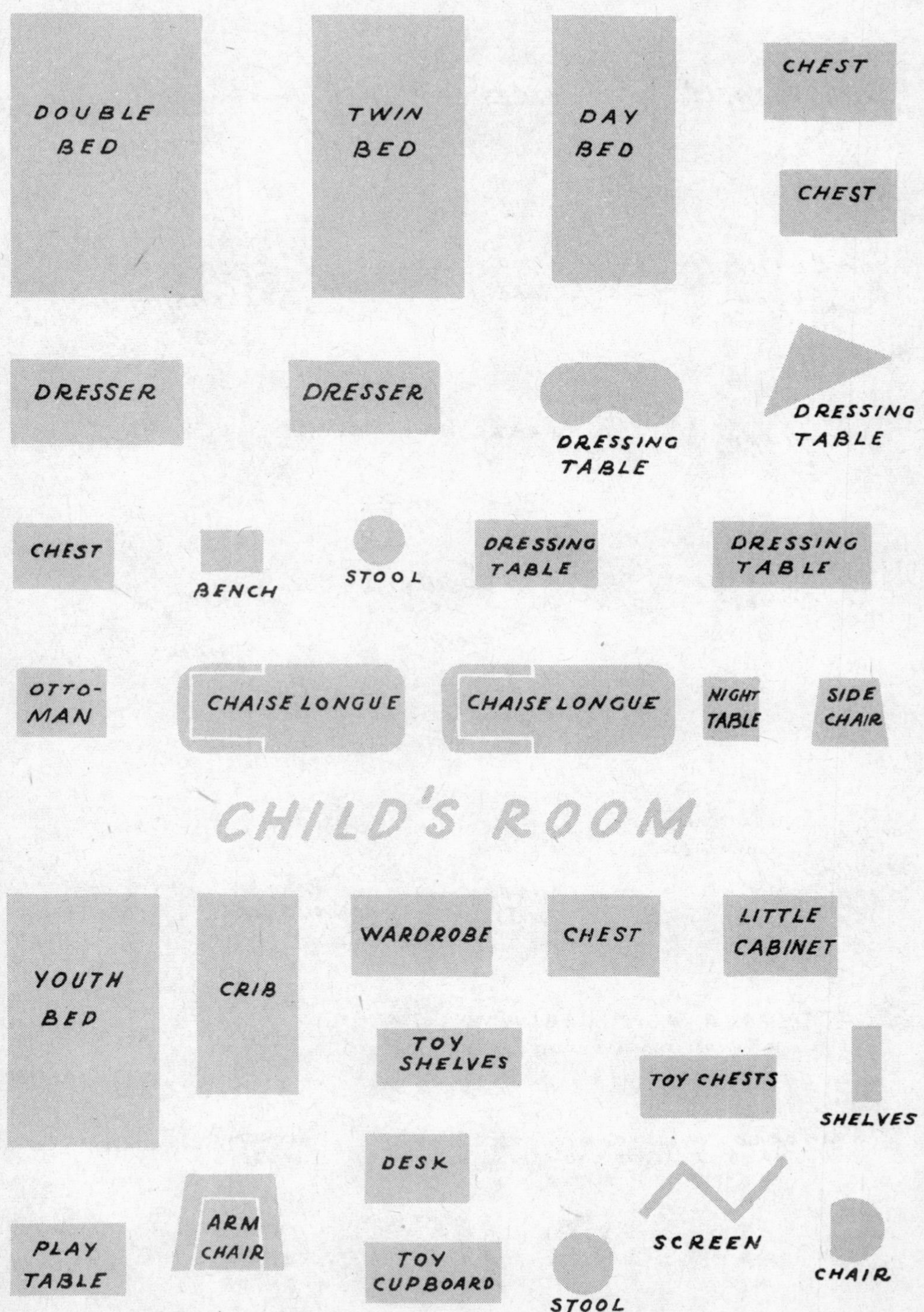
BEDROOM
DOUBLE BED
TWIN BED
DAY BED
CHEST
CHEST
DRESSER
DRESSER
DRESSING TABLE
DRESSING TABLE
CHEST
BENCH
STOOL
DRESSING TABLE
DRESSING TABLE
OTTOMAN
CHAISE LONGUE
CHAISE LONGUE
NIGHT TABLE
SIDE CHAIR
CHILD'S ROOM
YOUTH BED
CRIB
WARDROBE
CHEST
LITTLE CABINET
TOY SHELVES
TOY CHESTS
SHELVES
DESK
PLAY TABLE
ARM CHAIR
TOY CUPBOARD
STOOL
SCREEN
CHAIR

DINING ROOM

DINING TABLE

TRESTLE TABLE

ROUND DINING TABLE

WELSH DRESSER

ROUND BREAKFAST TABLE

CONSOLE END

DROP-LEAF EXTENSION TABLE

CONSOLE END

SIDE BOARD

BREAKFRONT

SERVER

SECTIONAL CHEST

SECTIONAL COMMODES

TEA CART

CORNER CUP-BOARD

CHAIRS

KITCHEN

WASHING MACHINE

AUTOMATIC WASHER

LAUNDRY TUBS

SMALL SINK

SINK

STANDARD BASE CABINETS
(ALL 36" FROM FLOOR. DEPTHS 25¼")

KITCHEN TABLE

30 GAL WATERHEATER

STANDARD WALL CABINETS
(DEPTHS 13" HEIGHTS 1' TO 4')

LINEN CLOSET

CHAIR

RANGE

RANGE

STOOL

RANGE

7 CU. FT. REFRIGERATOR

CORNER CABINET

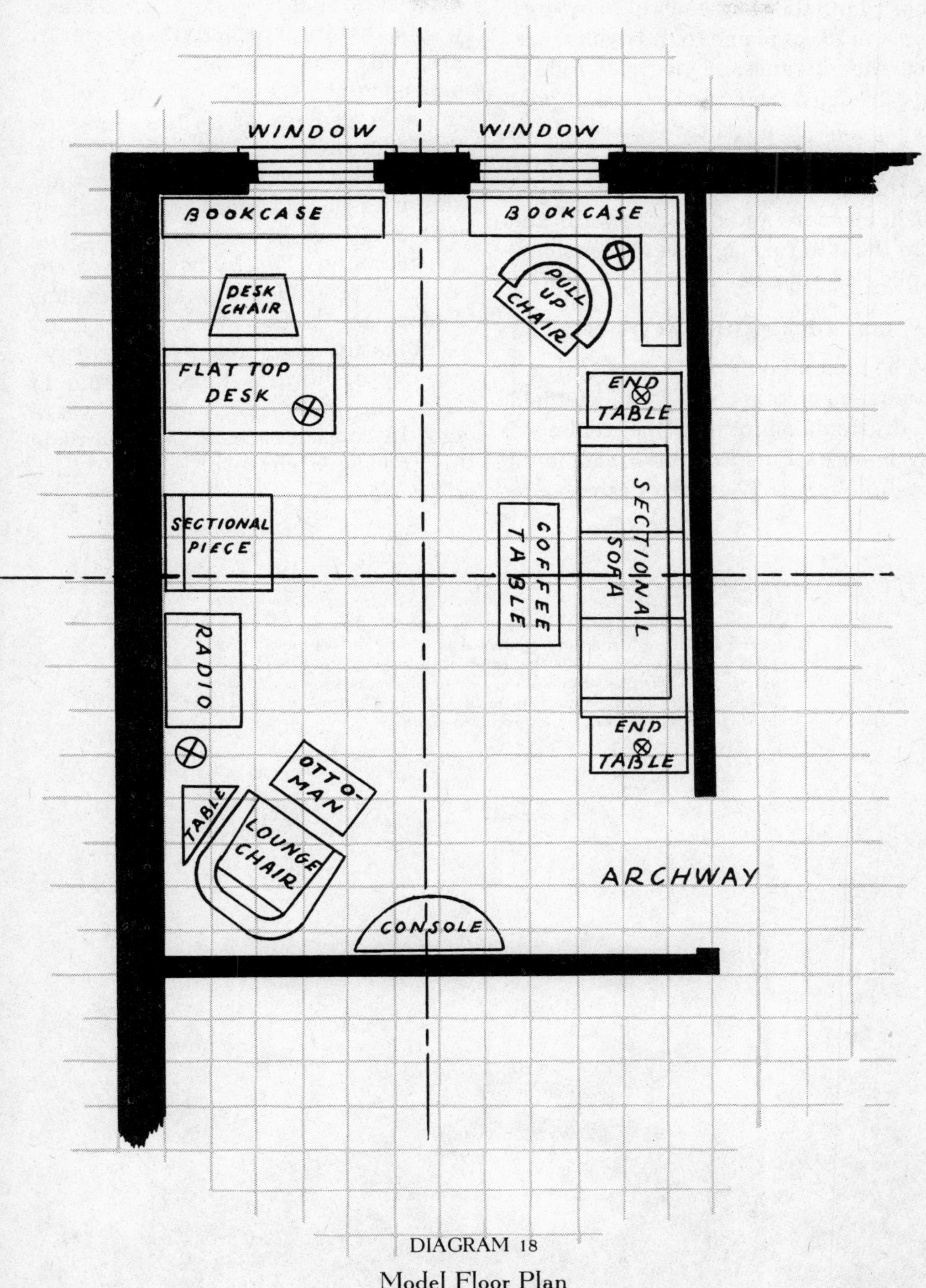

DIAGRAM 18

Model Floor Plan

from a straight line. You can then reproduce these irregularities on the floor plan, allowing each quarter-inch division to equal one foot. If you measure the distance of doors, windows and fireplace from the corners of your room, you can indicate these structural features in their proper places on the floor plan. You can also, if you wish, measure and draw the walls and fold them to form a three-dimensional replica of your room.

LIST YOUR FAMILY ACTIVITIES

The next step in planning furniture arrangement takes you from the field of draftsmanship into the realm of psychology! Furniture arrangements are *functional.* They are designed to serve the needs and wants of your family. Your family carries on certain activities, but what these needs, wants, habits and activities actually are, only you can determine. Much depends upon the size of your family, the ages and sex of its members and their interests.

You must, therefore, consider what activities the members of your family will carry on in the room that you are planning. The living room is the most diversified room of the home. Today, the living room is a happy combination of the front parlor, drawing room, library, music room and often the game room of fifty years ago. In consequence, it must provide for the lion's share of the activities of the family.

A circular sectional sofa that covers one entire wall marks this room as one dedicated to leisure and comfort. The curved shelves and the coffee table are in keeping with the spirit of this luxurious grouping. For spectacular effect, the silver wallpaper, patterned in chartreuse and green, and the huge sofa pillows "leap to life" under the irradiation of black light lamps secreted behind an overhead cornice.

It may have to provide facilities for any or all of the following doings:

Entertainment—from a few friends who drop in during the evening for an informal gathering to the more formal monthly club session or even a gala affair. You will need facilities for seating and serving, and possibly a table for games.

Refreshments—when you are entertaining. You may find a console-extension table, a drop leaf table, a tea table or a nest of tables satisfactory for your needs or you may use folding bridge tables and chairs.

Conversation—a sofa or love-seat, together with nearby chairs.

Relaxation—easy chairs for the members of the family, with perhaps an ottoman or hassock on which to rest one's feet.

Reading—again an easy chair is indicated, as well as a reading lamp, bookshelves and possibly a magazine stand.

Radio-listening—chairs for comfortable listening. You may wish to place the radio where the listener will not be disturbed by other activities going on at the same time. If you have a radio-phonograph combination, you may need a cabinet in which to store your collection of favorite recordings.

Music—if you have a piano, you will want to provide room for this instrument, suitable light for the pianist and perhaps seating facilities for listeners.

Studying—requires a desk or a table, some bookshelves with sufficient light and quiet.

Play area for the infant—a place for a play pen, with shelves or a chest for storing his toys.

Just list the activities of your family and the interests that you want the room to provide for. In this way, you can assure yourself that the room will really serve your family. If the room has to do double duty—as a living-dining room or a living-bedroom—be sure to include these activities in your list. Your list will vary, too, if you have a rumpus room downstairs in the basement or if play activities take place in the living room. As combination rooms and the one-room apartment present special situations, they will be discussed in the next chapter.

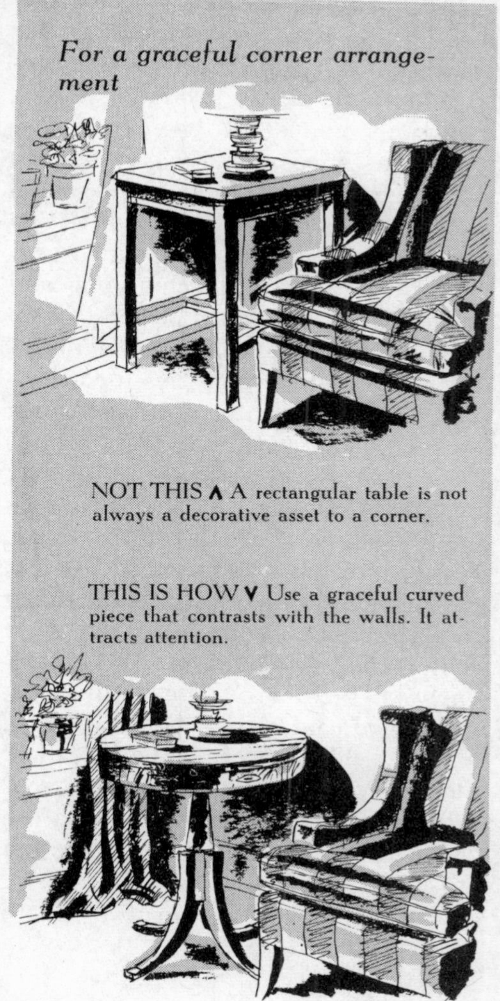

For a graceful corner arrangement

NOT THIS ∧ A rectangular table is not always a decorative asset to a corner.

THIS IS HOW ∨ Use a graceful curved piece that contrasts with the walls. It attracts attention.

All the activities that you list offer possibilities as centers of interest for your room. A center of interest consists of a furniture grouping that is dominant because of its intrinsic importance. A room may have several centers of interest, though one should receive the principal emphasis. You must, accordingly, decide which center of interest is the chief one and which ones are subordinate.

It is, of course, possible—and necessary—to combine facilities for activities. A reading center of interest may be integrated with the radio center of interest. A conversation center may be part and parcel of the entertainment center. The interests of your family indicate which centers are important and essential, and which may be eliminated or combined with other centers. The size of your room is similarly a factor in determining the number of centers that you may have, while its chief structural features will indicate where to place the centers of interest. The spirit that you wish the room to embody will also guide you in determining what centers of interest you will have and how these will be treated.

YOUR FURNITURE NEEDS

Your next step involves determining the pieces of furniture that are to be placed in the room. You must know which pieces are to go into the room and which pieces are to be grouped together. The number of pieces of furniture that can be put into a room is limited. The dimensions of the room, the kinds of pieces you are using and the way they are arranged are all determining factors. The kinds of pieces you require—such as tables, chairs, sofas, chests—depend upon the family activities for which you are providing.

The list of your family activities will guide you in making up your furniture list. Make your furniture list complete for each of the centers of interest you plan. If you already have furniture that you intend to use in the room, inventory these pieces and add any additional pieces that are

In planning a kitchen

NOT THIS < Dispersed work centers cost extra steps and inefficiency.

THIS IS HOW > Locate the stove, sink and refrigerator centers close together. And provide ample work surfaces and storage facilities.

A WALL OF BOOKS

A wall of books marks this room as a study. The armless chairs in pale green, with vivid red bolsters, are grouped on each side of a Modern tree of lights. The library table is grouped with a low champagne-toned bench which, like the chairs, is set on metal legs. Café curtains, which draw to one side, cover each section of the window wall to provide an attractive Modern treatment. The carpeting is a solid forest green.

ELEGANT EMPIRE CONVERSATION CENTER

A contemporary sofa in chocolate brown stands against a dark green wall to form an attractive conversation center with a pair of Empire armchairs upholstered in a vivid red and a contemporary cocktail table. An antique Empire desk, surmounted by a bust, stands against a rich drapery. Louvered doors in soft blue interrupt the drapery. Gold floor covering enhances the beauty of this elegant, dignified room

A FORMAL GROUPING WITH TRADITIONAL ELEGANCE

Rich, elegant and formal is this beautiful traditional living room The wall is a very dark brown set off with a white chair rail. The sofa is a deep rose velvet with emerald green toss pillows. The wing chair is an emerald green texture, the club chair a lively print. The carpeting is a sculptured broadloom in a sand tone. The picture arrangements are especially noteworthy, as are the furniture woods which vary attractively.

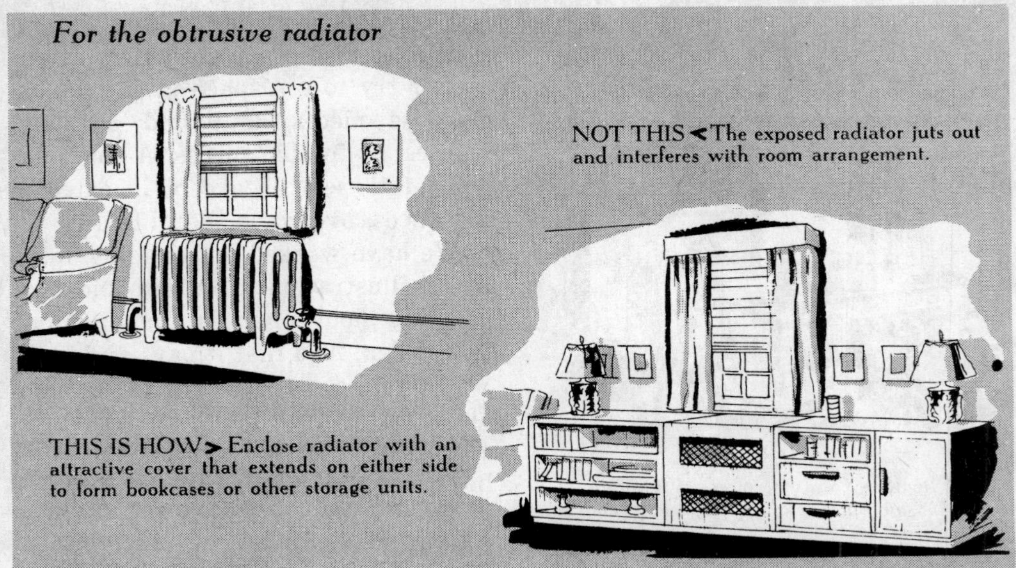

needed. In this way, you assure that you have not omitted any important piece, and that all your furniture is integrated in its appropriate grouping.

ARRANGING THE CENTER OF INTEREST

You are now ready to try out tentative room arrangements on the floor plan. Trace and cut out the pieces that you will need in the room, as determined by your furniture inventory. If you have pieces that are not illustrated, you can draw them. In making your own figures, let one-quarter inch equal a foot of the real piece. Place the pieces you intend to use for each group in a separate pile.

You will find it helpful, in planning your furniture groupings, to place your largest pieces first—cabinets, chests, sofas, love-seats, pianos, large tables, daybeds. These pieces are the ones that require the most space. In this way, you can see how much space you have available. Also, few groupings contain more than one large piece. By locating these pieces, you actually are deciding where your principal furniture groupings will be placed.

After you place your largest pieces throughout the room, begin with the grouping of your main center of interest. This center of interest usually consists of the principal piece of furniture in the room. For best effect, this center should be built around one of the chief structural attractions of the room. This may be a group of windows or a fireplace. It may be a long, unbroken wall or a corner that offers interesting possibilities. It may be a bay, French or picture window. Do you have a fine outdoor view on which you can capitalize? Any one of these structural features may readily be incorporated into your main center of interest.

After you group the pieces in the main center, proceed to the next grouping. Try to visualize the group as you place each piece, and consider how the group will be used. Feel free to shuffle the pieces around, trying out one arrangement, then another. Don't leave a grouping until you feel that you have attained the most sat-

Circular space-savers

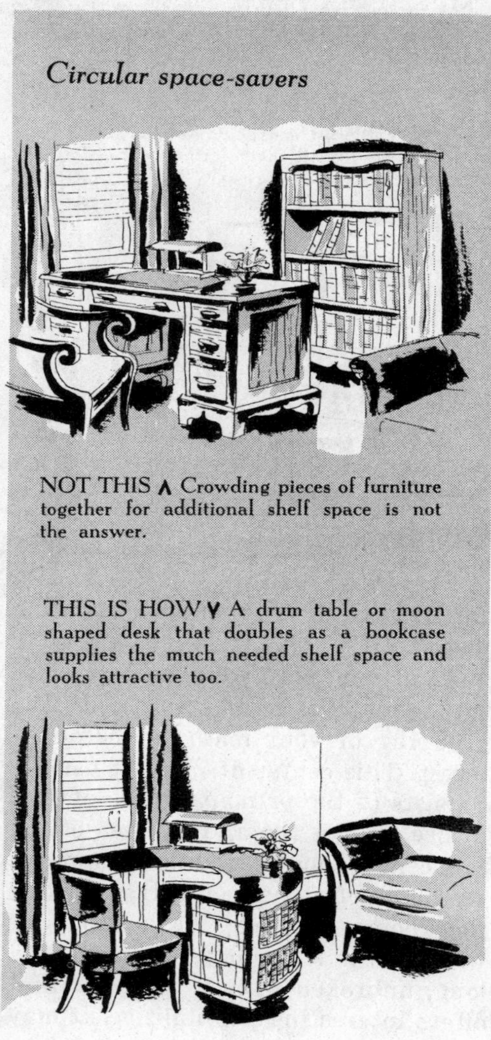

NOT THIS ∧ Crowding pieces of furniture together for additional shelf space is not the answer.

THIS IS HOW ∨ A drum table or moon shaped desk that doubles as a bookcase supplies the much needed shelf space and looks attractive too.

isfactory arrangement. When you achieve a pleasing arrangement, either paste the figures to the floor plan or fasten them with a snip of Scotch tape.

One advantage of your inventory may now be apparent. You may find difficulty in placing all the pieces that your furniture inventory calls for in the room. If this is so, there are several courses open to you. You can go over your list of family activities and reduce or combine the number that you tried to provide for. Or you can eliminate pieces not absolutely essential or try to use space-saving double purpose pieces, unit and sectional pieces, or folding pieces. A combination of these will, except in extreme instances, overcome the difficulty.

We have worked out one floor plan as an illustration. You will find that creating floor plans in this manner is real fun. And that it pays dividends when you come actually to arrange furniture in your home. In arranging furniture, the illustrations in this book will offer you many a useful suggestion. Magazines on home decoration are good sources of inspiration, as are the interiors you may see in motion pictures. Model homes and exhibits in furniture shops also offer many ideas for arrangement.

GUIDES IN GROUPING FURNITURE

There are a number of guides that will aid you in creating pleasing arrangements and in judging them. These guides apply to the arrangement of furniture in all rooms of the home. You must consider *balance* in making a furniture arrangement. The pieces in each group may be balanced formally or informally, as explained in chapter 2.

Bisymmetric balance, remember, is dignified and even reserved. It may give the effect of precision or aloofness. An asymmetric arrangement possesses more movement and liveliness. Unless you are aiming to create a wholly formal room, use both types of balance for your groupings. It will avoid monotony and introduce a pleasing variety.

As any grouping may use both large and small pieces, you may have to counterbalance a large piece within

A pair of windows frames an attractive setting for a love seat. The furniture is here arranged in bisymmetric balance and gives the feeling of formality. Such a grouping may serve as one of the dominant centers of interest in a room. The flowers on the chest brighten up the corner, while the irregular curve of the cornice board adds a note of charm to the draperies and the Venetian blinds of the background.

a group. A sofa, for example, can be balanced by two large chairs, by a chair and a table or by a large table.

Proper *scale* requires that the pieces in each grouping be in proportion to one another. Only in this way can you achieve a harmonious whole. Remember that furniture has height as well as width. Assure yourself that your groupings are not dwarfed by large pieces. Pictures, mirrors and other wall hangings may often be used to balance irregular heights. Avoid grouping very large and very small pieces together. A pair of small pieces, used together, may restore proper scale and balance. The furniture for children's groupings should be suitable to their size. Vary the spaces between pieces of a grouping for best effect and leave space around each grouping.

The *lines* of the large pieces in your groupings should parallel the lines of the room. This does not mean that pieces of furniture must necessarily be placed next to the wall. A sofa, placed at *right angles* to the wall, does often permit an interesting grouping. Nevertheless, the sofa is parallel to the wall behind it. Chairs in a conversation group should preferably face toward one another. Rugs or carpets should also parallel the wall, as should scatter rugs. Remember that for best effect, your large rug should extend underneath the large pieces that are placed near the wall. Wall-to-wall carpeting is an advantage in arranging furniture.

Placing large pieces, oblong in shape, parallel to the wall produces an effect of restfulness and harmony. Furniture placed close to the wall gives a small room the appearance of spaciousness. If it is not possible to place furniture near a wall because of irregularities or breaks in the wall, you might line up the furniture parallel to but away from the wall. Or you might create a center of interest around a window. Obtruding radiators also cause difficulty, but you can produce the effect of a continuous wall by flanking the radiator with bookcases or other unit pieces.

Capitalize on *corners* in grouping furniture. Nothing looks quite so forlorn in a room as an occasional chair all by itself in a corner. Corners invite the use of unit and sectional pieces that follow the angle of the walls. Sectional sofas and unit bookcases, either rectilinear or curved, are especially well adapted and make attractive corner centers of interest.

In placing large pieces near a corner, avoid a diagonal or cater-cornered placement. A small piece, such as a rocker or a chair, may, however, be placed at an angle to the wall. A group of small pieces may also be arranged in a semi-circle near a corner. In a room that must provide for activities such as studying or a baby's play area, corners may find especially effective use.

Don't have your groupings obstruct traffic or access to drawers or closets. Avoid narrow passageways between groupings. Allow room for doors to swing open. Allot each grouping an amount of space commensurate with its functional and decorative importance. Leave space around each grouping to produce an effect of spaciousness. There is no reason to think that wall space must be filled with furniture. A cluttered room lacks unity and orderliness, looks busy and distracting. Don't obstruct a pleasant view from a window. Use low pieces for window groupings or space the pieces so as not to block the view.

Try to separate activities that may interfere with each other. A conver-

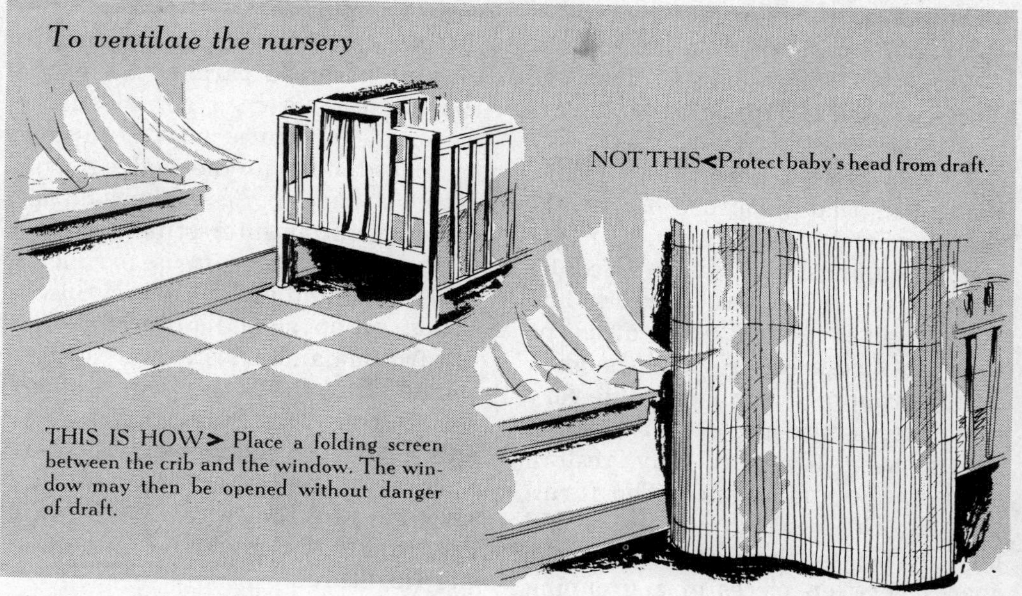

sation grouping may interfere with those who are listening to the radio. The radio may distract the youngster who is trying to study. Spacing your centers in this way is a matter of judgment, and depends upon the activities you plan for the room.

THE ROOM AS A WHOLE

Your purpose in arranging furniture is more than to produce a pleasing grouping. You want your entire room to produce an effect of harmony and beauty. This is possible only if all the groupings give the impression of belonging together. Line, texture, color scheme and furniture style all contribute to producing an effect of harmony.

Balance applies to the room as a whole as well as to the individual groupings. It is advisable to have two opposite walls in balance. One way you may assure balanced arrangement and placing throughout a room is to draw two lines on your floor plan, each one connecting the midpoints of opposite walls. These lines divide the room into four quarters. Check each quarter to see that no one quarter has a disproportionate share of large pieces. Make sure that colors and textures are distributed throughout the room, too.

If you have a fireplace grouping on one wall, you can secure balance by placing a large secretary or breakfront on the wall opposite it. If you have a corner arrangement in one section of the room, try to create another corner arrangement in the corner diagonally opposite it. Balance wood and upholstered furniture in the room, too. These add variety to a room.

To achieve good proportions, you will remember, avoid groupings that are in obvious, precise divisions. Don't divide your room into quarters, thirds or halves through placing large pieces at these points. The placement of pieces can also serve to change the apparent dimensions of a room. A broad piece against a narrow wall gives the wall an effect of greater breadth. A broad piece parallel to, but a distance from, the wall shortens or narrows a room. Line and color are also adjuncts in altering apparent size.

Check the entire room for unity and harmony. A group is harmonious if the pieces give a feeling of belonging together and blending with the room.

Unless the furniture styles mix well, you cannot produce harmony in your room. You can assure harmony in the room by seeing that balance is maintained among groupings and that each group is unified. Unity is further advanced if your groupings seem to merge with one another. If the groupings appear as individual clusters, then the over-all effect is one of disunity. Nevertheless, allow free space around each grouping. See that the predominating line that you have selected for your room actually predominates in each quarter of the room.

Next, check each grouping and the entire room for completeness and convenience. Does your main entertainment grouping have sufficient seating facilities, or will it be necessary to draw chairs from elsewhere? Have you provided for books and other accessories? Ashtrays should be strategically placed throughout the room.

Accessories help to give a grouping and the room an effect of completeness. They also contribute to balance and to unity within a grouping. In addition, accessories impart a touch of variety to a room. Often the difference between a harmonious, distinguished room and a room that lacks warmth and friendliness lies in the presence or absence of accessories.

Finally, see that your furniture arrangement accords with the *spirit* that you want your room to express. Through balance, your room may be formal or informal. The groupings may look hospitable and friendly, dignified and reserved, gay and blithe. The spirit that you create for your home is of prime importance in determining whether your home will be a livable and comfortable one. The placement of pieces and accessories does much to establish the spirit of your home. Make it one that you will enjoy living with.

Turning a corner is easy with versatile sectional pieces. The corner table, which combines straight and curved lines, permits a very handy arrangement. The ledge of the partition was drafted into service as a shelf, while the frames of the pictures continue this horizontal line on the adjoining wall. A scraggly rug, with a soft pile and fringes, adds warmth, color and textural variation to this inviting grouping.

Clever furniture arrangement here transforms an irregular attic into a comfortable living-study-bedroom. The sofa, placed under a sloping roof against a jut in the wall, is grouped with a bookcase that serves as an end table. Hanging shelves complete the desk center, the desk chair is decked with an easy-to make seat cover, a scalloped border decorates the wall, while a braided oval rug adds a touch of hominess.

CHAPTER ELEVEN

Combination rooms

THE past two decades have brought a twofold development in modern architecture. Large, many gabled homes have given way to compact, efficiently planned homes. The decrease in the size of dwellings has led to a reduction in the number of individual rooms, until today the twelve or fourteen room home is comparatively uncommon. A similar trend has also modified the design of apartment dwellings.

Like most processes of development, this twofold change did not proceed uniformly. At first, only the size of dwellings was decreased. Homes retained individual living and dining rooms, even though these rooms shrank to boxlike proportions. Eventually, the wall separating adjoining rooms was omitted, thus giving rise to the combination room.

The combination room may be a living-dining room, a living-bedroom, a recreation-living room, a guest-study room or a kitchen-dinette. With the designing of flexible space-saving furniture, combination rooms caught on. Now, guest rooms are often treated in this economical manner and bedrooms combine the sitting room, study or nursery function. The one-

To subdivide a large room

NOT THIS < When you modernize your house and want to subdivide a large room into two rooms —

THIS IS HOW > Consider building a divider that has clear, large panes of glass above a dado.

room apartment is a highly concentrated combination room that attracts many small families. As this tendency in architecture and home decoration continues, combination rooms will become even more popular.

FURNITURE FOR COMBINATION ROOMS

Two different attitudes prevail as regards the selection of furniture for the combination room or small apartment. To many persons, combination rooms are a temporary expedient. They plan in time to secure larger quarters that will provide a greater number of rooms for their needs and family activities. Guided by this view, these people buy odds and ends of pieces that are often frankly makeshift and which they intend later to discard. This attitude is a mistaken one. There are better ways of economizing than by skimping on quality, utility or comfort.

The other attitude is to buy furniture that is suitable not only to the present small quarters or combination room but to any future home. For very little additional outlay, it is possible to buy furniture that is flexible and permits making even a temporary home comfortable and attractive. In selecting furniture for the combination room, therefore, select pieces that answer your future needs as well as your present ones. Besides, your future home may itself be provided with combination rooms for which space-saving furniture will be required. In addition, a well built piece of furniture looks far better and makes possible an attractive, desirable home, large or small.

Space is usually at a premium in rooms that combine several functions. Especially is this true of the small apartment. The first step, therefore, in selecting furniture for a combination room is to see what space-saving furniture is available that will satisfy your needs. New pieces of space-saving furniture are designed almost every day, so that a visit to the furniture shops will offer you useful suggestions.

In choosing space-saving furniture, let both utility and beauty be your guides. Scale is another very important consideration where space is

A built-in unit for the studio couch

NOT THIS ∧ Do you need storage space for cushions or bedding?

THIS IS HOW ∨ A built-in unit with padded headboard provides storage space as well as extra comfort.

limited. Concentrate on streamlined pieces that offer the most usefulness in the least space. Pieces that fit snugly side by side can also save precious inches for the small room.

Space-saving furniture is manufactured in a variety of forms. Many of these pieces are just as suitable to the large room as to the combination room, and are especially designed as space-savers, while some are small-scaled versions of average-sized pieces.

Double-duty pieces are the earliest form of space-saving furniture, having originated with Sheraton. A piece that takes the place of two or more pieces also offers an opportunity for the budgeting homemaker. In fact, to call some of these piece *double duty* understates their utility. A *many-purpose* secretary may serve as desk, bookcase and bureau. A highly useful and decorative cabinet for the kitchen-dinette offers storage space, work surface for meal preparation and a drop leaf table for dining.

A nest of tables may be considered a many-purpose piece, as may a two-or three-tiered table. Even headboards of beds are designed to provide additional cabinet, shelf and table facilities. Studio couches that double as beds are well known articles of double-purpose furniture. Armchairs that similarly open up to provide a single bed for the occasional overnight guest are also obtainable. The living-bedroom should avoid presenting a "bedroomy" appearance.

Unit or *sectional* pieces are a second form of space-saving furni-

Unit pieces placed on either side of a headboard prove a convenient and practical arrangement for this study-bedroom. The drawers in the units provide welcome storage space. The quarter-circle end units are a decorative as well as a useful addition to a line of unit pieces. Instead of a wall, glass windows separate this room from its neighbor.

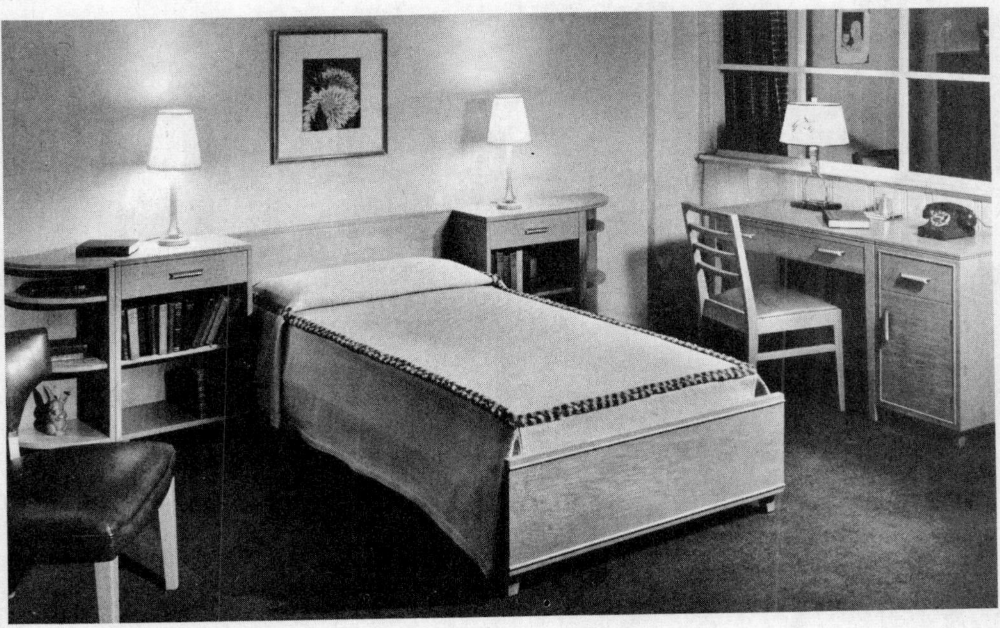

ture. The adaptability of unit pieces is often magical. Depending upon the amount and shape of space that is available, these pieces may be combined and arranged in a variety of configurations. They turn corners, may be placed horizontally or vertically, fit into odd spaces large or small. They may also be used individually or in ensemble. Unit pieces are suitable for any room, formal as well as informal. Many of these pieces give the appearance of custom-built furniture. They are made in both modern and period styles.

Unit pieces are built in both wooden and upholstered form. Sectional sofas are especially smart and popular, offering as they do many interesting possibilities of grouping. Unit end tables are manufactured that may be used individually or placed together to form one large table. One advantage of unit pieces is that they may be added to at a later time when more space or funds are available or they may be separated when space is reduced. Their versatility of grouping suits them to varying sized rooms, while demountable unit pieces are an added convenience in moving to different quarters.

The combination room may also conserve space through the use of *folding* pieces. Folding and extension bridge tables and folding chairs are useful and may be stored in a closet or cabinet when not in use. Extension console tables are especially useful space-savers. Tilt-top and drop leaf tables may also be considered under the heading of folding pieces. A

Five poses of one table, constructed of three bleached oak leaves and four rectangular frames, testify to the versatility of Modern furniture. Open, this table may serve for refreshments or coffee; with its leaves dropped, it may be used beside a chair; in pairs, it is suitable as end tables and, with its top tilted, it makes a reading stand. In addition, this table is a desirable space-saver and decorative too.

One piece that does duty for two is shown in this two-faced desk of bleached mahogany. Placement of the desk at right angles to the window assures good light and takes up a minimum of space. The leather upholstered chairs spell comfort. Note the decorative folding screen in the background, the sill length draperies and the rich incised rug.

double-purpose cabinet with drop leaf is similarly a folding piece.

A fourth type of space-saving furniture consists of *built-in* pieces. A ledge may be built at chair-rail height along the wall and swerve outward at one point, in a flowing curve, to form a table. A built-in bench may offer both seating and storage facilities. Built-in wardrobes, closets, cupboards and bookshelves may be designed to utilize every bit of space and take the place of chests, dressers and bureaus. Especially are built-ins useful as frames for daybeds if they are made to provide cabinet space for the bedding or the couch cushions. They may also offer shelf facilities for books and accessories. Built-in pieces may be decorative as well as functional.

Varied-shaped pieces may also be selected that fit conveniently into a room. Triangular cupboards, circular sofas, rounded cabinets, kidney-shaped or moon-shaped desks, odd-shaped tables—all economize space, are available in a variety of different sizes and permit interesting arrangements. If you are equipped with the dimensions of your room, know its jogs and juts, and have a list of your family needs, a shopping trip may reveal precisely the piece you can use to advantage.

The combination room may, accordingly, be furnished with a variety of space-saving furniture. Furniture selection is not difficult. It must, however, take into consideration your furniture arrangement. When space is an important factor, it is particularly necessary to plan your arrangement in advance. You can make arrangement-planning easier if you are acquainted with the space-saving pieces that are available.

SPACE-SAVING ARRANGEMENTS

The methods of treating furniture arrangement in combination rooms and small apartments reflect the history of the origin of these rooms. One way is to assign each function to a separate area, as though the wall originally separating the adjoining rooms still existed, and to treat each area as an independent room. A combination living-dining room, under this treatment, would consist of two distinct sections that may be separated in any one of a number of ways. The second method is to treat the entire combination room as a single unit, integrating its diverse functions and permitting each to capitalize on the larger area of the combination room as a whole.

Each of these methods has its advantages and permits the creation of an attractive room. To treat separate functions independently, in the living-dining room, has a house-cleaning advantage. In the one-room or small apartment, where the additional function of sleeping is added to the living-dining room, a separate treatment affords privacy and quiet. This method is particularly desirable if a youngster is a member of the family. The nursery may then be treated separately from the parents' bedroom, if these functions are combined in one room. If possible, it is better to have the youngster take over the bedroom and change the living room into a living-bedroom for the parents.

The unit treatment permits a more concentrated use of space. This type of treatment is therefore desirable in the small-sized apartment and combination room that must provide for a number of family activities. It is not usable, however, in the kitchen-dining alcove. The sitting-bedroom combination may receive unit treatment if the bed is of the studio type and serves for both sitting and sleeping. If used in the living-dining room, it is advantageous to cover the entire floor with linoleum. A unit treatment may take advantage of a foyer or an alcove of a room and give the effect of unity, harmony and spaciousness.

If you choose the first method of room arrangement, you must decide upon the kind of divider to use in separating the sections. You need not use an actual partition. Two rugs or carpets, separated by a few inches of bare floor, may very effectively divide the two areas without interfering with light, passage and the effect of spaciousness. Or you may use a screen, curtain or sliding door. These

For serving convenience

NOT THIS < A dinette separated by a wall from the kitchen means extra steps in serving.

THIS IS HOW > Use a low partition divider instead. A Lazy Susan turntable does the trick equally well.

A right and left pair of wing-shaped sofas in foam rubber offer many possibilities for ingenious room arrangements. The lacquered corner table matches the wood of the dining table, while the frame of the easy chair introduces a pleasant light wood contrast. Carpeting and lamp base add pattern to the room, the upholstery fabrics provide texture. Open spaces in all the pieces give a feeling of lightness despite the large size of this furniture. The dining chairs revolve, making them adaptable for games as well as for televiewing.

partitions are suitable since they may be opened or shut as desired.

Screens of bamboo that fold, lightweight Chinese lacquer paneled screens, mirrored screens or accordion-type folding doors are popular. You may choose a screen that may be painted or papered to match or contrast with your room. Curtains or draperies that run on overhead pulleys or tracks, or Venetian blinds, may also be used effectively. Sliding doors of glass or mirrors are becoming increasingly popular. These partitions need not be straight but may follow a curve.

Divider furniture is another form of partition. The divider may be a low counter, separating the kitchen from the dining alcove. Or a divider may be fitted with benches on the dining side and provide cabinet and shelf space for the living room. Special divider tables, chests and bookcases are available for this type of treatment. "Two-faced" furniture, which looks attractive from both front and back and often is dual purpose, makes an effective divider.

Still another way of dividing areas is through furniture arrangement. Bookcases may close off the dining area from the living section, the books facing the latter section. Cabinets, tables, chests and sofas may similarly be used, with the advantage that they may be shifted around the room when desired.

With either method of treatment, you may find it advisable to resort to space-saving furniture. In addition, it may be necessary to utilize every bit of floor space maximally. Corners, accordingly, will assume added importance. Unit and sectional pieces and built-in units are well adapted to corner arrangements. Corners, too, may readily be screened off to serve as a dressing or sleeping area. The entrance hall or foyer should also be used to advantage.

A few tricks of furniture placement and arrangement will save space. Two pieces placed back to back is one such arrangement. Chests may be arranged in this fashion if they are identical in size. If two different kinds of pieces are placed back to back, each one may be a part of a separate grouping.

Furniture placed at right angles to the wall often permits economy of space. A sofa, desk or bookcase so placed may also serve to divide two sections of the combination room. A table may often be placed in a corner without reducing its usefulness. Built-in corner cabinets or benches around a table may serve to create an attractive dinette. Tables that are attached to the wall and may be folded when not in use offer aid in treating the combination room. Circular or semi-circular tables similarly permit highly flexible and space-saving arrangements, as do circular sectional upholstered pieces.

Centers of interest may be arranged to serve several activities. A dining center may double as a reading, writing or recreation center. The radio center may be combined with the conversation center.

Rumpus and hobby room activities may readily be provided for in the living room. Especially is the recreation-living room a favorite in the family with teen-aged children. The children are then able to entertain their friends, hold parties and dances, which the parents may oversee without directly interfering. An extension table or portable folding table-top can serve for games, a movable buffet can

Designed for a modern bachelor apartment, this living-bedroom exemplifies the "half-and-half" technique, dividing the living section of the room from the sleeping end by a clever wall treatment of plaid and crackle wallpaper. Two large sectional chests screen the bed from view and help the division along. The Tunisian striped bedspread is a multitextured pile fabric in a soft honey beige color.

supply refreshments. Bar cabinets are also available in a variety of forms. You can choose a buffet or bar cabinet that will fit in well as a console table or end table for one of your groupings.

Studio beds often present a problem in the combination room or small apartment. The difficulty may be overcome if a cabinet is built around them in which bedding or cushions may be stored. Twin beds may be placed parallel and close to each other, they may be placed against opposite walls, or at right angles to each other in a corner. A corner table simplifies this last arrangement and adds convenience.

The steps that are followed in planning the combination room or small apartment are the same as those described in the last chapter. The better the planning, the better will be your results. The combination room and the small apartment may be beautiful and comfortable, and radiate a distinct personality.

A fully equipped, decorative closet encourages orderliness. Here, the walls and shelves are lined and fitted with garment bags, shoe bags, hat racks and hangers in fabric to match the decor of this pleasant bedroom.

STORAGE SPACE

The home that must make the best use of its space is also likely to lack sufficient closet, storage and shelf facilities. The amount of closet space that a home requires depends upon the size and activities of the family. Certain it is, however, that few homes can boast of a plethora of storage space. Closets are needed for clothes, linens, dishes, electric appliances and house-cleaning equipment. A pantry or cupboard is required, too.

Space may also be required for storing summer or winter clothes and bedding, as well as folding tables and chairs, carriages, sports gear, garden equipment and often business records and books. Fortunately, the basement or the garage often furnish some of this space, as does the attic or the apartment building storeroom.

One step toward the solution of insufficient space is the provision of auxiliary facilities. Cabinets that attach to the walls and hanging shelves may be installed. Chests may be added and, if space is limited, substituted in groupings for end tables. A breakfront also provides added storage space, as do built-in and unit pieces. Fiberboard closets are also available and may be placed in an inconspicuous spot. Ready-made built-in closets, often used in pairs, may easily be installed even in a finished room. They can fit into a corner, a recess in the wall or be placed into or against a flat wall.

Another step toward meeting this

problem is to make the most efficient use of available closet, shelf and bureau space. Orderly arrangement can often help. Placing all the short clothes together on the horizontal bar may permit using the free space beneath for boxes or drawers. Hooks, racks and shelves may be added to the inside of closet and cupboard doors, providing facilities for many items. Dishracks store dishes vertically in a minimum of space. Cleaning equipment may be held by hooks against a wall or against the inside of a closet door. Special enclosed closet door attachments are available for this purpose. Infrequently used apparel and linens may be stored in boxes, trunks or valises. A very deep closet may be provided with parallel rods, two feet apart.

As a last resort, pantries and cupboards may be reconditioned. Additional shelves may be placed between existing shelves or the shelves may be better spaced. Upright vertical dividers may be arranged between pantry and cupboard shelves that permit placing pans and cooking utensils on edge. Dividers and trays may also be built for drawers. The width of the shelves may be varied—cut-out shelves or stepped shelves often provide better storage facilities. Closet accessibility may be increased through widening the door opening and installing double doors.

The best planned closets allow a two foot depth for clothes, are equipped with a rod from which clothes may be hung, contain shelves and are entirely accessible. The rods, shelves and hooks in children's closets should be adjusted so that youngsters can store their effects in an orderly manner. For cleanliness, the closet should be painted or papered with a DDT preparation or cedar lined, and the floor covered with linoleum. An electric light, garment bags, hat boxes, tie and shoe racks, and drawers add to the usefulness of a closet.

CHAPTER TWELVE

SELECTING FURNITURE

BESIDES being one of the greatest furniture designers of all times, Thomas Chippendale was a forward-looking business man. He opened a tea room in the London of 1749 where he exhibited pieces of his furniture. In addition, he issued a book advertising two hundred of his designs. The fashionable world swarmed to his shop, sipped tea and — purchased Chippendale furniture. Thus it was Chippendale who initiated the practice, which we like to consider a distinctive modern trait, of displaying and advertising furniture. His business prospered and his customers benefited.

Before Chippendale took these steps, it was necessary to seek out a cabinet maker and tell him what furniture was wanted. Furniture then was entirely custom built. But its style, quality and appearance depended upon the ability of the cabinet maker, upon the materials with which he was acquainted and which he could obtain, and upon the traditions of the times and of the locality. Chippendale's clientele, however, could inspect the furniture, compare it with other pieces and decide in advance whether it suited their needs, wants and purposes.

Today, fortunately, furniture buy-

Added utility for the one room apartment

NOT THIS < A dining or dinette table takes up a large proportion of the space.

THIS IS HOW < A versatile extension table seating 2 to 10 persons can serve as an attractive console when closed.

Good proportion in your groupings

NOT THIS ∧ Avoid the simple, precise ratios of halves, thirds and quarters in furniture grouping.

THIS IS HOW ∨ The most pleasing proportions are in the ratios of 2 to 3, 3 to 5 and 5 to 8. Observe them in your furniture grouping.

ing is patterned after Chippendale's innovations. You can look over different pieces and inspect their construction and their fabrics. Very often shops display furniture in groupings you can adapt for your own home. Trained salesmen are at hand to advise and help you make your choice.

Furniture today is almost wholly a product of quantity manufacture. This feature has many advantages. You are presented with a wide variety of possible choices. Furniture is far less costly than if it were wholly custom made. And it is available at every price level, for every purpose and in every style that finds use in today's homes.

GUIDES IN SHOPPING

When you have planned your furniture arrangement and prepared your shopping list, you will know exactly what items of furniture and accessories you need. There are a few standards that can guide you in making your actual purchases. The design of the furniture is your guide in determining its beauty. Your furnishings should be in scale to your room. Their line, form, color and texture should be such as will carry out the effect that you intend to achieve in your home. These are art principles which we have already discussed. If you know the dimensions and the architectural features of your room, you will be able to decide whether the furniture, rugs, curtains and draperies that you select are in scale to your room. Take your floor plan with you when you shop.

The furniture that you select should offer good value for its cost. *Quality* is an important element in wise buying. It includes both beauty of design and comfort. To determine the quality of a piece of furniture or of an accessory, it is necessary to know something of its construction, something about the fabrics of upholstered pieces, and something about wood finishes. This knowledge will enable you to select furniture that will be a good investment for your money.

Quality is a feature that we have come to take for granted, so high is the level of American workmanship. But an understanding of construction, fabrics and finishes will explain to you why two pieces, outwardly similar in size and form, will differ markedly in price. You may not be playing the part of a good consumer merely by selecting the cheaper of two pieces. Penny-wise often means pound-foolish.

Another standard that you apply in selecting your furniture is — good taste. Of all things, this is one of the most important. It is of course true that good taste is neither fixed nor immutable. And it is especially true that it is difficult, if at all possible, to reduce its tenets to black and white. Yet it is an important consideration. A knowledge of period styles in furniture will assist you in appreciating the requirements of good taste. Restraint in decoration and in color is a property of good taste. And an awareness of beauty stands at its core. Good taste, in this sense, consists of moderation, a sense of fitness and an appreciation of the beautiful. These should be your standards in selecting and arranging your furnishings.

A figured mahogany cabinet and desk, designed by Hepplewhite in the 18th century, exemplifies the fidelity to detail and beauty of scale characteristic of the noted master craftsmen.

BUDGETING

Your budget will direct how much money you can afford to spend for your furniture. The wisest course to follow in allotting your money to your purchases is to spread it evenly. By this is meant that you avoid spending a disproportionate amount on one piece—the sofa or radio-phonograph, for instance—and then be forced to stint on other essentials. The best practice is to have all your furnishings in one price class. If you have a moderate sum for your furnishings, then all your pieces should be moderate priced ones. The reason for this is one with which we are already familiar in another guise—the matter of contrast.

One expensive piece of furniture in a roomful of moderately priced furniture will tend to emphasize the disparity in quality. Thus, a cheap, poorly designed upholstered sofa would look incongruous in a roomful of good furniture. With a better-balanced apportionment of the same outlay, the entire room can look attractive and integrated.

An expensive antique among a roomful of medium priced reproductions will not show to best advantage either. You could have procured better results if the difference in cost had been applied to all the pieces, or used on accessories. Many home decorators, nevertheless, commit this error, perhaps with the mistaken notion that one piece upon which they have splurged will magically give distinction to their room. Or, possibly, they may be indulging one of their secret longings in purchasing a rich Oriental rug and economizing on all the other furnishings in the room. If you must satisfy such a longing, do so—but realize that it is a splurge that will not contribute its proportionate share to beautifying your room.

The person with a limited budget is likely to feel that her results will not equal those of another with a more liberal sum at her disposal. This is not invariably so. The person of limited means may key her home so that it will secure a pleasing and beautiful effect. If her effect is one that can be attained with maple, birch or country-styled furnishings, she can achieve beauty, even though her budget is very small.

The person of limited budget is wise to buy at first only the most essential pieces and accessories that she needs. Later, she can add the other pieces to her room. Meantime, the pieces that she has bought will bring satisfaction. Home furnishings are an investment that lasts for many years. For this reason they may seem expensive. Viewed over the years, however, the amount expended for them is quite small.

There is much to be said in favor of the current practice of completely refurnishing one's home periodically. Formerly, it was felt that the furniture that a newly married couple bought should last them, with the proper additions, until they celebrated their golden wedding anniversary. This view is now largely outmoded.

It is like a refreshing breeze for husband and wife to decide, "We've lived long enough with this furniture. It's long past time that we refurnish our home." The very act of planning a new home, of working out its details together, serves to draw man and wife closer. It gives their spirits a fillip, it gives them a new

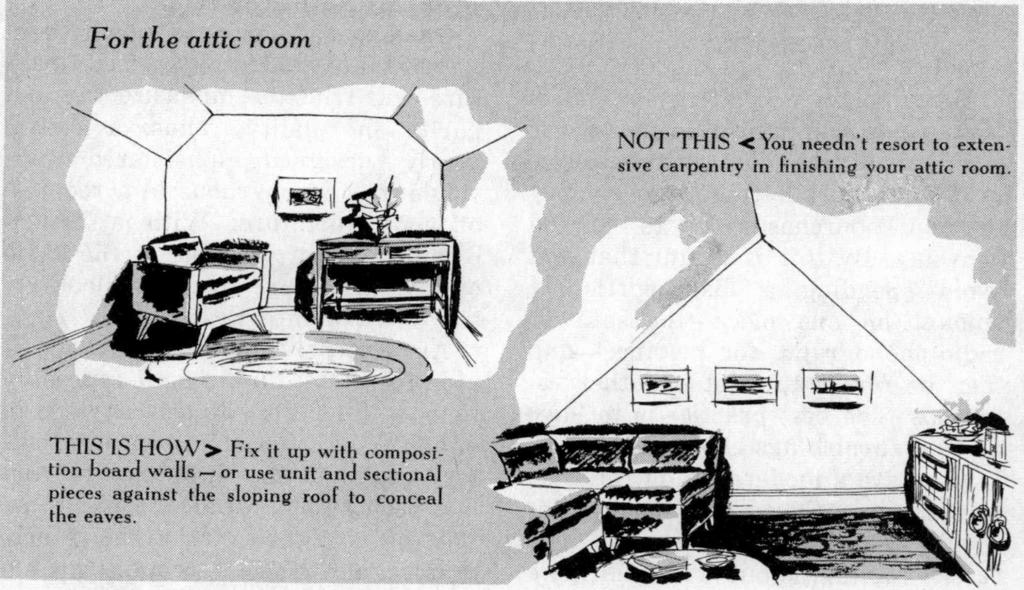

For the attic room

NOT THIS < You needn't resort to extensive carpentry in finishing your attic room.

THIS IS HOW > Fix it up with composition board walls — or use unit and sectional pieces against the sloping roof to conceal the eaves.

For between-meal snacks

NOT THIS < Are you forcing your child to drink his milk on the run?

THIS IS HOW > Provide a convenient snack bar in the kitchen. It makes an excellent dinette, as well.

goal toward which they can work together. Pieces that hold a high sentimental value can be retained. But just as new accessories brighten a room, so new furnishings revivify and freshen a home.

A home — it cannot be repeated often enough—is not something that is created and endures forever after. It involves a genuine, constant growth. It should reflect the growing richness of life and experience. It should mirror new interests, new feelings and deepening values. Only in this way can an old home remain truly young and fresh in spirit. The adventure of re-furnishing a home is one that brings spiritual reward.

FURNITURE WOODS

Over fifty different kinds of woods enter into the construction of present-day furniture. These woods vary in their suitability to different purposes. One wood may be strong, like ash, but lack beauty of grain. Another wood may be extremely rare and expensive, like satinwood. A third—gumwood—may be too soft for surface use.

A single piece of furniture may therefore consist of several different woods. One wood may be used for the exposed surfaces where beauty of grain and of finish is important. A second wood may be used to impart strength and durability to the inside frame, while a third may be used for its lightness. As a result, a well built piece of furniture will use the woods best fitted to secure good results. This also reduces the cost of the furniture even though its quality is improved.

Good quality surface woods possess certain properties. They should be sufficiently hard so as to resist dents, cuts and scratches. The harder the wood, the better it can withstand bruising of this nature. But very hard wood requires good workmanship if it is to avoid splitting through the use of nails and screws. Woods must be well seasoned to avoid warping, shrinking, swelling and twisting.

If wood is to meet the stress and strain of use, it must possess high

Good in construction and in design, these maple bookcases and chest form a pleasant bedroom grouping. The plaid wallpaper panel introduces a decorative touch, while the well proportioned mirror completes the grouping and gives a feeling of spaciousness. The strength and beauty of maple make it a favorite both in period and Modern styles.

bending or tensile strength. This quality is most important in frames and underbracings, the parts that absorb most of the strain. Beauty of grain or figure is another important quality in wood, especially in those woods used for outer surfaces. A highly figured grain is less desirable for certain purposes and finishes than is a well modulated grain.

The best quality furniture is likely to be constructed of imported mahogany or native walnut, hard maple or oak. Mahogany and walnut are both used as solid woods and veneers. They may be identified by their visible pores that resemble small dots on the end surfaces. Oak and maple are used almost entirely as solid woods.

Red gum is the most widely used furniture wood in America. It is mainly used for concealed parts and in inexpensive furniture. It may be stained to match mahogany, walnut or maple. Red gum nevertheless has the disadvantage of splitting rather easily and of denting. Red alder is another wood that may be stained to simulate mahogany and walnut. It is used for flat surfaces, kitchen furniture and inside parts.

Yellow poplar ranks below red gum and red alder in desirable qualities. Tupelo is also used for frames and concealed structures. With modern bentwood construction, birch has again become a popular furniture wood. It is used in both solid and veneer forms and is often bleached. Red birch resembles mahogany, while

Figured satinwood, one of the richest of rare woods, is here used as an inlay with walnut in a Regency sofa table. Satinwood is obtained from Ceylon. Such rare woods are restricted to use as veneer and inlay.

unselected birch resembles walnut and oak. A third variety, curly birch, finds use in veneers.

Furniture is usually designated by the name of the wood used for its exposed surfaces. An oak table is one whose table surface, apron and legs consist of oak. If the exposed surfaces consist of more than one wood, the piece is designated by the names of the principal woods—e.g., a mahogany secretary with red birch legs. Solid wood construction denotes that the exposed surfaces consist of the particular wood or woods named—a solid maple desk has a maple top, front, sides and legs, while its drawers and its back may consist of another wood. The maple used is not veneered.

VENEER

A veneer consists of a thin facing wood glued under high pressure to a core of wood underneath it. The art of veneering is so ancient that its origin is lost in antiquity. The process of machine manufacture of veneer is, however, a development of the 19th century. A veneer is itself a very fine layer or ply of an ornamental wood. In thickness, a plain veneer may vary from 1/1000th of an inch to 1/40th of an inch, while figured veneer varies from 1/32nd of an inch to 1/16th of an inch.

The number of plys in a veneered construction—or plywood construction, as it is also called—may vary from two upwards. The more plys, the stronger the plywood. Three and five ply stock are widely used for furniture. *Diagram* 19 illustrates the makeup of plywood. Adjacent plys are *crossbanded*—i.e., the grain of each ply runs in a different direction. Crossbanding adds strength to the plywood and prevents warping. The core or center piece consists of a wood that absorbs glue readily, such as yellow poplar, chestnut and basswood.

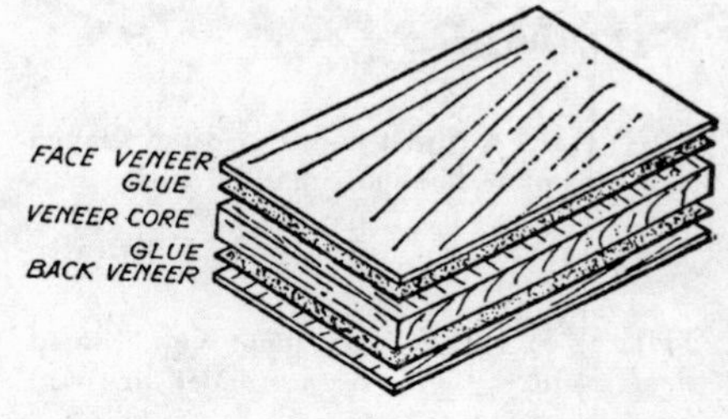

DIAGRAM 19

Plywood Construction

Both solid and veneered furniture possess good and bad features. Solid wood runs less danger as a result of poor workmanship, for a poorly bound veneer will chip, peel off, or blister. If its surface is marred, solid wood may be sandpapered down and refinished, while veneer reveals a different wood. Solid wood is heavier and gives a feeling of being substantial. Solid wood, moreover, may be carved. The lack of humidity in many modern homes may cause solid wood to check or split. The wider the surface, the greater is this danger. It can be avoided by gluing together narrow strips of wood into the desired width and sealing the pores on both sides of the wood. Solid wood is less resistant to warping and swelling than is veneered construction.

The widespread use of plywood in the construction of airplanes during the war is evidence of its great strength. On wide surfaces plywood can withstand warping, splitting and cracking better than can solid wood. Plywood can achieve beautiful finishes. Its patterns are very attractive, particularly in large panels. Veneer is more economical than solid wood, especially in the utilization of rare woods such as crotch mahogany and burl walnut. Strong, sound wood that could not otherwise be usable for furniture is used for the core of plywood construction.

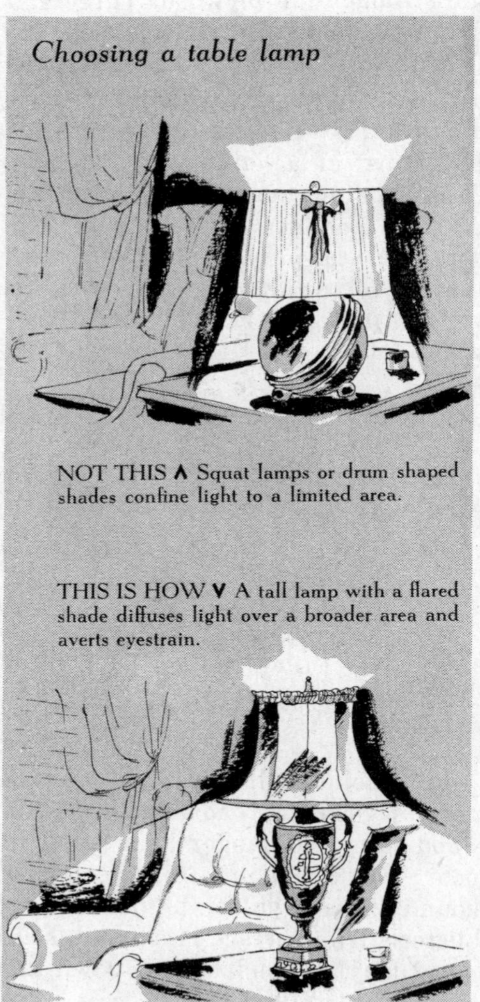
Choosing a table lamp

NOT THIS ∧ Squat lamps or drum shaped shades confine light to a limited area.

THIS IS HOW ∨ A tall lamp with a flared shade diffuses light over a broader area and averts eyestrain.

The disadvantages of plywood result principally from poor workmanship, inadequate seasoning and inferior glue. The best glue is a heat and water resistant phenolic resin, though animal casein glue and vegetable starch glue are used in less expensive furniture. Veneer panels that are faultily aligned sometimes occur as the result of inferior workmanship.

The most expensive furniture consists of solid mahogany or walnut. Veneer is less expensive and stained woods are the cheapest. In buying, assure yourself that you are actually obtaining solid wood construction when you pay for it. Veneers of mahogany and walnut may be detected by inspecting the surface edges.

CONSTRUCTION

The best wood, if poorly put together, is of little avail. Construction is as important as material in securing quality in furniture. Because so very much of the workmanship in furniture, especially upholstered pieces, is concealed from view, it is not easy to determine quality of construction. However, there are certain points of construction that you can inspect. If the furniture scores well on these points, the likelihood is that it is well made.

Inspect all the wood surfaces—top and bottom, front and back—of the furniture. Do you notice any woods that are warped, cracked or swollen? Are the exposed surfaces hard enough to withstand bruising? Are the parts that bear the brunt of the strain sufficiently strong for this purpose? Do you see any signs of splitting around nails and screws? Does the grain of the wood look attractive? Is the finish a pleasing one?

If you are buying a light wood chair, there is nothing that can prevent your picking it up and turning it upside down. Try to peer under table and sofa surfaces, if possible. In good furniture, these wood undersurfaces are shellacked or stained. If only one surface is finished, the piece may warp because of unequal absorption of moisture.

Framework has joints. Inspect these joints where arms, legs and bracings are attached. The poorest

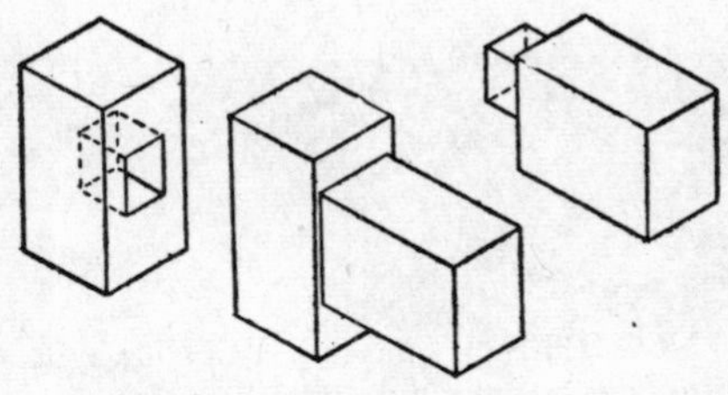

DIAGRAM 20
Mortise and Tenon Joint

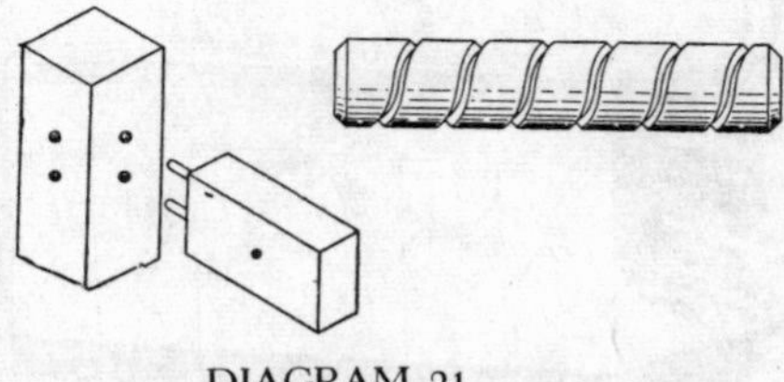

DIAGRAM 21
Dowel Joint

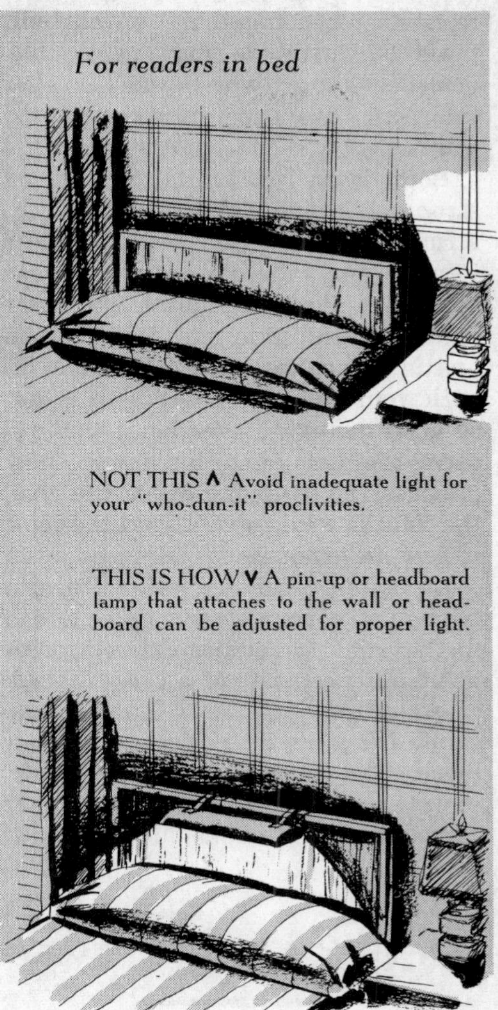

NOT THIS ∧ Avoid inadequate light for your "who-dun-it" proclivities.

THIS IS HOW ∨ A pin-up or headboard lamp that attaches to the wall or headboard can be adjusted for proper light.

grade of furniture merely relies on nails and screws, with perhaps a daub of glue, for strength. Far superior to these are the mortise and tenon or the dowel joint. These are illustrated in *diagrams* 20 and 21.

In the mortise and tenon joint, the piece that is inserted is shaped into a tongue that fits snugly into a pocket. The dowel is a cylindrical peg, preferably of wood and often spirally grooved, that is fitted into matching holes in each of the pieces of wood to be fastened together. A well built piece of furniture may be double-dowelled—i.e., two dowels, rather than one, are used in securing the joints.

Both types of joints depend on strong, adhesive glue to bind the construction. When you inspect these joints, note whether any glue has oozed out along the joints or corner blocks. If the glue has dried into a brittle lump that you can flake off with your fingernail, the glue is not of good quality. If the holes that receive the tenon or the dowel show crevices due to drying out of the glue, the joint is weakened. Tug at the joint to test its firmness.

In better constructed furniture, a triangular corner block may be added to the joint for additional reinforcement. This consists of a shaped block of wood that acts as a brace to the joint. *Diagram* 22 pictures a corner block. The bentwood type of chair, however, in which the wood is not joined but continuous, does not require corner blocks in its construction.

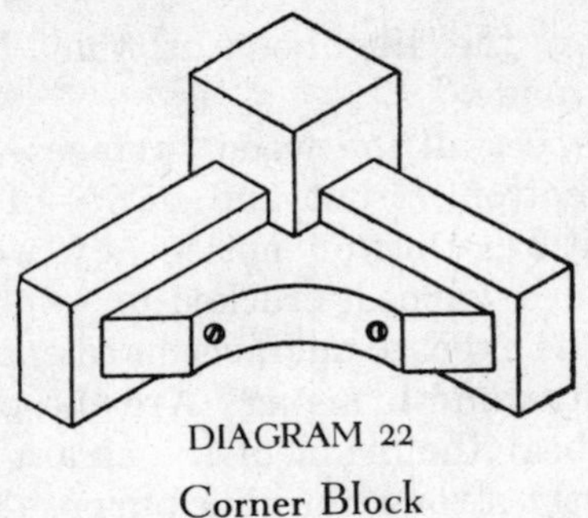

DIAGRAM 22
Corner Block

You can test any piece of furniture for firmness and rigidity simply by shaking it. If it wobbles, then the furniture is not substantially constructed or the legs are uneven in length. Be sure that the legs of sofas, chests and similar pieces are high enough to permit cleaning underneath the piece. Look at the rungs of chairs. Are they securely in place? Certain types of chairs, such as Duncan Phyfe or Sheraton, do not use stretchers. Good pieces in these styles compensate for this by especially strong braces underneath the seats. Metal

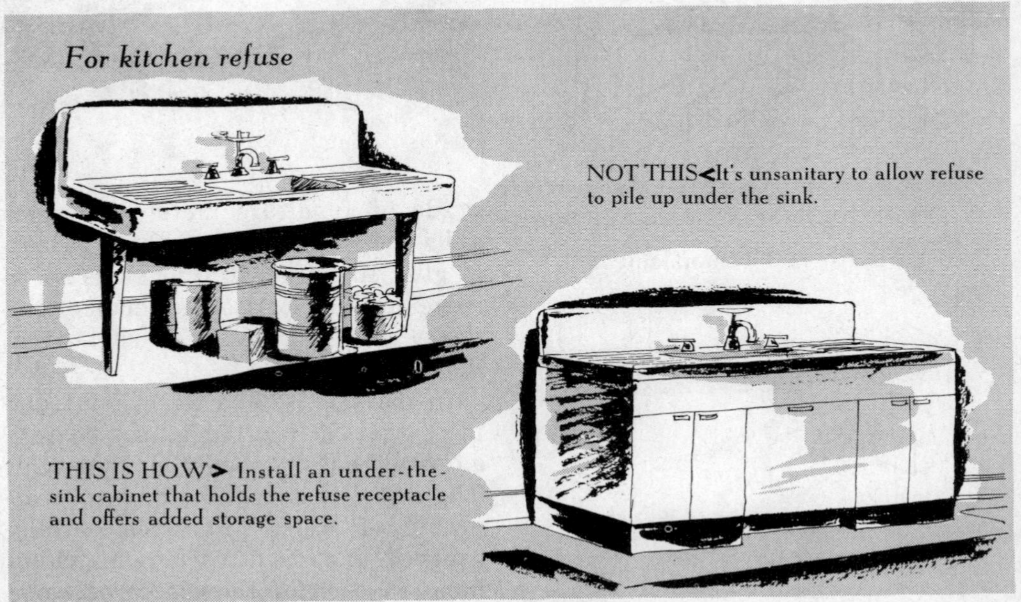

For kitchen refuse

NOT THIS< It's unsanitary to allow refuse to pile up under the sink.

THIS IS HOW> Install an under-the-sink cabinet that holds the refuse receptacle and offers added storage space.

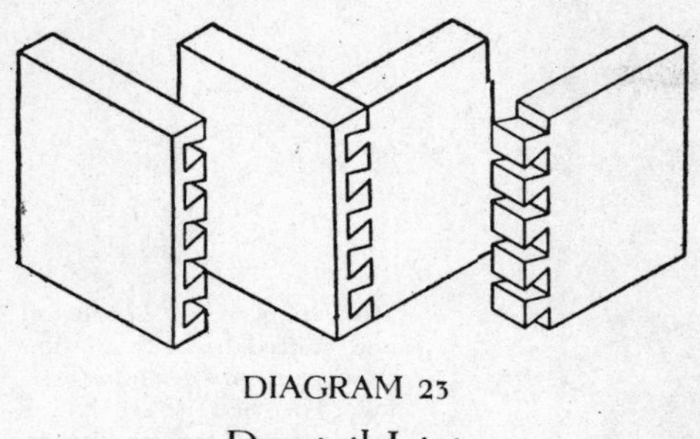

DIAGRAM 23
Dovetail Joint

stay braces, which may be tightened by a turnbuckle, are sometimes used in chair seats and bed springs.

If you are selecting a desk, dresser or chest, pull out the drawers. The best construction for drawers is the dovetail joint, shown in *diagram* 23, which should be used at all four corners. A drawer whose sides are unevenly nailed together is of cheap construction. The dovetail joint is superior to a slotted joint. Is the bottom of the drawer strong? Look for signs of splitting, warping and swelling. Slide the drawer in and out several times. Look at the slides upon which the drawer rides. Notice the bottom of the drawer. The best type drawers have bottoms that set into grooves and are reinforced with small blocks. This type of joint, called a *dado,* is also used for shelves of chests and cabinets. Drawers should be separated by dustproof panels for cleanliness.

Run your finger along the edge of flat surfaces. Is the edge smooth and even? On high grade table surfaces, a solid edging strip is used, which improves the appearance of the table. Test the piece you intend to buy for comfort. It should fit the member of the family for whom it is chiefly intended. Are its arm rests comfortable? Is the desk at a comfortable level? For typewriting, the desk surface should be lower than for writing. End tables should match the height of the upholstered pieces with which they will be grouped.

Mirrors are produced in a variety of grades. Common defects to look for in mirrors are bubbles, wavy lines and bull's eye disfigurations. The

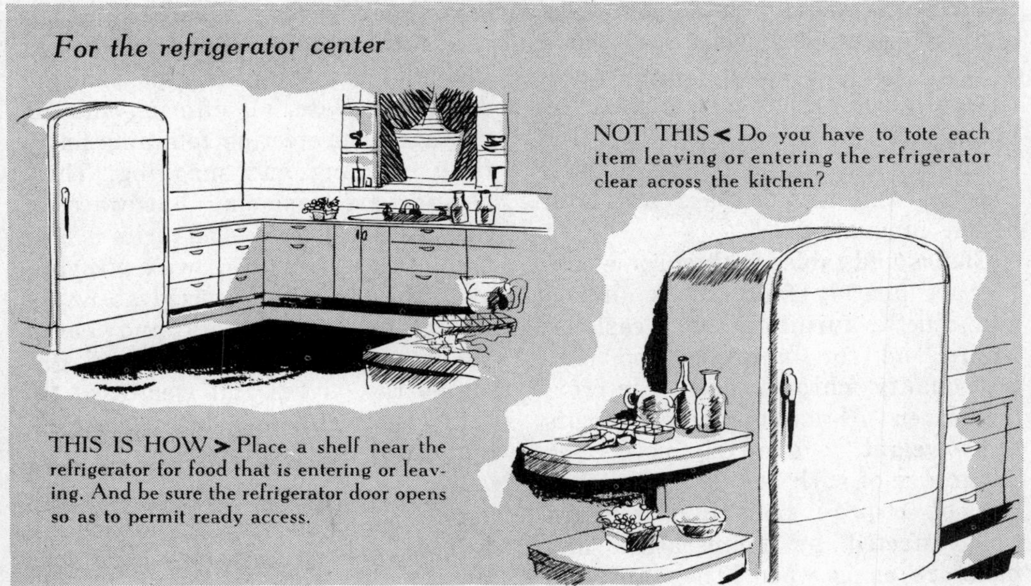

An upholstered headboard and shirred bedskirt give this Modern room a feminine feeling. The bed is set into a mirrored wall recess which reflects the opposite wall. Inbuilt niches afford space for decorative objects as do the mirrored glass bedtables. A fabric valance, which matches the bedspread, runs across the wall recess and adds attractively to the room.

mirror should be securely fastened to the bureau or vanity, if it is an attached mirror. The frame of a hanging mirror should be substantial enough to support it.

OTHER FURNITURE MATERIALS

Besides traditional wood, new materials are being adapted to furniture use. Mirrors and plate glass are becoming increasingly popular. Tables and shelves of these substances have a rich, sophisticated appearance. Crystal glass has long been used for lamps and chandeliers as well as for decorative bowls and flower holders. Frosted and tinted glass are both recent innovations.

Chairs and tables with chrome tubing are already familiar as kitchen and dinette furniture, as occasional chairs and for bathroom use. The best-quality chrome has a mirror-like sheen. Aluminum, noted for its light weight, is similarly used. One advantage of such metals is that they do not require polishing, nor are they affected by temperature and moisture as is wood. They are cold to the touch, which makes them especially desirable for summer use. However, they lack the softness and tradition that we associate with wood. Still, they do possess an air of modernity and lend a note of distinction to the room in which they are used.

Plastics, too, are growing in popularity. Transparent plastics, like lucite and plexiglas, are finding new uses. They already have been widely used for lamps, tables and accessories. Plexiglas has made its appearance as a drawer material, offering the advantage of protecting feminine finery from catching and snagging. These plastics are replacing hardware on chests and cabinets. And lucite is used for desk accessories as well. Vinylite, like other plastics, is used as woven straps for chair seats and backs. Vinylite is elastic and resilient, giving to the curves and weight of the body and returning to its original taut form when released.

UPHOLSTERED FURNITURE

It is unfortunate that furniture manufacturers do not usually provide a series of photographs showing the careful step-by-step construction of typical good quality upholstered pieces. The consumer has little by which he may judge these pieces and appreciate the very fine workmanship that enters into many upholstered pieces. The amount of handwork largely distinguishes the superior piece and accounts for the difference in price between outwardly similar pieces.

Upholstered pieces of the best grade usually have a hard wood frame of ash, birch or hard maple. The principles of joinery that apply to case goods also apply to joints of these frames. The base for the springs, in the best quality upholstered furniture, consists of textile webbing. This webbing is in the form of strips, at least 3¼ inches wide, that are interwoven closely for firmness and tacked securely to the frame. The finest grade of webbing has a red stripe near its edge; cheaper grades have a blue or black stripe.

Substitutes for webbing are used in medium and low grades of furniture. Sagless construction consists of a heavy jute material stretched across the seat of the chair and attached to the frame by means of small springs. Supersagless construction adds two heavy metal wires below the sagless construction for added strength. Wires or flat steel bands are used in the lowest quality furniture instead of webbing. Wooden slats occasionally are used, but are accompanied by smaller, less resilient springs.

The comfort of a chair depends upon its springs. Double cone springs are superior to single cone. A good quality chair uses nine to twelve springs in an ordinary chair seat, while sixteen or more are found in sofas. The springs should be close enough to provide firmness and prevent sagging, yet not so close as to lock together when the seat is occupied. The springs must be securely fastened in place for best results. Strong hemp or flax twine is used to fasten the springs to the front and rear frame. Wire is less suitable than twine. In good quality chairs, each spring is tied with eight knots. Four knot construction is definitely inferior. As a test, press the springs down. A well constructed seat will resume its shape as a unit.

NOT THIS ∧ Why succumb to the drab, the listless and the non-committal? Forego neutral, "safe" finishes.

THIS IS HOW ∨ Take advantage of texture possibilities along with pattern and color.

The springs are covered with burlap which serves as a foundation for the stuffing. If no springs are used in the chair, the burlap is stretched over the webbing. In the best grade furniture, the stuffing is in two layers, separated by burlap, and sewed to the burlap to prevent the formation of bumps in the upholstery.

The best stuffing is long, curled horsehair. Medium grades of furniture use Spanish moss, cheaper grades of cattle hair, or a combination of moss and hair. The poorest stuffings are palm-leaf or coco fiber, sisal, tow and excelsior. Many states have laws that require labelling the type of stuffing used in upholstered pieces and bedding. Stuffing in these should be sterilized for cleanliness and health.

For the low ceilinged den

NOT THIS ∧ Low ceilings give a feeling of claustrophobia.

THIS IS HOW ∨ Hang floor-length curtains from the ceiling line. A small patterned wallpaper helps out, too.

Padding is placed over the frame to give the piece an attractive shape and to prevent frame and springs from wearing through the outer upholstery. In best quality furniture, firm rolls of cotton felt are used, tacked and sewed to the frame. These are covered with a layer of cotton felt to present a smooth surface.A grayish felt or cotton batting, if substituted for this layer, is a sign of inferiority. Before the outer cover is placed over the entire piece, an inner heavy muslin cover is attached.

Cushions in the best grade are stuffed with down and feathers, protected by an inner downproof ticking. Goose down and feathers are best, followed in order by duck, chicken and turkey. Spring cushions are found in medium priced pieces, while kapok, cotton, cotton linters or a mixture of these are used in inferior pieces.

Upholstered pieces are covered in a wide variety of fabrics, in many colors, textures and patterns. You should select the fabric that accords with your color scheme, decorative purpose and style of furniture. Texture is important in fabrics and interesting results may be produced through texture variation. Coarse textures usually wear better than smooth textures and tight weaves are more durable than loose weaves.

Printed textiles, such as linen and toile de Jouy, decorative damasks, brocades, brocatelles, reps, denims, friezes, pile fabrics such as mohair,

A game center for Canasta or Bridge provides pleasant relaxation for family and guests. Here the black lacquered furniture with a raised Chinese pattern in color finds an attractive corner niche at a window. The plant stand, with an alcohol-resistant marble top, doubles as a serving bar. The scroll pattern of the light-toned carpeting simulates a sculptured effect and contrasts with the dark walls and furniture.

velvet and corduroy are widely used. Crewelwork and needlepoint, silk and satin and many rough textured fabrics are also used for upholstery.

In addition to the animal and vegetable fibers, synthetics are enjoying increased use as upholstery fabrics. Rayon is widely used, alone or in combination with other fibers. Koroseal and foam rubber are washable and stain resistant synthetics, which make practical the use of such colors as eggshell and creamy white. Rubber-lined mohair is a recent addition to the family of fabrics. Leather and fabrikoid are also used for upholstery.

BEDDING

Closely related to upholstered furniture is bedding. There are three types of mattresses — solid, innerspring and latex. The solid mattress may be stuffed with curled horsehair and lined with a layer of lambs' wool. Cotton mattresses are similarly of solid construction, the best grade of this kind using long staple cotton with felted top and bottom layers. Kapok is also used for mattress stuffing, but is perishable and requires frequent airing and sunning.

The innerspring mattress is today's most popular type. Though this type varies widely, there are two main classes. In one, each coiled inner spring is enclosed in a muslin or burlap pocket and fastened in place. This type may use 800 or more individual coils in a mattress. The other class of innerspring construction uses

For kitchen storage space

NOT THIS ∧ Crowding everything into one small closet makes it hard to get anything out.

THIS IS HOW ∨ Add unit floor, wall or base cabinets. In enamel or stainless steel, they are decorative and easy-to-clean as well.

180 to 360 larger coils. These coils are held in position by wire ties, metal clips or small springs. The coils are covered with a layer of curled hair or cotton felt. In the more cheaply made innerspring mattresses only the center is furnished with springs, the outer edges being stuffed with cotton felt.

The latex or rubber mattress is a comparative newcomer. The sap of the rubber tree is frothed up to capture air within its cells. Latex mattresses do not sag or mat down, do not require periodic turning, are hygienic and a protection to persons suffering from certain allergies.

Mattresses, like other types of furnishings, should be tested before purchase. In this way it is easy to determine the resilience, buoyancy and softness of a mattress. A good mattress gives readily when pressure is applied, but springs back into its original form when the pressure is removed. It is sufficiently buoyant to prevent the body from sinking too deeply into it, yet soft enough for comfort.

Inspect the tailoring of a mattress. Mattresses may be button tufted or raw cotton tufted, the former being more desirable. Or they may be quilted to the ticking. The poorer grade is tuftless and unquilted. The mattress edges are also variously finished. Borders should be reinforced. The lowest quality has plain stitched edges. The rolled edge is better, while the square imperial edge, with its four rows of stitching, is best. Mattresses should be provided with handles by which they may be moved. Ventilation is another requisite of a good mattress.

Ticking should be at least eight ounces in weight—that is, a yard of 32 inch wide ticking should weigh at least eight ounces. Mercerized cotton damask and sateen are often used, as well as plain cotton cloth. Ticking may be rendered dust and germ proof. Hair filled mattresses should have hair proof ticking. Inspect the ticking for wrinkles and durability.

Bed springs come in a variety of forms. The box springs are designed for the innerspring mattress. This spring consists of heavily coiled springs set into a slat of wood or steel, covered with hair or cotton felt and enclosed in ticking. The coils, in the best type, cannot be felt through the padding. The best frames are made of spruce, screwed and doweled together. Pine frames are used in the cheaper construction.

The other type of bed spring is known as the metal unit. The cheapest type of metal unit is the link fabric spring which consists of a metal frame with linked wire fabric. This type has a tendency to sag in the center. Nevertheless, it may be used with an innerspring mattress. Open coil springs consist of cone springs set in a wire frame and are intended primarily for solid mattresses. This type must be heavy, with springs secured by wire ties, for satisfactory service. The open top is not suitable to an innerspring mattress. The closed top spring is designed for use with the innerspring mattress.

Good bed springs are noiseless and rustproof. A good coil spring is fitted with two steel braces to prevent sagging and swaying. Springs must be strong enough for support and must be adapted to the mattress. The grades of pillow stuffing correspond to those of cushions of similar construction. Bed headboards are often upholstered today. Some of this upholstery is quilted or tufted. It is desirable that the upholstery fabric be one that can be wiped clean with a damp cloth. The same considerations of stuffing, ticking and tailoring apply here for quality as to upholstered chairs.

For the under-the-window sink

NOT THIS ∧ You don't have to clutter up the window sill with cleansing items.

THIS IS HOW ∨ Put up corner shelves on either side of the window. They're fine for holding plants, too.

WOOD FINISHES

Woods of better grade furniture go through an involved process in acquiring a finish. The wood is first sponged, to remove loose fibers and depressed core matter, then thoroughly dried. Next, the entire surface is sanded and dusted with an airgun. The wood is then stained by brushing, wiping or spraying, methods that secure uniform absorption. The stain is sandpapered and then filling, in the form of paraffin wax, varnish or linseed oil, is applied to the wood, the surplus being wiped off. After this preliminary preparation, the wood is ready for the final finish.

Finishes may be of two kinds, in a wide variety of colors. *Dull-rubbed*

A light wood occasional table in a pickled finish. Blonde wood furniture is growing in popularity and permits striking contrasts in groupings with dark woods or with accessories.

finishes involve the application of an undercoat of shellac, followed by several coats of varnish. Each step is followed by additional sanding. The final undercoat is rubbed with fine pumice stone and paraffin oil. The *high gloss* finish adds another step. The finish is rubbed still further with rotten stone powder and linseed oil in a circular motion. The final finish may be varnish, lacquer, oil, or wax and shellac.

Blonde furniture consists of both unbleached woods that are naturally light in color and bleached woods. The colors run from white through eggshell and cream to silvery gray, light yellow, beige, tan and light brown. Blonde walnut and mahogany are both popular bleached woods, their beauty depending upon their natural grain. Maple, light oak, birch, satinwood, avodire, myrtle burl, and zebrawood are also bleached. The finish is obtained with a transparent stain or shellac that is rubbed to bring out the grain. Pickled woods are first bleached, then coated with light gray paint that is rubbed down later with steel wool to produce its distinctive appearance. Blonde woods are very effective in brightening a room and giving it a gay, cheerful air. Combined with trimmings of dark wood, they achieve very effective contrasts.

In addition to these processes, furniture woods may be painted, enamelled or gilded. Decalcomanias and stencils are also applied. Highlighting or antiquing produces an effect of age and use through a burnt umber stain finish. Two tone finishes appear very rich and are used with mahogany and walnut. Japanning uses a black varnish.

In selecting furniture, see that the finish feels smooth to your touch. A poor finish becomes powdery or sticky when rubbed briskly until warm. Finish should be applied to the undersides as well as to the outer surfaces. The color of the finish should be attractive, of course. With the varied finishes available today, you should readily be able to conform to your color scheme and procure an attractively finished piece of furniture.

CHAPTER THIRTEEN

YOUR EFFICIENT KITCHEN

ONE of the sharpest breaks with the home of yesteryear has occurred in the planning and equipping of the present-day kitchen, laundry and bathroom. These rooms now profit by modern devices and facilities. The terrific drain on time and energy that meal preparation and laundering formerly entailed is abolished. Efficient equipment and arrangement can save your energy and health, make the tasks pleasant and easy and give you increased leisure for relaxation and recreation. Moreover, these rooms now embody a beauty and an attractiveness that are appealing.

PLANNING THE KITCHEN

In its initial stages, kitchen planning is a matter of efficiency engineering. According to scientific research, the two most fatiguing activities in the kitchen are the endless retracing of steps and the back-breaking involved in continually bending, stooping and stretching. You can avoid much of this wear and tear by adopting an efficient arrangement for the kitchen work centers and by adjusting them to suit your height and work habits.

The one principle involved in plan-

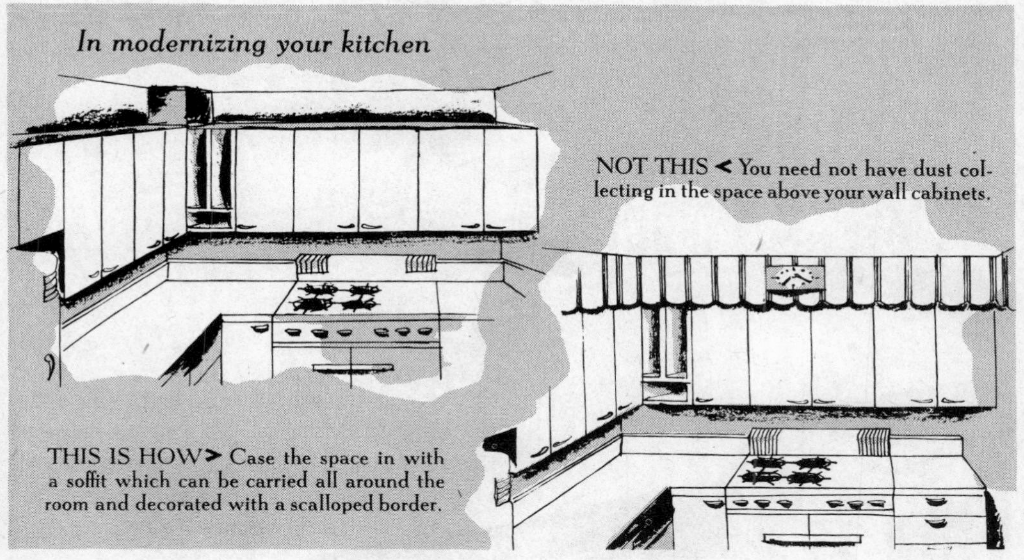

In modernizing your kitchen

NOT THIS < You need not have dust collecting in the space above your wall cabinets.

THIS IS HOW > Case the space in with a soffit which can be carried all around the room and decorated with a scalloped border.

ning an efficient kitchen arrangement is to contrive to group your work centers conveniently close to one another. The main work centers in a kitchen are the stove, refrigerator, sink and work counter. If these centers are well coordinated, with ample work surfaces and ample storage facilities conveniently located, your kitchen will be efficiently planned.

There are a number of kitchen arrangements that permit locating the work centers efficiently. The most economical arrangement, both in space and in cost of installation, is the *straight-wall* kitchen. In this arrangement, the four work centers are compactly aligned against one wall, with the refrigerator to the left of the sink and the stove to the right. The work counter is located next to the sink.

The *L-shaped* kitchen, in which the work centers are placed against two adjacent walls, is the most widely used arrangement. The four work centers are arranged in the form of a triangle. The housewife, working within the bounds of this triangle, is within easy reach of her kitchen facilities and equipment.

The *U-shaped* kitchen is the ideal labor-saving kitchen. This style of arrangement permits locating all four work centers most closely together and yet provides ample storage facilities. Three walls are required for this type of kitchen. If one of the three walls is interrupted by a door, low window or an arch, a modified

This L-shaped kitchen provides well placed base and wall cabinets, a snack bar and work surfaces topped with linoleum. A twin bowl cabinet sink, with double drainboards, includes five drawers, sliding shelves, breadboards and a compartment for refuse. The L-shaped kitchen arranges the four work centers against two adjacent walls, within easy reach, and is a convenient arrangement adapted to the small kitchen.

The U-shaped kitchen has three unified work centers — refrigeration and preparation center; sink and dishwasher center; range and serving center — which correspond to the three distinct processes involved in meal making. Each work center has its own mechanical "servant" and is serviced by cabinets and counter surfaces. Kitchens of this type require three walls and permit locating all work centers close together.

form of the U-shaped kitchen is still possible.

A fourth type of kitchen arrangement is the *peninsular* type. In this design, the sink and stove are placed back to back in a custom-built unit that flows out from a wall. So placed, these two work centers are both very close to the refrigerator. The peninsular design also provides ample work and storage space. While a most attractive and novel arrangement, peninsular design is not so efficient as the U-shaped kitchen.

The factors that decide which one of these kitchen arrangements you adopt are, mainly, the size, shape and architectural openings of the room and the amount of money earmarked for kitchen equipment. Whether you use your kitchen for canning and freezing foods, dining and laundering, will also be considerations. The up-to-date kitchen is amply provided with storage cabinets. Since these cabinets are manufactured as individual units, they may be installed and added to as desired. Unit cabinets are also an advantage to the homemaker who wants to remodel her kitchen. These cabinets are easy to clean, both inside and outside. Drawers and shelves are removable, and warm water and soap suffice.

Cabinets are usually made of enamelled or stainless steel and come in several types that match and interlock. Floor cabinet units are one type. The tops of these units may be covered with linoleum or wood to

In the attractive peninsular kitchen the sink and range are placed back to back in a custom-built unit that flows out from a wall, and permits a functional two-wall placement that leaves one wall free for several full height cabinets for dishes, glassware and serving equipment. The fourth wall has wall and base units, the latter with maple counter top, for storing utensils and foods needed in preparing meals.

The corner closet of this attractive kitchen has revolving shelves for ready access. The scalloped soffit adds a pleasing decorative note, as does the contrasting linoleum which repeats the scallop pattern.

provide a convenient work surface. These base units are equipped with drawers for cutlery storage, pullout tables, vertical dividers for trays, adjustable shelves, ventilated fruit, vegetable and flour bins, bread and cake receptacles, and even towel driers. Wall cabinets, which may be attached at a height convenient to you, afford storage for dishes and food. Tall, narrow units permit the storage of housecleaning equipment. Revolving closets are an additional convenience.

All these cabinets are produced in a range of widths so that it is possible to cover an entire wall and utilize space to the utmost. In addition, both base and wall cabinets are manufactured for corner installation. Rounded-edge open shelves are also available for corners. Undersink cabinets that enclose a refuse receptacle also offer additional storage space.

Accessories still further lighten kitchen chores. Spice shelves, drainboard mats and bread boxes are among the more common accessories. Stoves are supplied with hoods and ventilating fans that remove odors and smoke. Electric ozone generators, chemical deodorizers and deodorants are also used to purify the air. Movable work tables, provided with rubber wheels, are useful additions.

A number of other facilities are now being manufactured for the kitchen. Air-conditioning maintains an even temperature in the kitchen as well as in the other rooms of the home. Quick-freezer lockers that match the other units in size and construction may be purchased for the storage of frozen foods and for home freezing. An automatic dishwasher is an especially welcome addition to the kitchen. Combination automatic clothes and dishwashing machines are obtainable for the kitchen. These combination washers, however, require storage space for the unit not in use.

The items needed for each work center should be placed close by for efficiency and convenience. The sink should have storage space at hand for utensils and pots, cutlery and dishes. If the sink is placed beneath a window, corner shelves may be installed on either side of the window to hold cleaning articles often used,

To reduce kitchen labors

NOT THIS ▲ Stooping, bending and stretching increase kitchen fatigue.

THIS IS HOW ▼ Store your most used pots and pans in convenient spots. Place door handles low on wall cabinets and high on base cabinets.

or storage space for these items may be provided under the sink. The sink base should be recessed to provide toe space.

The stove center should have convenient racks for pots, ladles and lids. The cooking and serving utensils should find a place near the stove, too. The spice shelf similarly should be within easy reach. A work table near the stove is an added convenience. The refrigerator door should open so as to permit ready access from the sink. A clear shelf should be close by for food leaving or entering the refrigerator. The fruit and vegetable bin, as well as the freezer unit, should also be near the refrigerator.

You can easily determine the most convenient height for work units and surfaces. Stand in a relaxed, normal position and measure the distance from the floor to your hands when they are in a comfortable, kitchen-working position with elbows crooked. A woman five and a half feet tall will usually find that 34 or 35 inches is the most suitable height for her work counter, sink and range.

You can then select base cabinets in the most suitable height. Stoves and sinks may similarly be adjusted to conform to your height. Your work bench, too, should be so regulated. For accessibility, the top shelf of your wall cabinet should be within reach when you stand a foot in front of it. By placing your most-used items in the bottom section of wall cabinets and in the top section of floor cabinets, you can avoid much of the stretching, stooping and bending that plague the kitchen worker.

As an added convenience, kitchens are often provided with a desk in which recipes and cook books are kept for ready reference. A chair at the desk invites relaxation. A recent innovation is the addition of a living area in the kitchen, permitting the housewife to listen to the radio or take a short refreshing nap.

Many kitchens have breakfast nooks or dining alcoves, separated by a divider counter or other partition.

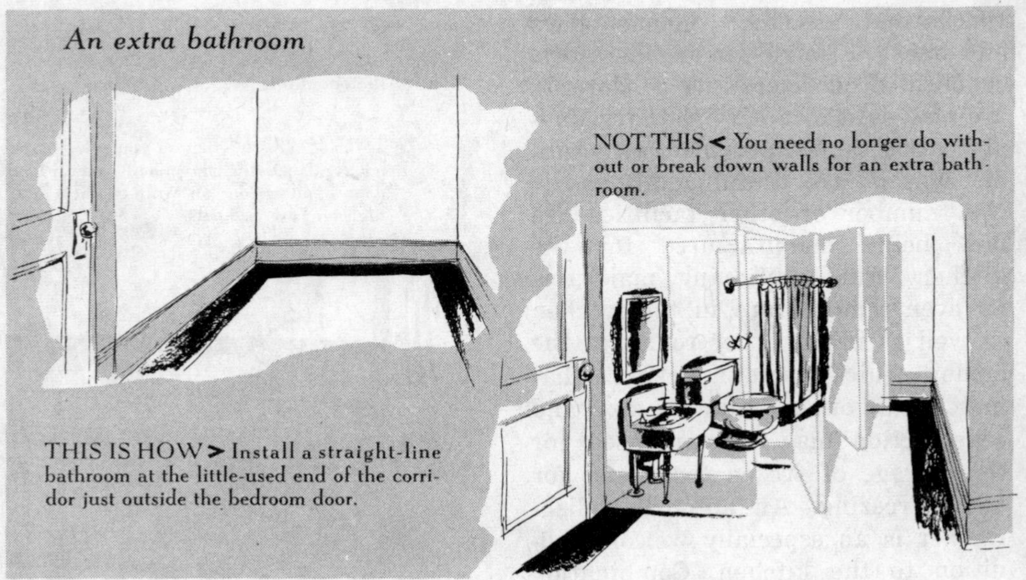

An extra bathroom

NOT THIS < You need no longer do without or break down walls for an extra bathroom.

THIS IS HOW > Install a straight-line bathroom at the little-used end of the corridor just outside the bedroom door.

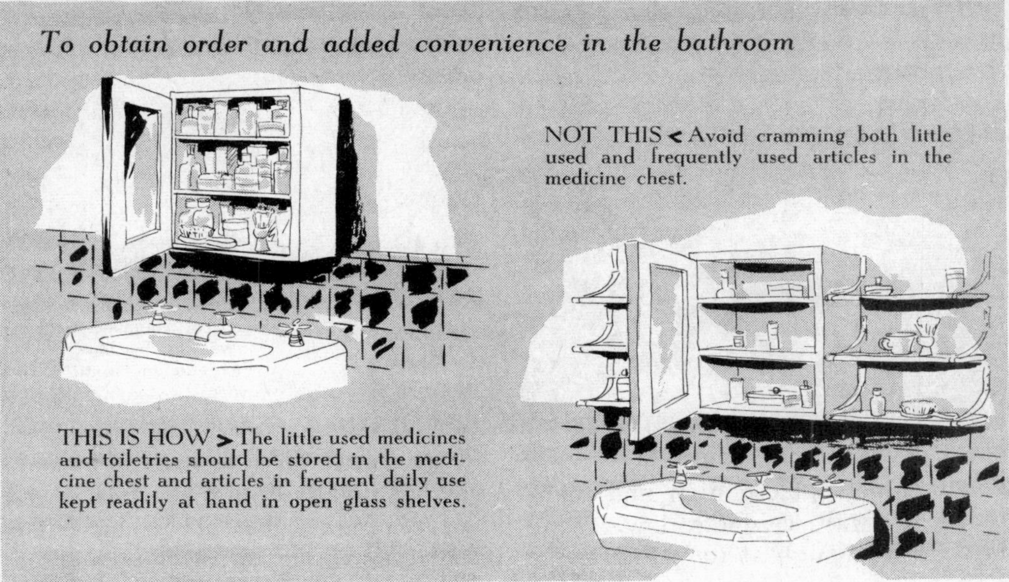

To obtain order and added convenience in the bathroom

NOT THIS < Avoid cramming both little used and frequently used articles in the medicine chest.

THIS IS HOW > The little used medicines and toiletries should be stored in the medicine chest and articles in frequent daily use kept readily at hand in open glass shelves.

A variation for the small kitchen is the snack bar. Such a bar may be the work counter fitted with stools. A Lazy Susan turntable, set in a partition, is attractive and a practical step-saving method of serving the dinette.

Good light is an essential in the kitchen. Windows contribute to this, but artificial illumination is also required. Each work center should be provided with light. Cove lighting gives a soft diffused light. Fluorescent lighting is especially well adapted to the kitchen, avoiding the heat of incandescent lamps. Fluorescent tubes may easily be placed under wall cabinets. The use of structural glass brick as a divider between kitchen and dining alcove serves to seclude the kitchen without cutting off light from the alcove.

The color schemes for kitchens are gay, spirited and lighthearted. Even the metal cabinets come in a variety of colors. Linoleum, too, is obtainable in a wide range of colors. Colored tile or scrubbable wallpaper are popular wall coverings. Windows sport pert, crisp glass curtains. Stencils and decalcomanias also impart a cheerful air. Wall cabinets, if used to cover an entire wall, are provided with soffits or furring from their top outer edge to the ceiling. This gives the cabinets a built-in appearance and adds to the cleanliness of the room.

In planning your kitchen, you draw up a floor plan as in planning other rooms in the home. The size of your family, your habits of entertainment and food preparation all indicate activities for which the kitchen must provide. In planning, avoid placing your sink in a corner. Allow ample room for cabinet doors to swing open. Let air and light suffuse your kitchen. Don't place cabinets above the stove. Select a floor covering that is easy to keep clean. A patterned floor covering is less likely to show footprints than a solid-colored one. For easy opening, have the door handles of

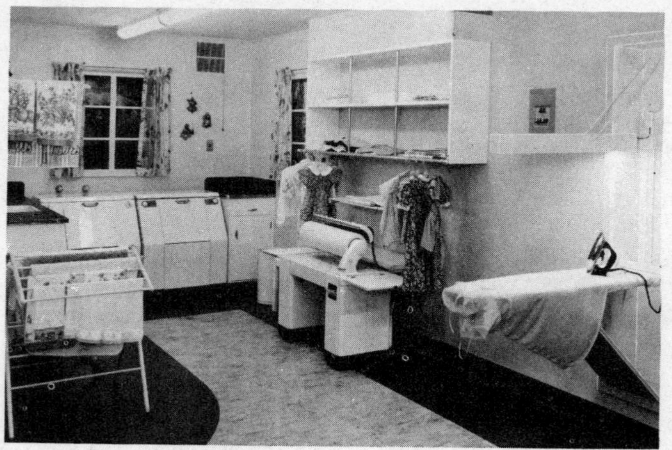

Fully automatic facilities are provided in this laundry for the four major tasks of sorting, washing, drying and ironing. The equipment includes a washing machine, clothes drier and an electric clothes ironer.

floor cabinets placed high and place those of wall cabinets low. Your kitchen will laugh at its chores.

THE LAUNDRY

The laundry may be combined with the kitchen, assigned to an adjoining alcove, or placed in the basement. The placement of the laundry depends, of course, upon the size of the home and location of its plumbing. It is considered preferable, however, to locate the laundry on the same floor as the kitchen, if possible.

As with the kitchen, the efficiency of the laundry is in direct ratio to the facilities it provides and to its arrangement. Modern facilities have revolutionized the laundry. The automatic washing machine has eliminated nearly all the drudgery and toil of laundering. Artificial driers have freed the housewife from dependence upon the sun. Air-conditioning now adds greater comfort.

The well planned laundry is fitted with tubs placed at the best height. The washing machine is located close to the tubs as is the storage hamper. The electric or gas drier is within easy access of the washing machine. The ironing board is adjusted to the correct height and folds into a flat wall cabinet when not in use. The board is firm, broad, well padded and provided with overhead illumination. Electric ironers are available that simplify one major task of laundering. A rod and shelves should be provided near the ironing equipment to take care of freshly ironed laundry.

Floor and wall cabinets as well as shelves afford convenient storage facilities. The floor is covered with a washable surface that is easy to clean and easy to stand on. A broad window, curtained in the same manner as the kitchen window, admits light and sun. The walls may be covered with wallpaper, moisture-resistant asbestos panels, or they may be painted. The color scheme is often the same as the adjoining kitchen. So arranged, the laundry provides for the four major activities—sorting, washing, drying and ironing.

THE BATHROOM

Modern bathrooms are gayly colored affairs. Pastels and dark colors are used. Paneled mirrors, washable patterned wallpaper, natural woods, tile, glass brick and fiber board are employed decoratively in the bath-

Carrara glass forms the walls of this attractive and functional bathroom with its many shelves. A full length mirror built into the wall doubles the apparent size of the room and adds to its over-all richness.

room as are stencils and decalcomanias. The floor is usually covered with linoleum or tile. A cotton scatter-sized rug should be placed near the tub.

The planning of a bathroom depends upon the size and shape of the available room. The bathroom contains four centers—bath and shower facilities, a dressing section with make-up accoutrements, a lavatory and a toilet. A towel cabinet, medicine chest, shelves and racks supply storage facilities. A full-length mirror is an added attraction, while an electric outlet convenient for the electric razor is desirable. The bathroom may be further fitted with a scale and even with a waterproof sunlamp over a reclining chair for health-giving vitamin D. A tub with high sides is available that obviates the need of shower curtains, though you may prefer the added color of a curtain.

The bathroom may provide all these facilities in one individual room or the room may be compartmentalized. This latter arrangement permits privacy during joint use. Compartmentalized bathrooms are divided into three centers—bath, toilet and lavatory. The dressing section is usually combined with the bath center. The compartmentalized arrangement is possible in a square area as well as in a long, narrow area. Such a bathroom may even be installed in an unused end portion of a hallway.

Set against a striking background of Chinese wallpaper, this pleasant bridge corner consists of a blonde mahogany table with a blue leather surface, rough-textured upholstered chairs and amber unit wood cases with shelves, drawers and sliding doors. An interesting decorative touch is provided by the shade of the floor lamp which is made of the same fabric as is the upholstery. The carpeting is a monotone brown.

CHAPTER FOURTEEN

SELECTING LAMPS AND LIGHTING FIXTURES

IT IS hard to imagine the Mauve Decade of the 1890's without calling to mind a picture of gas lights and flickering Welsbach mantels. Perhaps in years to come our own time will evoke images of the incandescent electric lamp. For today we similarly stand at the end of an era. Already the fluorescent lamp, invented in 1938, is gaining widespread acceptance. Eventually, this type of lamp will entirely replace the lamp that we owe to Edison's genius.

In an incandescent lamp, an electric current passes through a filament. The resistance offered by the filament to the passage of the current produces a white-hot glow that gives off light. Actually the incandescent lamp is an efficient heat generator, the glow of a 60-watt lamp reaching a temperature of over 4300°F. To withstand this temperature, filaments are made of tungsten, a metal with the highest melting point known. Incandescent lamps are manufactured in a wide variety of shapes, sizes and colors for both utility and decoration.

The fluorescent lamp, on the other hand, is an electronic device, at one with radio, television, x-ray and the electric eye. A tungsten filament

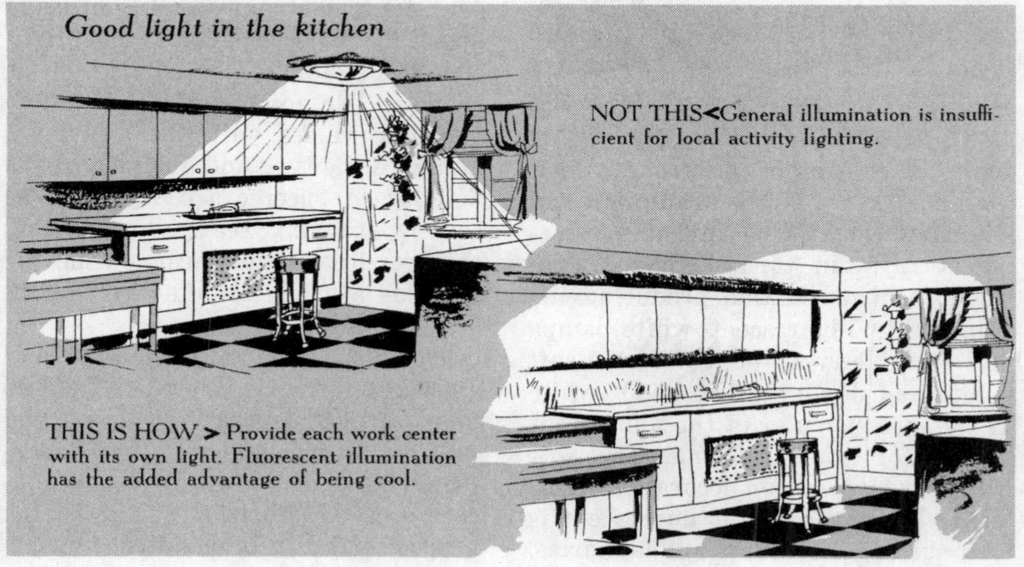

Good light in the kitchen

NOT THIS < General illumination is insufficient for local activity lighting.

THIS IS HOW > Provide each work center with its own light. Fluorescent illumination has the added advantage of being cool.

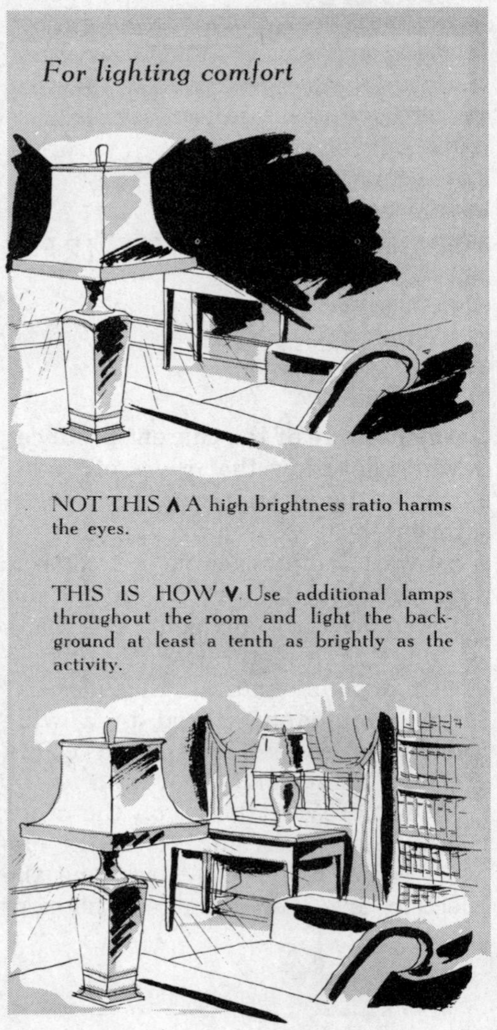

For lighting comfort

NOT THIS ∧ A high brightness ratio harms the eyes.

THIS IS HOW ∨ Use additional lamps throughout the room and light the background at least a tenth as brightly as the activity.

emits a stream of electrons which produce ultra-violet radiation in mercury vapor. The invisible ultraviolet rays, in turn, bombard fluorescent chemicals, thus producing visible light. Fluorescent white lamps are of three types—3500° white, soft white and daylight. The 3500° white is the most popular of the fluorescent lamps for home lighting. The soft white is favored for decorative lighting, while the daylight fluorescent is best suited for kitchens and laundries.

Fluorescent lamps are more economical of operation than are incandescent lamps and yield a softer light that approaches the qualities of natural daylight. Fluorescent lamps provide a better distribution of light and their illumination is cool—an advantage in kitchens, laundries, game rooms, or for desk and summer use. They are not, however, produced in the adaptable shapes and sizes of incandescent lamps and they require additional devices—special sockets, a ballast that controls the amount of current flowing through the lamp and a starter switch for other than instant starting circuits.

LIGHTING COMFORT

In planning home lighting, you should consider the twin aspects of comfort and decoration. Lighting comfort takes into account the amount of light, its distribution in the room and its quality. Decoration considers the role of lighting in the creation of attractive interiors.

Lighting comfort should aim to protect and preserve eyesight and prevent nervous strain. Good lighting is essential to good health. The light should be ample, without glare or shadow. The amount of light that is adequate varies with the individual and with the type and duration of the activity. A specific activity, such as sewing, studying, reading or shaving, requires local illumination, while the room as a whole should receive general illumination.

The distinction between local and general lighting is related to the two types of lighting fixtures—*direct* and *indirect*. Direct lighting focuses nearly all its light downward and concentrates illumination. This is the type of lighting best suited for specific tasks. Indirect lighting sends its light upward to be reflected from the ceiling. It produces a broader area of diffused illumination, well adapted for general lighting. Two other types of lighting combine both direct and indirect features in varying degrees. The *semi-direct* is principally a direct type, with a small portion of its light reflected from above. The *semi-indirect* reverses this procedure.

You must consider both quantity and quality of light for each room. In illuminating a specific activity, eye comfort requires the avoidance of too great a disparity between the amount of light supplied to a task and the amount of general illumination. The reason behind this brightness ratio is physiologic. If the eyes have to readjust themselves continually to varying degrees of brightness, fatigue quickly results. In a room, the background should be lighted at least one-tenth as brightly as is the activity itself.

A Modern desk deserves modern lighting. This fluorescent desk lamp has swivel arms which permit focusing the direct rays of light where they are needed.

The use of indirect forms of lighting requires close attention to the color and texture of the ceiling if you are to assure a pleasant over-all result. Glossy surfaces produce glare. Mat finishes, however, distribute light evenly with a minimum of glare. Light-colored surfaces reflect a greater percentage of light than do dark-colored surfaces.

Since different colors reflect different amounts of light, the quantity of light in a room depends in part upon the colors of its surfaces. White paint reflects up to 85 per cent of the light that strikes it, a light green 65 per cent, a medium green 52 per cent, while a dark green reflects only 7 per cent. Wood finishes similarly vary in the amount of light that they reflect. A maple finish reflects 42 per cent of the light, walnut reflects 16 per cent, while mahogany reflects only 12 per cent. Blonde finished woods reflect more light than do dark-colored woods.

Glare and shadow indicate that the lighting is of poor quality. Glare results when light shines into the eyes, distorting the visual image. Unshaded or poorly shaded lamps produce glare, as do glossy surfaces. Shadow reduces the amount of light reaching the eyes and places an added strain upon them.

It also increases the disparity of illumination. Both these defects can be avoided through distributing suitable lamps properly throughout a room.

You can assure sufficient, well distributed light by providing a lamp with a proper sized bulb for each of your centers of activity, in addition to providing for general room illumination. An activity that is forced to depend upon general room illumination is seldom adequately lighted. Your electric company will check the quality of illumination in your room with a light meter and recommend desirable changes, if necessary.

A good quality lamp is tall enough to diffuse light over a broad area and to make it unnecessary to move the lamp about in order to focus its rays. It should not be too tall, however, or you will have difficulty integrating it with your furniture grouping. It should be furnished with a flared shade that is broad at the bottom and tapers toward the top. The top of the shade should be open so as to direct light upwards. The shade should have a highly reflective inner lining, preferably white or a very pale tint. The light bulb should not be visible through the shade. Reflector bowls of glass or plastic should surround the bulb to diffuse and soften the light. For indirect illumination, silver lined or metal reflectors are highly desirable.

For reading and study, floor lamps should be placed beside and slightly behind chairs. Lamps should be placed near the piano so as to light the music without glare or shadow. Clamp-on fluorescent lamps are available for music racks. For sewing, the light should be placed opposite the hand that is used. A right-handed person, accordingly, would have the lamp placed to the left. A table or study lamp should similarly be placed toward the rear of a desk or table directly opposite the hand used. Desk and table lamps should be of the semi-indirect type to avoid glare. For reading in bed, pin-up bracket lamps may be used. Fluorescent lamps are especially good for bed lighting and desks,

For the breakfast nook

NOT THIS < You needn't work in the kitchen and miss breakfast with your family.

THIS IS HOW > Install several electric outlets in the breakfast nook. They're convenient for the toaster, waffle iron and coffee maker.

as well as for illuminating mirrors and kitchen and laundry work centers. End table lamps of good quality are designed for both general and local illumination. Extensible swivel-arm lamps are highly decorative and flexible.

Wall and ceiling light fixtures are most suitable for providing soft background illumination. Concealed cove and fluorescent lights are well adapted to this purpose. For best results, a ceiling fixture should be at least seven and a half feet above the floor. Wall brackets should shoot light upward as well as downward.

DECORATING WITH LIGHT

Aladdin had only to rub his lamp to get his wish. You can make wishes come true that Aladdin never dreamt of. The secret lies in the fact that lighting can unify a room, highlight a grouping or a wall, impart color and glamor, and create a mood through the use of portable lamps and built-in fixtures.

General room lighting suffuses the entire room with light and thus produces unity. Localized lighting, on the other hand, creates contrasts between areas of the room. This latter type of illumination may be used to accent a grouping or an object. Gradations of light throughout a room produce a pleasing over-all effect. Sharp contrasts of light usually are disturbing or restless though their skilful use may achieve interesting dramatic effects.

Subdued lights and soft shadows create a mood of hospitality and intimacy. Direct lighting, with contrasting areas of light and shade, is gay and vivacious when the contrasts blend harmoniously together. For a quiet, restful effect, indirect illumination is preferable, while cove lighting is sophisticated and modern, though it may be used with rich effect in rooms done in the traditional manner. Colored lamps also create dramatic effects in a room, but they may be difficult to live with and they are not adapted to activity illumination.

Clever lighting here finds use in an attractive bedroom. The linen bedspread is bordered with a broad band of yellow satin, on which is superimposed a narrow ribbon of coral. This trimming is repeated at the bottom of the linen draperies which are semi-sheer. The textured linen rug, with coral loops, lies on a navy blue carpet. The yellow cushion matches the border of the bedspread. Walls are a pure white.

At your beck and call are such built-in genii as cove, panel and spot lighting. *Cove lighting* consists of a series of bulbs or a tubular bulb set in a recessed reflecting trough, usually concealed by a molding, shield or louvre, that provides indirect lighting. Fluorescent tubes and lumiline incandescent lamps are both well suited to this type of lighting. Cove lighting may be used around a door, under a valance, behind draperies or cornices, alongside mirrors, around a mural or behind the pediment of a cabinet. It is especially effective around a mirrored wall recess, edged with a valance, into which the headboard of a bed is set. Cove lights on opposite walls give a particularly pleasing effect.

Panel lighting is lighting installed behind panels of frosted, etched or otherwise decorated glass. The glass panel is usually installed flush with the wall or ceiling. Luminous panels may be placed around a piece of furniture, such as a bookcase, cabinet or mirror, around a fireplace or in an alcove. Placed over a mantel, panel lights may be used to cast a soft glow over decorative accessories. Like cove lights, panel lights may be used over windows and doors.

Spot-lighting is a form of direct lighting. These lights may be installed in a ceiling to focus upon any object. Lenses can limit the light to a picture or a piece of furniture, highlight a furniture arrangement or attract attention to an object. The spotlight may be placed within a glass shelved cabinet. Spotlights—or downlights, as they are also called—create dramatic effects in a dining room where they can focus light upon the table setting.

Colored bulbs may be used in any of these built-in fixtures, as well as in portable lamps. Amber lamps, installed over windows, can create the illusion of sunshine during bleak winter days. A gold fluorescent tube may be placed behind a breakfront, silhouetting its pediment. Black-light (technically, ultra-violet light) can be used to achieve unique sophisticated effects together with fluorescent wallpaper and fluorescent treated fabrics. Glass brick may be flooded with a soft light for a distinctive effect.

Lighting does affect color and texture. It is important to test rugs, wallpaper, upholstery material and paint colors under the type of lighting your room uses. The incandescent lamp emphasizes reds and yellows in a room, while toning down blues and greens. For example, under incandescent illumination, a dark blue is dulled and grayed, while a tint of blue appears greenish-yellow. These color changes vary with different textures. Two fabrics of the same color but of different textures will vary under the yellowish-red effect of filament lights.

The white fluorescent lamp intensifies blues, greens and yellows, while toning down reds and oranges. For example, under daylight fluorescent lighting, a dark blue becomes a vivid royal blue, while a tint of blue also gains in brilliance. The other two types of fluorescent lamps affect light and dark blues with grayed and purplish casts. The incandescent lamp produces a warm effect, the fluorescent a cool effect.

A color scheme that is pleasing by daylight but is distorted by incandescent lighting, may be improved through the use of fluorescent lighting or colored bulbs. As colored bulbs alter colors perceptibly, it is advisable to test the effect they will exert upon your color scheme before resorting to them. Remember, too, that colored bulbs produce varied color changes with different textured materials.

Colored translucent lampshades also change the colors in your room. Especially do translucent blue, purple and green shades exert an unflattering effect upon the occupants of a room. In addition, colored shades when illuminated may contrast too markedly with the color scheme of your room. For these reasons, white, eggshell and rosy-beige are especially recommended for translucent lampshades. White or pale tinted shade linings will also prevent these undesirable effects.

Lighting fixtures, wall brackets and lamps are available in a wide range of types, many of them well adapted to period styles. Portico lanterns, fumed brass chandeliers with etched glass chimneys and pewter lamps

"Hightlighting" here receives a literal interpretation. Lights beneath a shelf highlight the accessories within the cabinet while lights atop the cabinet contribute a novel interplay of light and shadow to the effect.

A pair of table lamps take their place among the many delightful accessories shown here which permit use in the well decorated home of today.

with homespun shades are as distinctly Colonial as crystal chandeliers with colored satin shades or classic urn bases with parchment shades are formal traditional. The spirit of the period will direct you to select the proper lamp for your room. In fact, a lamp can contribute to creating a mood. A dark leather lamp has a masculine feeling, a delicate crystal lamp is feminine.

Modern floor and table lamps are manufactured in a wide variety of materials. Metal, wood, glass, plastics, porcelain, earthenware and leather are all used as lamp bases. Shades similarly are made of a wide range of materials — fabrics, parchment, paper, plastics and metal. The trend in modern lamps is toward broader bases, higher shafts and larger shades. Another modern tendency is to use lampshades of one color throughout a room. The shades may repeat or blend with a color of the background, or contrast with it. Whatever lamp you select should be in scale with your room. Lamps are one of the most important accessories and should fit the mood and enhance the decoration of your room.

NEW ELECTRIC DEVICES

Closely allied to the incandescent lamp is the *drying lamp*. This type of lamp takes advantage of the fact that the incandescent lamp converts 90 per cent of the current it consumes into heat. Instead of light, however, the drying lamp emits infra-red radiant heat. Much used in industry to perform a wide range of jobs, the application of infra-red lamps to the home is growing fast. These lamps are already used to remove the chill in a room, protect tender plants from cold, dry fingernail polish, freshly shampooed hair and laundry, as well as to provide therapeutic heat treatment.

The *ultra-violet* lamp will doubtless in time be combined with conventional artificial illumination. At present, ultra-violet lamps are manufactured as units or combined with infra-red lamps. The ultra-violet lamp generates rays through an electric bombardment of mercury, much as these rays are produced in the fluorescent lamp. The erythmal energy is about triple that of the action of the summer sun, so that a year 'round suntan may now be obtained by turning a switch. The ultra-violet lamp is also used to produce a fluorescent glow in wallpaper and fabrics treated to respond to activation by black-light.

Another adaptation of the ultra-violet lamp is the bactericidal Sterilamp. This lamp kills bacteria within range of its rays. Used in the nursery, the Sterilamp will safeguard a youngster from bacteria-borne diseases. The night-light is another safety device consisting of a one-watt fluorescent lamp, designed with two prongs to fit into an electric outlet. It serves to light steps, halls and other potentially risky spots, and burns for an entire year at an electric current charge of only a few cents. A neon lamp is also available for the same purpose.

All is grist to the mill of the present-day lamp maker! Here a beautifully wrought Chinese figurine has been converted into a smart, practical lamp.

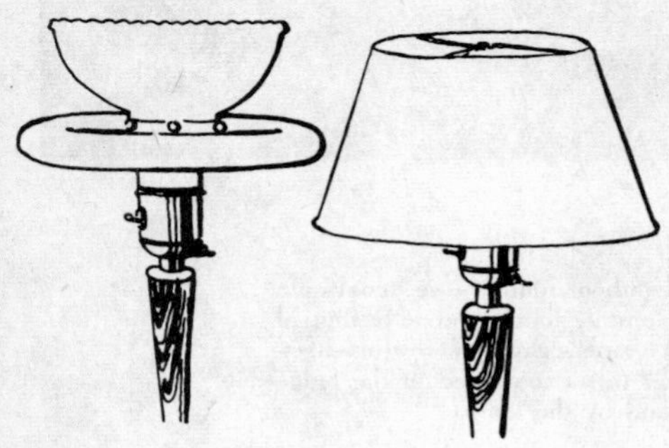

DIAGRAM 24

Circline Fluorescent Lamp

A forecast of things to come is contained in a new type of lamp that adds a circle of fluorescent lighting to the conventional incandescent lamp, as shown in *diagram* 24. In time, research will doubtless develop the fluorescent tube for all types of portable lamps. And lamps will be manufactured that preserve the true value of colors. Until this is done, it remains necessary carefully to test the effects of lighting upon the decoration of your home.

A border of Chinese prints, framed in bamboo, follow a sectional sofa around a corner. The pictures add a decorative touch and a feeling of completeness to the grouping, as well as emphasizing the restful effect. The pictures are illuminated by fluorescent tubes concealed in the ledge behind the sofa and in the ceiling cove, and by the lamps.

A pair of large prints, framed to contrast with the deep cordovan of the Mr. and Mrs. chests, accent this grouping and give it the proper scale and balance. The tambour doors roll into the sides of the chest to expose the English drawers of varied sizes.

CHAPTER FIFTEEN

PICTURES AND OTHER WALL HANGINGS

LIKE OTHER accessories, pictures contribute much to the decoration of a room. A well-chosen picture may complete a furniture grouping, introduce a pleasing variety of line and color, or attract attention to a center of interest. Especially are pictures versatile in the moods they create. Gayety, quaintness, serenity or dignity can be conveyed so persuasively by pictures as to establish the atmosphere of a room.

SELECTING PICTURES

Pictures may be chosen in a wide range of media, for artists create their effects through the use of many different means and techniques. You may choose water colors or oil paintings, etchings, lithographs or linoleum blocks. You may decide upon woodcuts, steel engravings or mezzotints. Or you may prefer photographs, murals, metal work, silhouettes, papier mache figures or mounted maps. Indeed, you may incline to other types of wall hangings. You may use mirrors to advantage, as well as tapestry, petit point, samplers and decorative china plates. You may even select serapes, Navajo rugs or tapa cloth as wall hangings.

For the room in the Chinese spirit

NOT THIS < Are you finding it hard to mix other styles with your pieces having Chinese fretwork, pagoda motifs and bamboo legs?

THIS IS HOW > The twain can meet! Chinese Chippendale, for instance, goes well with Hepplewhite, Sheraton, Duncan Phyfe or Modern furniture. Japanese prints are indicated, too.

Your point of view in judging a picture differs from that of the art critic. He evaluates pictures as works of art on the basis of color, form, pattern or composition, and technique. The subject matter of a painting is usually secondary to him. As a home decorator, you consider pictures not only as works of art but also as decorative accessories. They must harmonize in spirit and theme with the over-all effect you wish to create. A picture may be a work of art, but unless it accords with your purpose it is not decoratively suitable to your home.

For inexpensive picture framing

NOT THIS ∧ Framing many individual pictures of temporary interest is expensive.

THIS IS HOW ∨ Use two long horizontal moldings with a glass insert. This holds several pictures and permits easy changing.

If you intend to create a gay-hearted, buoyant home, a warm, bright colored picture may keynote this spirit. Landscapes, seascapes, pastorals and scenic photographs may introduce the feeling of quiet and restfulness you wish for your living room, entrance hall or stairway. Or pictures of still life, attractively designed floral arrangements, Japanese prints, etchings or aquatints may underscore the very effect you seek.

Godey fashion prints, framed papier mache characters, floral prints or samplers suit the feminine room. A masculine room deserves a sporting print, a surging seascape, a winter view or perhaps photographs of dogs and horses. Or, you may prefer to have a favorite photograph finished in sepia tone, mounted on a cream colored mat and framed in a narrow natural wood frame. Such photographs go well with hammered copper plates.

Children's rooms may display historical or genre pictures. Highly colored pictures uniformly appeal to children, as do silhouettes, posters, decorated maps and colorful magazine illustrations. Children particularly like drawings done by themselves or by other children. Provide the child's room with a bulletin board placed low enough for the child to tack up pictures that he likes.

Pictures should harmonize with the type of furniture you use. Colonial New England style furniture goes well with paintings of Colonial life and scenes, monochromes, etchings, Currier and Ives prints, samplers, pastorals and artistic floral pictures. Such decorations add a note of authenticity to a room and point up its period furnishings. Reproductions of Greek classic paintings belong in a classic period room, as do reproductions of the Old Masters. Eighteenth century rooms may use oval or oblong portraits, formal landscapes, classic paintings, cameos, medallions, tapestry and statuary. Often such rooms have as their center of interest an imposing portrait done in oils and hung above the fireplace.

Scenic prints may be used to decorate a living room in the Duncan Phyfe tradition, while silhouettes may be used in the traditional bedroom. Southwest American style is very flexible, permitting both classic and modern paintings, frescoes, metal work and statuary. Deep rich colors are readily adaptable to such rooms. Mexican and Indian art work are especially appropriate to provincial and Modern rooms, and modern art goes well in theme and spirit with the home furnished in the Modern manner.

Since color is one of the most distinctive elements in pictures, care must be taken that your selection of a picture does not clash with your color scheme. In fact, you can plan your entire room around the colors of a painting. A room or corner lacking in color may be brightened through the use of a highly colorful picture. If your room already abounds in color, you should select etchings, lithographs, photographs or black and whites as a counterbalance.

The colors of your upholstery, rugs and draperies may be repeated in the colors of the picture, or contrasting colors may be used to give zest and gayety. Warm, bright colors give the impression of bringing walls nearer to the observer, thus producing a feeling of intimacy in a large room. On the other hand, cool blues and greens of sea and landscapes have a receding effect. Pictures can heighten the over-all effect you wish to achieve. If you make the acquaintance of pictures through visits to museums and art galleries and through consulting illustrated magazines, selection will be easier.

ARRANGEMENT

Your selection of pictures should be made with their arrangement in

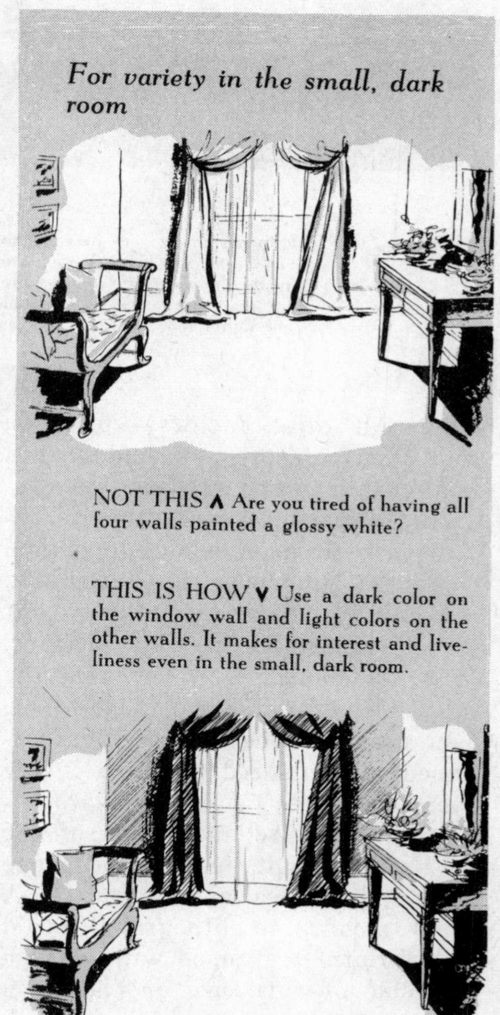

For variety in the small, dark room

NOT THIS ∧ Are you tired of having all four walls painted a glossy white?

THIS IS HOW ∨ Use a dark color on the window wall and light colors on the other walls. It makes for interest and liveliness even in the small, dark room.

Extremes in size are here harmonized and unified through the use of small prints. Without these pictures, the large mirror would dwarf the fragile drawer table over which it is hung. The arrangement of the pictures is especially decorative and serves to fuse the grouping together. The mirror reflection adds spaciousness to the composition.

mind. All three factors — pictures, wall and furniture — should bear a relationship to one another that produces a pleasing composition. In arrangement, color, line and proportion, balance and emphasis are your guides.

You have already given due weight to color in selecting your pictures. It is not enough, however, that the colors blend into a harmonious whole. You cannot achieve a well-proportioned and balanced grouping if any one of the three factors is disproportionate. The size and shape of the picture must suit the size and shape of the wall area and furniture. A small etching or lithograph would look forlorn if grouped with a large ensemble of furniture or placed on a large wall area. Instead, use a large picture or several small ones. Similarly, a massive oil painting would not go well with a delicate console table.

The shape of the wall space will often indicate the shape and size of the picture. A tall, narrow wall requires a picture of these proportions, while a horizontal wall space calls for a broad picture or grouping. The lines of the furniture and of the room will specify the desirable lines of the picture. Variety, however, may sometimes be introduced with flattering results.

Your pictures should be arranged with an eye to rhythm and balance. Balance is sacrificed if your picture is not well centered and is out of alignment with the main vertical axis of the unit. Formal balance is not the only means at your disposal. Asymmetric arrangement requires attention to spacing and the use of other accessories as a compensating factor.

A picture that leads the eye away from your grouping through its design or theme, is unsatisfactory. This fault may be corrected through the use of another picture or decorative accessory. It is for this reason that two portraits of right and left profile respectively should be hung facing each other if both are used in the same grouping.

Emphasis may be secured by leaving ample free space around a picture. Patterned wallpaper may distract attention from oils and water colors, though photographs, lithographs and etchings will usually stand out. Emphasis may be achieved through eliminating other attention-competing elements, through mounting the picture on an over-sized mat and framing it attractively, through using a clever arrangement of lighting or through grouping two or more pictures together as a unit. Contrast of color also serves to heighten the effectiveness of a grouping.

When you desire to group two or more pictures together, not only must you consider their arrangement with your furniture and wall but you must also consider the value or decorative weight of each picture. Because of their value, oil paintings rarely group well with black and whites such as etchings, steel engravings, linoleum blocks or pen and ink drawings. Though each may be an excellent example of its kind, reproductions of a Renaissance master and of a modern impressionist differ too widely to group well together. An especially fine picture should keep good company. Individual pictures often gain in meaningfulness when grouped together.

Though the proportions of each

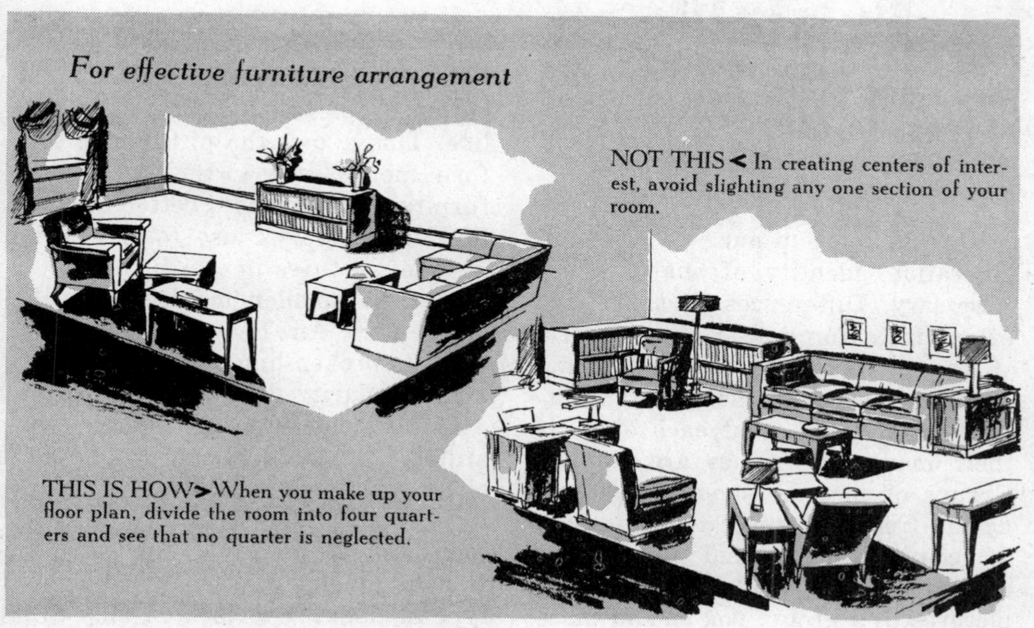

For effective furniture arrangement

NOT THIS < In creating centers of interest, avoid slighting any one section of your room.

THIS IS HOW > When you make up your floor plan, divide the room into four quarters and see that no quarter is neglected.

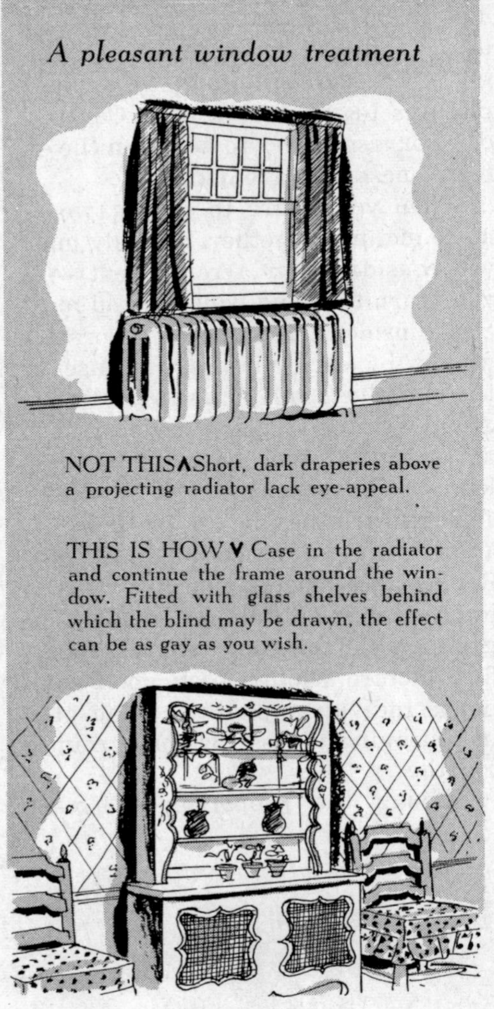

A pleasant window treatment

NOT THIS ▲ Short, dark draperies above a projecting radiator lack eye-appeal.

THIS IS HOW ▼ Case in the radiator and continue the frame around the window. Fitted with glass shelves behind which the blind may be drawn, the effect can be as gay as you wish.

picture in a group must receive consideration, identity of shape is not necessary. Differences in shape can often make for a desirable variety, if the pictures are properly hung. Pictures diverse in theme and treatment may complement each other if their mats and frames are similar. Groups of pictures should have sufficient free wall space around them to secure emphasis and permit concentrated enjoyment. In hanging pictures in a group, you should place them close enough to one another to avoid a scatter-shot effect.

HANGING

All pictures in your room should hang at a uniform height, between five and six feet above the floor. This rule may be modified in hanging a picture over a high mantelpiece or in unifying it with low furniture. The tendency in Modern interiors is to hang pictures unusually low, sometimes only three feet above the floor.

Pictures and mirrors should hang flat against the wall, not tilted away from it. And they should, of course, hang perfectly straight. You will find that concealed picture hooks are best for hanging pictures. You may prevent pictures from tilting by placing the screw eyes, to which the picture wire is fastened, high in the back of the frame. If you must hang pictures from the molding, use parallel wires for all but oval shaped pictures. Use the inverted V-shape for oval wall hangings.

If two or more pictures of varying size are grouped together over a broad horizontal piece or group, the bottom frames should form a straight line. This allows the pictures to conform more closely to the line of your furniture and permits better integration. This applies also to the group of three pictures in which the center picture is smaller in size than the outer two. An H-shaped grouping, with its broken-line effect, introduces an irregularity difficult to overcome.

If your pictures are widely separated, or on different walls and above varying sized pieces of furniture, then it is best to line up their top borders. In any event, avoid a step or oblique effect. This diagonal type of hanging looks well only over a stairway. In hanging pictures vertically, the larger picture should be hung above.

Unless pictures are hung close together they cannot comprise a group. The space between pictures in a group is regulated by the dimensions of the wall, furniture and pictures involved. If your sofa extends six feet in length, three pictures twelve inches wide should not be spread so as to cover this entire distance. Rather, you should center this grouping, allowing only a few inches between frames. Close hanging of pictures in a group increases the degree of integration and produces a better over-all effect.

MOUNTING AND FRAMING

The pictures you select may come already mounted and framed—that is, provided with mat, glass and frame. You may, however, wish to have this mounting altered. Or you may wish to decide upon the mounting and framing of unframed photographs, etchings, water colors, prints or magazine illustrations. If so, you will have to know something of the rules of balance and proportion that relate to picture mounting.

With the exception of oil paintings, which are most often framed without margins, all pictures have mats as borders surrounding the picture.

A picture is the center of interest of this attractive Modern bedroom. The colors of the room are taken from the picture. In turn, the wallpaper is designed to focus attention upon the picture. The pair of bedside tables and lamps are decorative and useful, while the shaggy rug adds textural interest as well as a feeling of warmth to the room.

These mats allow for margins or borders between the picture and wall. Whether a picture should have a wide or narrow border is relatively independent of the size of the picture itself. A large mat gives added importance to small pictures and adapts them for arrangement with large and important pieces of furniture. Broad mats and plain frames are best with patterned wallpaper, for otherwise the picture might be overshadowed by the design of the paper. A wide mat is preferable, too, if the picture gives an impression of movement.

For your plants

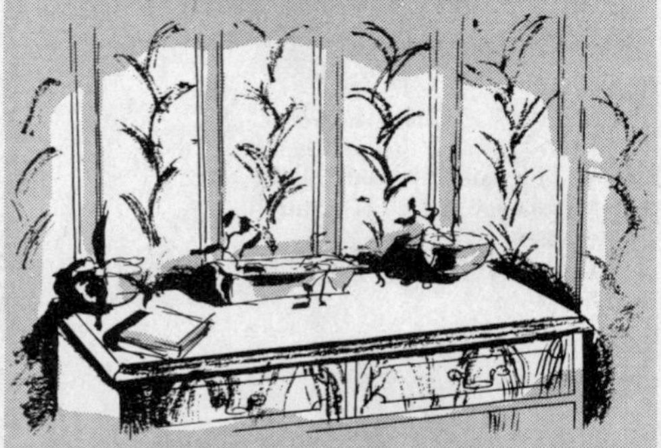

NOT THIS ∧ Plants can't thrive without ample natural light.

THIS IS HOW ∨ Place your plants below a long mirror that catches every bit of light. You can then keep plants on the inside wall.

In any picture mounting, whether the picture is square, horizontal or vertical, the bottom margin should be the broadest of the four borders. Only in this way will your picture look well proportioned. The borders on each side, moreover, should usually be of the same width. The top border may be the same width as the side margin, or the top margin may be slightly narrower for a horizontal picture or slightly wider for a vertical picture. The simplest and safest treatment is to have sides and top equal in width and have the broad margin at the bottom.

Mats and frames afford ample scope for felicitous color choice. The mat may be plain white, solid colored or patterned. Simple white mats tend to emphasize the colors of the picture, while gray mats tend to subdue these colors. The colors of the mats can harmonize or contrast with the pictures. You can repeat colors found in your wall or your furniture and thus secure greater unity in your arrangement. You may even adopt the colors of your draperies for the mat and frame.

The mat, in fact, need not be of regular mat paper. It may be of textiles, colored wallpaper, silver foil or linoleum. Copper foil mats are widely used with abstract art and floral designs. A plain mat may be decorated by drawing shaded pencil or ink lines on it. Pencil lines of varying shades are especially decorative with photographs and Japanese prints.

As with mats, the variety of frames is great. Oil paintings, which are usually framed without mats and glass, can take heavy, ornate frames.

These frames would, however, look grotesque on steel engravings, etchings, water colors or woodcuts. The present tendency is to keep frames simple. In this way attention is not diverted from the picture itself. Even so frames are available in a myriad of shapes, weights and woods.

Etchings and woodcuts are often framed with narrow strips of wood finished in a glossy black. Natural woods are widely used in scoop, fluted or shadowbox forms. Bevelled frames may be painted in two colors —the inner surface a different color from the outer surface. The inner surface may take its color from the picture or be a creamy white for emphasis, while the outer surface may be colored to blend wtih the wall or the furniture. Two long horizontal moldings with a glass insert may be used to hold several pictures at once. Bracket clasps of metal or plastic, adjustable to fit the top and bottom of different sized mats, are widely used instead of frames.

An ornate gilt period mirror is flanked by two identical floral prints. The flower stands, while tall, carry out the air of delicacy of the love seat.

OTHER WALL HANGINGS

Many other wall hangings may be used with highly decorative effect. Textiles — embroidered, screen or block printed — suggest themselves, as do tapestries, brocades, toiles and India prints. The designs may consist of all-over patterns or pictorial representations. The effect is rich and luxurious, combining well with traditional furniture in formal homes. The informal home may use Mexican serapes, Navajo rugs, tapa cloth or gay cotton prints.

Metals provide many decorative accessories and are especially attractive in rooms with figured wallpaper. The masculine room may be decorated with lustrous navigational aids — compasses, chronometers, mariner's wheels — which go well with maps, charts and seascapes. Rifles and war trophies similarly may be used.

Plaques of metal, glass or pottery as well as sculptured work offer decorative possibilities. Masks of metal, wood and clay are also used. Patterned china dishes, metal trays and semi-precious stone slabs framed in rare woods form interesting wall hangings. Hanging shelves, wall sconces, clocks and flower holders are pleasing decorative additions.

Murals and photomurals are widely used, as are wallpaper panels. Floodlighting may accent these wall hangings and create highly decorative effects. Picture windows may also serve as wall decoration, permitting the natural outdoor scene to serve as a backdrop for the room. Even draperies or decorative screens are used to cover an entire wall.

Mirrors answer needs that can be met in no other way. They bring light and gayety into a room and give symmetry through reflecting the opposite wall. They also create an effect of spaciousness. Mirrors may be framed or fastened by clips. They are often used to cover an entire wall or as hangings over fireplace and furniture. Mirrors are available to suit every period style. The *Cavalcade of Furniture Styles* on the front and back covers illustrates different period mirrors.

The standards of good taste involved in selecting and arranging pictures also apply to the selection and arrangement of mirrors and other wall hangings.

A Modern two-faced desk here is set against a traditional background. The placement of the desk and the two scenic water colors lends added attraction.

CHAPTER SIXTEEN

You can make your own

You can make your own curtains, draperies, bedspreads, dressing table skirts and slipcovers. Making these items yourself has several advantages. It permits you to suit your own taste and attain effects not readily purchasable. Fabrics, colors, patterns and finishes are available in far greater variety than are their ready made counterparts. And, of course, making these items yourself is a sure way of saving money. It permits more frequent changes, the use of more material for fuller effects and achieves results often possible only with expensive custom made products. In addition to the joy of the actual doing, there is much satisfaction in viewing and using what you have actually created with your own hands.

CURTAINS

The effect you want determines the type of material you select and the style of treatment. Remember that curtains should hang so that they just touch the sill or the floor or they may stop at the lower edge of the window apron. Tie-backs are measured to apron or floor length, not sill length.

You must also decide upon the type of curtain rod you will use and its

For the feminine room

NOT THIS < Dark shades are strong and masculine, emphasizing the effect of straight lines and rough textures.

THIS IS HOW > Use soft, light tints with smooth textures and stress curved and horizontal lines.

exact placement. Next, decide whether the curtains will have a heading, since this must be allowed for in your measurements. If you use a cornice or valance, the curtain needs no heading. If you omit cornice or valance, you may omit or include a heading. Usually a shirred or pleated heading is used when the curtains are hung without draperies, but a heading may be used even with draperies.

Once you have decided upon the type of curtain, its length, the kind of heading, and the type and placement of the curtain rod, you are ready to take the measurements for your curtains.

MEASURING

Length of curtains

1. Use a stiff measuring ruler; preferably a metal one, for accurate measurements.
2. Measure window length from *bottom* of curtain rod to bottom edge of window apron or to 1 inch above the sill or floor. This permits the curtain to drop and stretch a bit when hung.

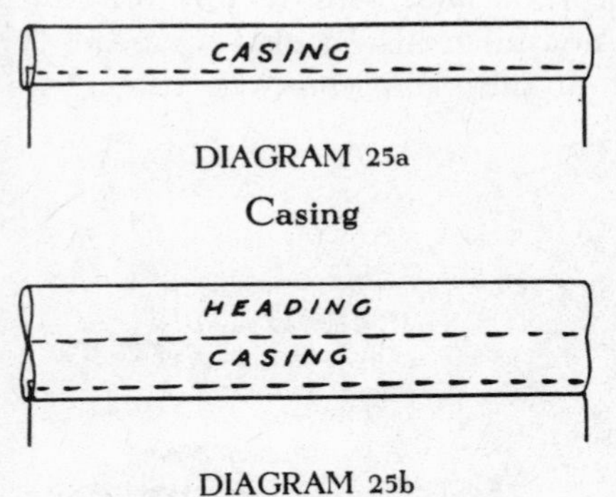

DIAGRAM 25a
Casing

DIAGRAM 25b
Casing and Heading

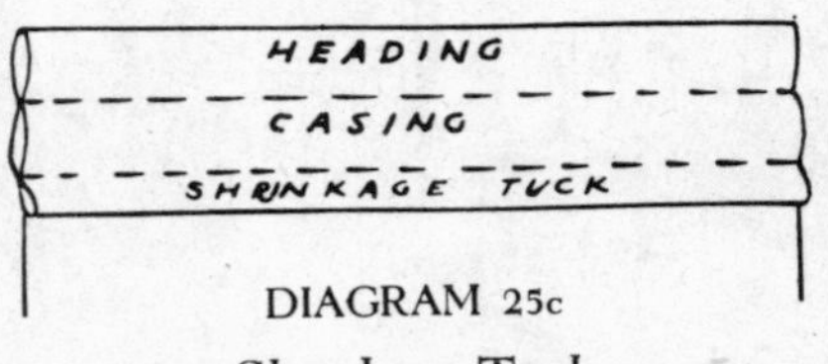

DIAGRAM 25c
Shrinkage Tuck

Dressing up the side chair

NOT THIS ∧ In slipcovering your furniture for the summer, did you omit decorating the side chair?

THIS IS HOW ∨ Cover the seats of side chairs with gay, easy-to-make cotton print. Use the leftover material as curtain tiebacks.

3. Add allowance for top hem. This allowance varies. Allow ½ inch seam allowance in addition to the following:

For *casing alone*—2 inches for a 1 inch casing or enough to permit the rod to slip through easily.

For *casing and heading*—usually 4 inches. This allows 2 inches for a 1 inch casing and 2 inches for a 1 inch heading. For a wider heading, allow 2 additional inches for each extra inch of heading desired.

Under a valance, without heading or casing—allow 1 inch for hem. If casing is desired, allow 2 inches for casing in addition to 1 inch for hem.

Beutanol, a washable plastic coated fabric, is here used for headboard covers, box pleated bedspreads, all-around ruffled draperies and slipcover with ruffled skirt in a bedroom with a distinct feminine feeling.

4. Add 2 inch *allowance for shrinkage.* Shrinkage allowance is concealed through double hem at the top or through a tuck on the wrong side close to the top hem line, as in *diagram* 25c. On French headings, an extra turn is made at the bottom of the curtain.

5. Finally, add allowance for bottom hem. This is usually 4 inches, providing a 2 inch double hem. If curtain is to be trimmed with ruffle, fringe or other edging, omit the hem allowance and add only ½ inch seam allowance.

Width of curtains

Allow sufficent width. Don't skimp. Preferably, plan to use at least double the width of the window to emphasize fullness.

Allowance for ruffles

1. Measure center edge and lower edge of curtain. Add lengths.

2. Then multiply this sum of length and width by 2 for soft fabrics like voile, by 1½ for stiff fabrics like organdy. This gives you the ruffle length for each curtain.

3. Allow strips 2 to 5 inches wide for ruffles, depending on the width desired. Divide the yards of ruffle length for each curtain by 18 for 2 inch ruffles, by 12 for 3 inch ruffles and so on. This gives you the yardage of 36 inch material needed for ruffles for each curtain.

Allowance for tie-backs

1. For plain band tie-backs, allow strips 4 inches wide by 12 to 18 inches long.

2. For band with ruffle, allow strips 3 inches wide by 12 to 18 inches long plus the ruffle allowance. The ruffle on the band is usually the same width as the ruffle around the curtain, while the ruffle length allowance before gathering is 1½ to twice the length of the band.

Allowance for ruffled valance

1. For fullness, use a strip twice the width of the curtain.

2. The depth of the valance varies from the width of narrow ruffles to any width desired

For the child's toys

NOT THIS ∧ Toys should not be scattered about on the bedroom floor.

THIS IS HOW ∨ Teach your child orderliness. Place a chest at the foot of the bed for the toys. It can be used as a seat, too.

—usually not more than 8 or 10 inches.

3. Allow for top hem as in 3 under *Length of curtains.*

CUTTING

1. Smooth out fabric first. Iron if needed.

2. To straighten end of fabric, pull a horizontal thread and cut on this line.

3. Measure length of curtain along one selvage. Mark by pulling a horizontal thread and use this as cutting line.

4. Trim off all selvages or clip them at 2-3 inch intervals. This is important if curtains are to be smooth and even.

5. Use this curtain as a pattern for the remainde of the pair or pairs.

HEMMING

For sheer fabrics, use double hems. Be sure center hems face each other. If the curtain edge is to be trimmed, omit lower and center hems, allow ½ inch seam allowance instead.

1. Hem outside edges first, using machine or hand rolled ¼ inch double hems, i.e., turn raw edge in ¼ inch, press, fold again, stitch and press. For reversible curtains, make outside hems same width as center hems.

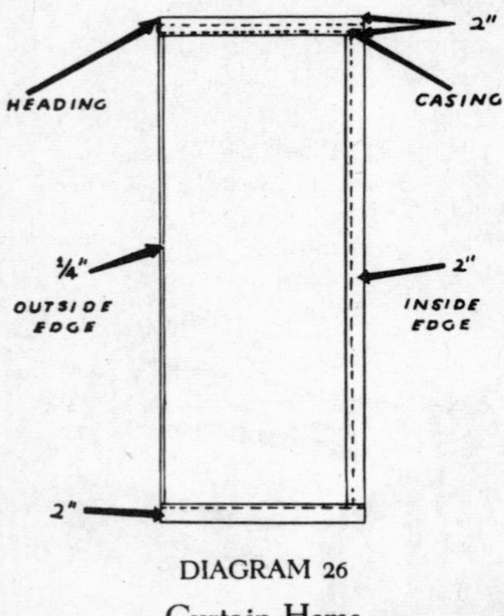

DIAGRAM 26

Curtain Hems

For an orderly closet

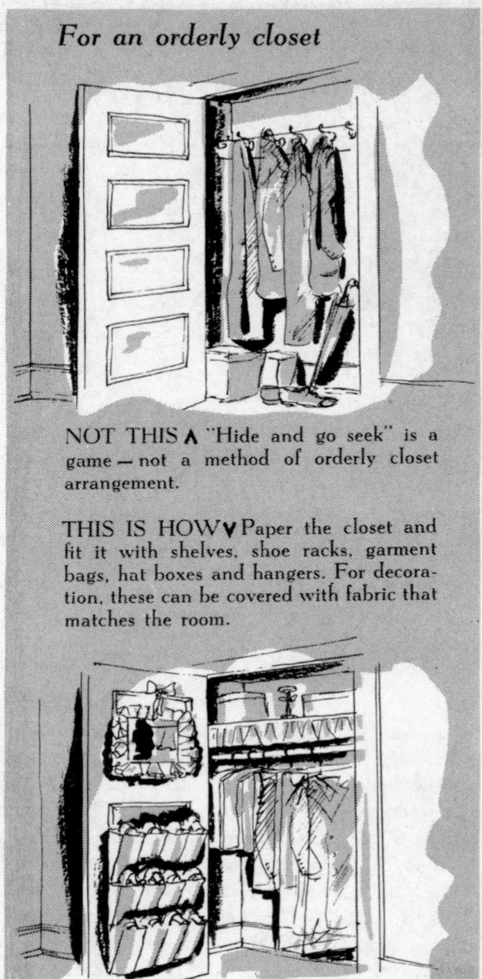

NOT THIS ∧ "Hide and go seek" is a game — not a method of orderly closet arrangement.

THIS IS HOW ∨ Paper the closet and fit it with shelves, shoe racks, garment bags, hat boxes and hangers. For decoration, these can be covered with fabric that matches the room.

2. Next, hem center edges. Make 2 inch double hems, i.e., turn raw edge in 2 inches, press, fold over again, baste, stitch and press.

3. It is more desirable to make the *top hem* before the bottom hem so that curtains can hang in place before you turn up the lower hem This assures correct length.

For top hem, turn under ½ inch, then fold over half the balance of the top hem allowance, baste, stitch and press. This forms a casing through which you may slip the curtain rod.

For a heading, make an additional line of stitching far enough above the hem line so that the curtain rod can slip with ease through the slot formed. Usually, the second line of stitching is ¾ or 1 inch above the first line. See *diagram* 25b.

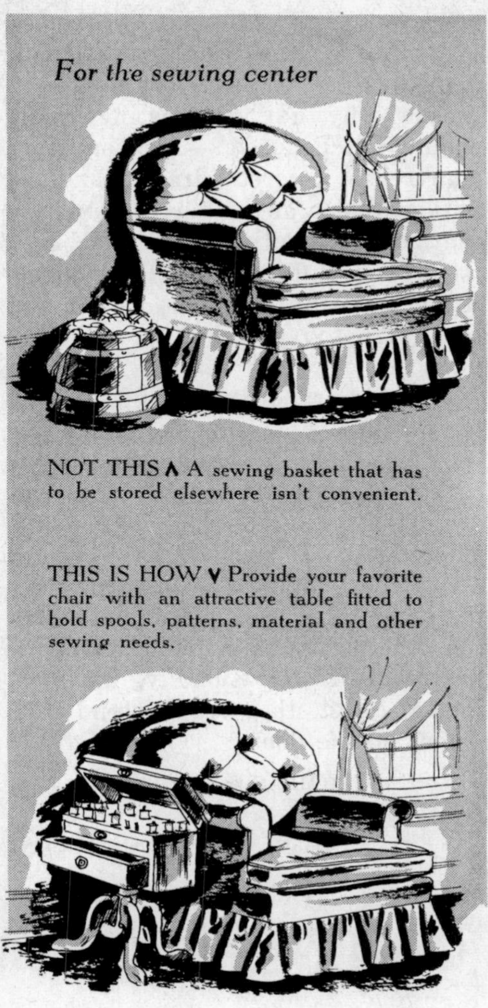

NOT THIS ∧ A sewing basket that has to be stored elsewhere isn't convenient.

THIS IS HOW ∨ Provide your favorite chair with an attractive table fitted to hold spools, patterns, material and other sewing needs.

4. Make *lower hem* the same width and in same way as the center hem.

5. For trimmed edge, allow only ½ inch seam allowance. If decorative edge of trimming is to show on the right side, turn raw edge of curtain toward the right side, then apply trimming over it. If the decorative edge of the trimming is to be concealed, turn raw edge of curtain to the wrong side, then stitch over the edge of the trimming.

6. For ruffles, use narrow French seams to join strips together for ruffle length of each curtain. Make narrow hand rolled or machine stitched hems on one long edge and both narrow ends of ruffle length.

Make rows of gathers ¼ and ½ inch from raw edge by hand or machine. Turn raw edge of curtains, baste and stitch to edge of ruffle. Be sure to full ruffle around corners.

7. For plain tie-backs, seam long edges of band together with right sides facing. Then turn to right side, fold in ends and stitch. Sew loops or small rings to short ends.

For ruffled tie-backs, hem and gather ruffle as for ruffles in 6 above. Stitch right side of ruffle to one long side of band, fold in ends of band. Then fold band in half lengthwise, turn in raw long edge of band and sew over seam line of ruffle. Finish as for plain tie-backs.

8. For ruffled valance, make narrow hems on one long side and two short sides of valance piece. Make top hem for heading and casing as in 3 above.

PLEATED HEADINGS

1. Pleats start at the inside edge of the curtain and continue across to within 2 inches of the outside edge. There should be 2 inches of plain, unpleated curtain at the outside edge.

2. For pinch or box pleats, the usual allowance is 4 inches for each pleat and 4-6 inches between pleats. The 4 inch allowance forms pleats 2 inches deep on the right side of the material. Stitch each pleat down from top edge, the width of hem.

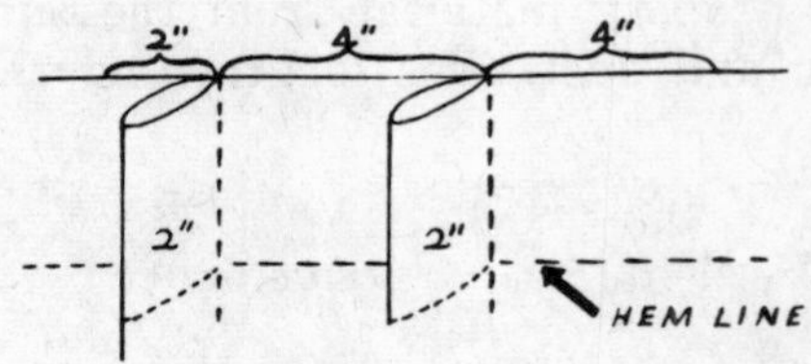

DIAGRAM 27a

2-Inch Pleat

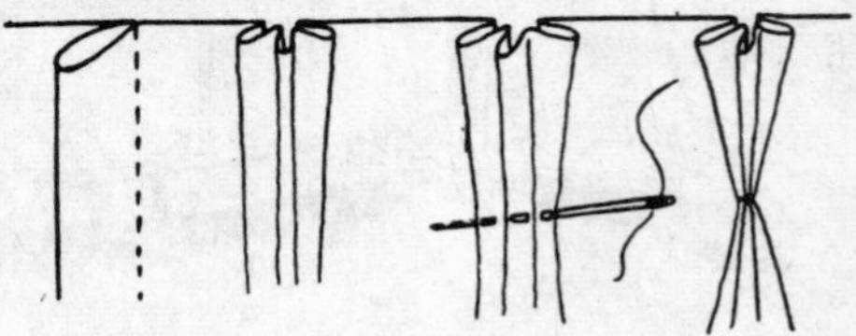

DIAGRAM 27b

Pinch Pleats

For pinch pleats, on right side divide each 2 inch pleat evenly into 3 small ones and stitch in place by passing needle through and over several times as in *diagram* 27b.

For box pleats, flatten each 2 inch pleat on right side and tack at center and outer edges.

3. You may purchase ready made self-pleating facings. Simply stitch to top of curtain on wrong side and slip curtain rod through the slots on the facing. Arrange curtain in pleats as desired.

DRAPERIES

As with curtains, the effect you desire determines the fabric you choose and the style of treatment. *Harmonizing Furniture and Backgrounds,* in chapter 9, suggests appropriate fabrics for period rooms, while *Suggested Window Treatments,* in chapter 7, indicates appropriate styling. Whatever the style, be sure to use ample material.

Unlike sheer curtains, draperies are usually lined. Linings give body to the draperies so that they hang and look better. Linings also protect the drapery material from the sun, rain and dust, thus lengthening the attractive life of your draperies. While linings have usually been made of neutral colored sateen, there is no reason why gay contrasting colors should not be used — for example, chartreuse colored draperies lined with coral or any other combination that goes well with your color scheme. Satin and taffeta linings are sometimes used for luxurious effects. Interlinings, too, are used for the same purpose.

Usually draperies are hung from the window frame or from molding level but today, to create the illusion of spaciousness or height, draperies are often hung from the ceiling line. Valances and cornices are placed above the window frame to produce the same effect. Draperies extend to the bottom of the window apron or to the floor. Occasionally, for rich, formal effect, they may extend 6-12 inches on the floor.

MEASURING

Length of draperies

1. First determine the kind and placement of the drapery rod.

For entertaining convenience

NOT THIS < You needn't go to the expense of installing a bar in your home for drinks.

THIS IS HOW Cabinet bars on wheels give all the pleasure — except for the brass rail.

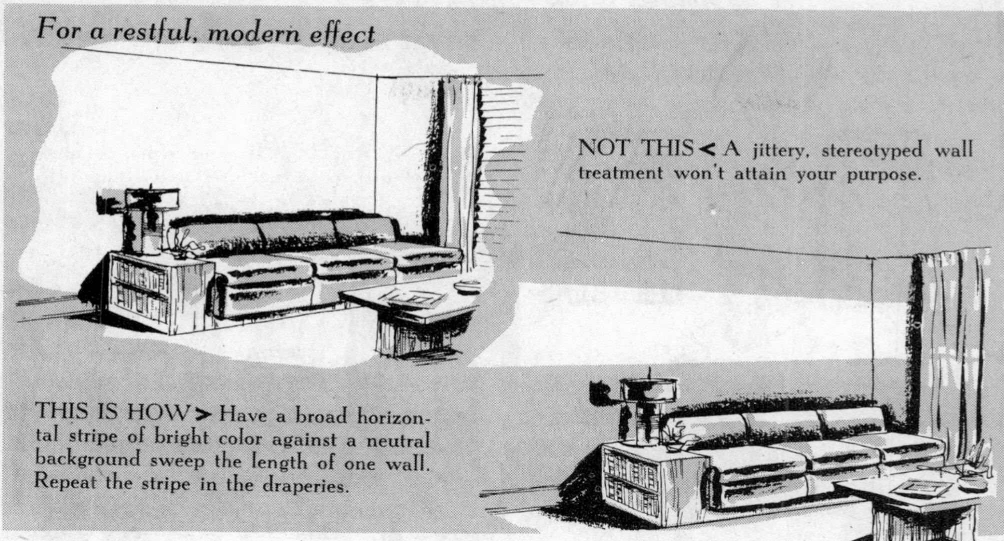

2. Use a stiff ruler, preferably a metal one for accurate measurements.

3. Measure window length from *top* of drapery rod to floor or lower edge of window apron unless draperies are to be hung on decorative rings from a pole.

If hung from decorative rings, measure from *bottom* of pole.

If drapery is to extend on floor, add 6-12 inches.

4. Add allowance for top hem. Usually 4 inches is allowed for a 2 inch heading, but if deeper headings are desired, allow additional inches. Allow 1 extra inch for turn-in if drapery is unlined.

If drapery is to hang under a cornice or valance, no heading is needed. Just allow 1 inch for top hem.

5. Add allowance for bottom hem—usually 3½ inches.

6. Be sure to allow for matching patterns. The larger the pattern, the greater the allowance needed.

Width of draperies

Preferably, allow twice the width of the window or a minimum of 1½ times the window width. Of course, the greater the wall area you wish to cover, the greater the quantity of material you need. Whatever the space the drapery occupies and whatever the style, be sure there is ample material with no suggestion of skimping.

Draw draperies require more than double the window width in order to hang full when draperies are drawn closed.

Allowance for valance

The allowance depends on the type of valance and the effect desired. While ordinarily the valance allowance is about 1/6 the length of the drapery, it is wise to determine the allowance from a pattern. You may purchase a pattern for the style desired or you can make your own pattern from heavy paper.

1. Simple swag valance pieces—Use a straight piece of material ½ yard wide and 2 yards long, or width of fabric with ends cut diagonally. Hem or line and drape over tie-back pins or pull through decorative rings attached to the window frame. As a variation, sew ruffles to 3 sides of the straight piece, then pull through loops of fabric attached to window frame.

2. Stiff valances—shaped straight or curved—Buy or cut a paper pattern the shape desired.

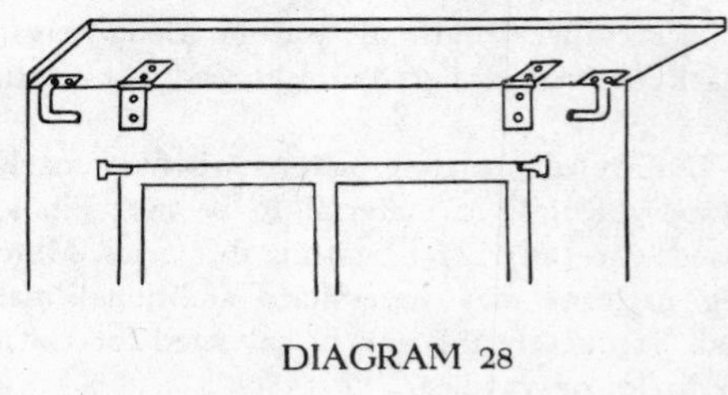

DIAGRAM 28

Valance Board

Try out the paper shape in place and alter to suit. Cut fabric 1 inch wider than the finished valance.

Stretch fabric over buckram cut to the desired shape. Turn raw edges of fabric over buckram on all sides, baste. Cut lining to fit valance, turn in edges and slip stitch to valance. Attach tape across top of valance and tack to valance board.

3. Ruffled valance—Same as ruffled valance for curtains.

4. Cornice boards may be used instead of valances. The cornice boards may be stained, painted or covered with mirror or fabric.

CUTTING

1. Smooth out fabric first. Iron if needed.
2. To straighten end of fabric, pull a horizontal thread or mark a straight line and cut along the line.
3. Measure length of drapery along selvage, mark or pull a horizontal thread for cutting line.
4. Carefully match pattern of first marked drapery length to material to be cut. Pin and match carefully *before* cutting draperies. Matching patterns may necessitate additional material. Frequently this can be salvaged for ruffles, tie-backs or valances.
5. Cut lining same width as draperies and 4 inches shorter than cut drapery length.
6. Cut off all selvages or clip at 2-3 inch intervals.
7. Cut buckram same width as top hem of drapery.

LINING DRAPERIES

Cut lining same width as draperies and 4 inches shorter. When draperies are lined, the hem is turned in only once since the lining hides the raw edges. Hem the drapery material as follows, making sure center hems face each other.

1. On wrong side, turn narrow ½ inch hem along outside wall edge. Press and catch stitch in place as in *diagram* 29a, using heavy duty thread.
2. On inside center edge, turn in 2 inches. Press and catch stitch in place as in *diagram* 29b.
3. Turn up 3½ inches for lower hem, baste, catch stitch and press, as in *diagram* 29c.
4. Turn upper hem down 4 inches over a 4 inch strip of buckram as in *diagram* 29d. For a wider heading, turn down 5 inches over a 5 inch strip of buckram and so on. Baste and catch stitch in place, fastening buckram firmly for stiffness and support.
5. Lay lining on hemmed drapery fabric, wrong sides together. Turn all edges under and smooth to fit the drapery fabric just covering raw edges at top and sides. Pin in place. Now unpin half of top, fold back lining

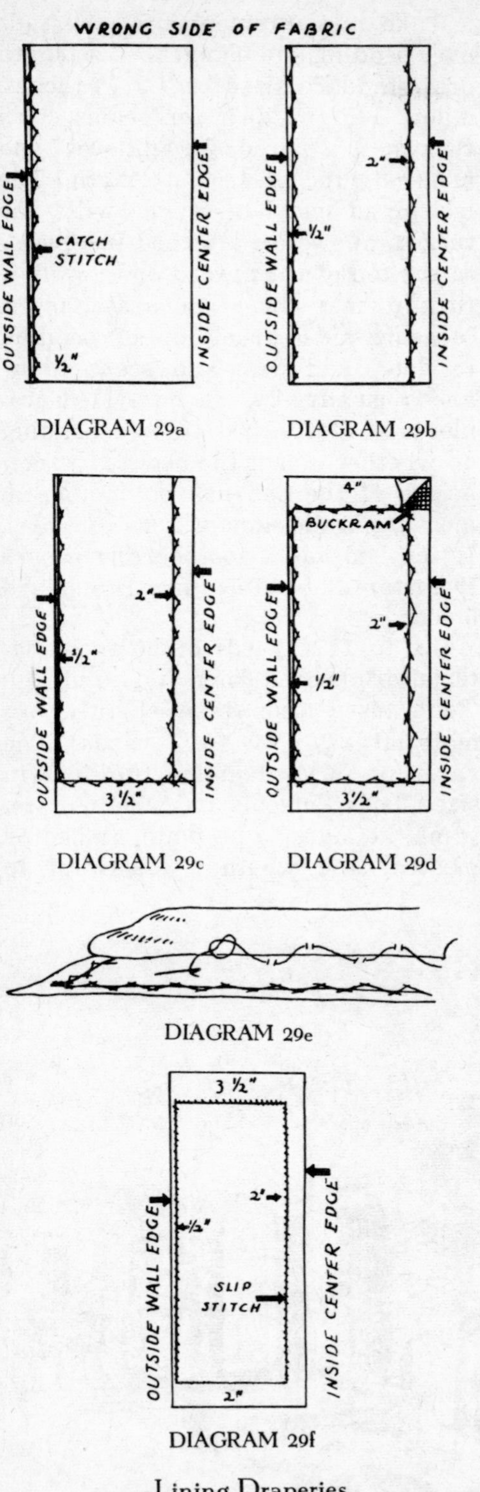

DIAGRAM 29a

DIAGRAM 29b

DIAGRAM 29c

DIAGRAM 29d

DIAGRAM 29e

DIAGRAM 29f

Lining Draperies

and tack loosely to drapery fabric down center line, as in *diagram* 29e. Do not permit stitches to show on right side of either material.

Smooth lining and pin or baste around top and sides. Hem lining at bottom, making lining 2 inches shorter than drapery. Finish lining and drapery with separate hems, and attach both hems together about every 6 inches with loose chain stitch or French tacks.

Slip stitch lining to drapery fabric around top and sides as in *diagram* 29f, or outside wall edge may be turned in even with drapery fabric, basted and then machine stitched.

6. For pleated headings, use buckram strips for stiffness and support and follow directions under curtains. Or purchase buckram heading

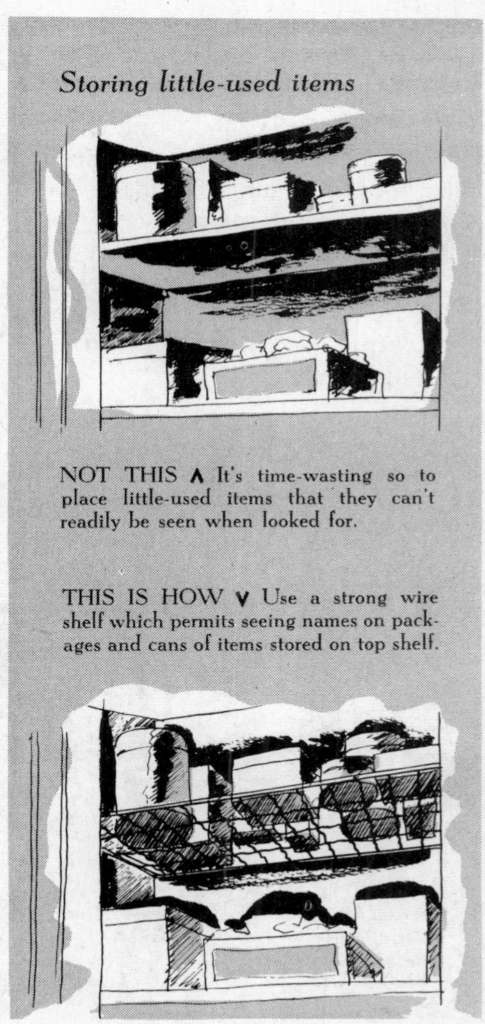

Storing little-used items

NOT THIS ∧ It's time-wasting so to place little-used items that they can't readily be seen when looked for.

THIS IS HOW ∨ Use a strong wire shelf which permits seeing names on packages and cans of items stored on top shelf.

strips that have snaps attached to the buckram at regular intervals. Insert in the top hem in the same way as ordinary buckram strips. For pleats, all you need do is press the snaps together to make pinch pleats or box pleats. They give a smart tailored effect, make pleating far simpler and permit you to alter the type of heading or the spacing of the pleats merely by varying the snaps you press together.

7. Behind each pleat of the heading, sew or pin concealed hooks 3 or 4 inches below the top edge of the drapery. If you are using decorative rings that you want to show, sew the rings to the top edge of the drapery, spacing the rings about 4 inches apart.

BEDSPREADS

Bedspreads are an important part of your room decoration. They may set the spirit of the room through fabric, color, pattern, texture and styling. Bedspreads may match draperies or dressing table, chairs or walls, or they may be made in a contrasting solid color and trimmed with patterned material. They may be severely tailored or frivolously frilly. In any case they are easy to make, especially if you use 50 inch width material.

Take measurements for spreads over bedding and blankets. Top length of a standard sized bed is 78 inches. Allow 1 extra inch for seams. If a tuck-in is desired for pillows, add about 30 inches to the length. The bedspread may be made with the tuck-in allowance attached in reverse to the top of the spread or the pillow tuck-in may be a separate piece. Measure sides from top of bedding to floor, add hem and seam allowance, usually 2½ inches. Measurements at foot of bed differ depending on whether or not the bed has a footboard. If the bed has no footboard, measure in the same way as for sides. If the bed has a footboard, measure from top of bedding to rail and add 5 inches.

Six to 11½ yards of 50 inch material are needed for a full sized bed. Twin sized beds take slightly less material—5½ to 10½ yards. The variation in yardage for full or twin sized beds depends on whether you want the sides to be plain, ruffled or pleated, and whether you want to

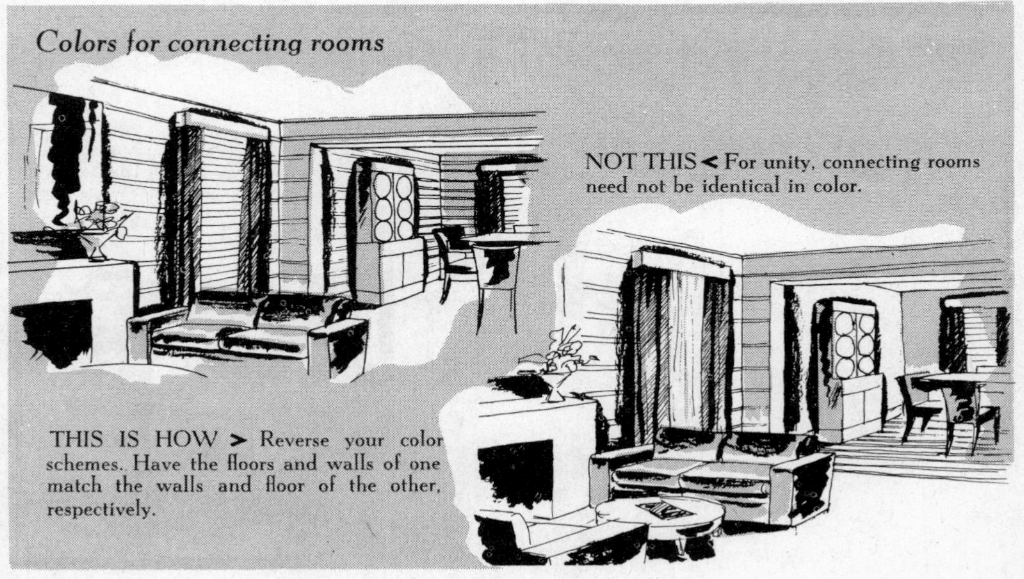

allow for a tuck-in under the pillow. Ruffled sides take twice the length plain ones do, while pleated sides take 2-3 times as much as plain ones depending on how closely the pleats are spaced. The minimum yardage given for each allows for spreads with plain sides and omits any allowance for pillow tuck-in at the top. The maximum yardage given allows for pleated sides and pillow tuck-in at top.

Colors for your telephone

NOT THIS ∧ The usual ebony phone may clash with your color scheme.

THIS IS HOW ∨ For a fee, the phone company will furnish a phone to match your room colors.

DRESSING TABLE SKIRTS

Skirts for dressing tables may be varied in treatment, fabrics and spirit. They may be very frilly or strictly tailored, pleated or ruffled, quilted or draped with swags. The possibilities are endless. Many stores sell dressing table skirts separately or in sets with matching draperies and bedspreads.

Measure height of table from floor. Allow for bottom hem and heading. If no heading is desired, allow only ½ inch at top for turn-in. For sheer materials, narrow rolled hems are used. For heavy materials, allow ½ inch to 2 inches for lower hem.

Measure width around front and sides of table. For a flat fitting skirt, add 6 inches for a 3 inch back extension on each side. This is also the way to measure for plain linings to which the top skirt will be attached. For a gathered or pleated skirt, however, allow at least twice the distance around the front and sides of the table and add 6 inches for a 3 inch back extension on either side.

If ruffles are to be attached to the skirt, measure material for ruffles as for curtain ruffles, usually allowing twice the skirt width.

Use 3 inch strips of buckram for a sturdy band that fits at the top around outside of the table and extends in back on either side. Cover the buckram with lining material. Baste skirt to buckram and tack buckram to table. Or use snap-fastener tape to hold dressing table skirt in place. Tack one strip of tape to the table and sew the other strip of the tape to the top of the inside band of the skirt, as in *diagram* 30.

If the dressing table has arms that open out, make the skirt in two sections. This is usually done whenever there are drawers in front, too. When the skirt opens at the front, measure two bands of buckram to go around the outside of the table from center front to a few inches in back on either side. Cover each strip of buckram to form firm bands, baste skirt to buckram and tack or snap to table arms.

With sheer materials, a straight sateen lining is used under a ruffled skirt. Attach the lining to the buckram bands, make narrow hems along ends and bottom of ruffles and stitch the gathered flounce or flounces to the sateen lining or foundation. Then tack to the table through the buckram band or use snap-fastener tape as suggested above.

For a full gathered skirt, hem the bottom, make two rows of gathers at the top and fasten securely to the buckram band. Tack to table. Cover top of table with fabric, turning in raw edges ½ inch. Stitch over edge of skirt and apply band of trimming over line of stitches attaching top to skirt. Cover top of table with glass cut to measure.

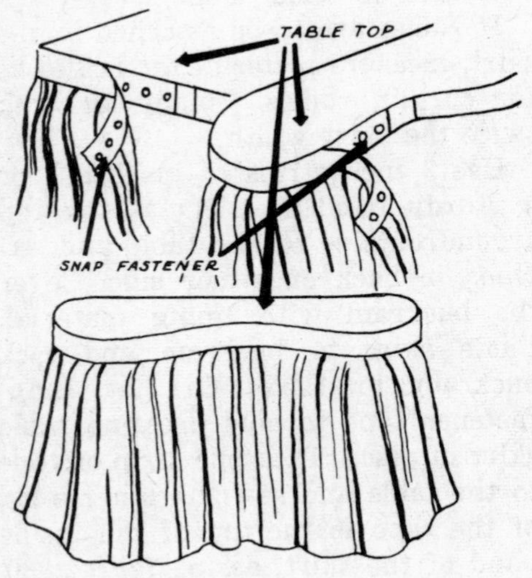

DIAGRAM 30
Dressing Table Skirt

For a pleated dressing table skirt, hem first. Then pleat the flounce, using box pleats or pinch pleats according to the effect desired. Two inch pleats ordinarily have 2 inches of plain material between each pleat. Baste and stitch each pleat about 4 inches from the top is in *diagram* 27a. Press.

One interesting dressing table skirt has groups of pinch pleats at the corners and center of front and sides,

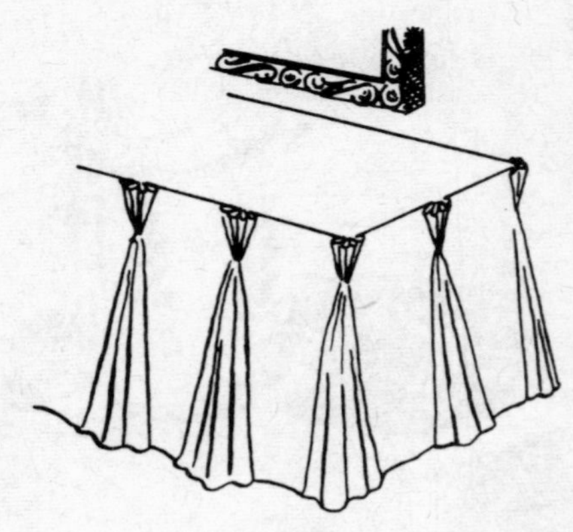

DIAGRAM 31
Grouped Pinch Pleats

while the material in the space between is stretched taut. The top of the table may be painted or covered with fabric or glass. Unless the fabric is so treated that it can be wiped clean with a damp cloth, it is advisable to paint the top or cover it with glass. Some of the new plastic film fabrics have textured surfaces producing a filmy lace-like effect feminine enough for the frilliest of dressing table skirts.

SLIPCOVERS

Well made slipcovers are smart and pleasing. Slipcovers save wear and tear on upholstery, introduce color

Print and plain fabrics with a brushed fringe trimming are combined in the slipcover of the chair. These materials are picked up in the sofa pillows. The gay print is repeated in the sofa and in the long, straight draperies. Decorative china plates are used to flank the large scenic picture which gives a feeling of spaciousness and repose.

and permit seasonal re-decoration. They also can be used to change the apparent proportions of furniture, conceal poor lines or construction and camouflage worn or faded upholstery.

You can style them to produce any desired effect — pert or dignified, simple or elaborate, tailored or frilly, period or modern. You may select patterned material, plain material or both. Since too much pattern produces a confusing effect, combine patterned covers with solid colored ones, or use only solid colored material and rely upon contrast in color or texture for interest. The patterns and colors should be in keeping with your decorative scheme and in scale to your room and furniture.

The fit and tailoring of the slipcover are as important as the color, pattern and fabric you select. The most beautiful material cannot overcome poor tailoring, while well fitted and smartly styled slipcovers can make inexpensive materials an effective part of your home decoration. Select strong fabrics that will hold their shape and tailor well. In addition, be sure material and trimmings are preshrunk and colorfast.

Slipcovers should fit smoothly. However, they should not be too tight as they may burst at seams. With care and accuracy in measuring, cutting and fitting, you can make slipcovers that have a professional air. For the amateur, it is wiser to select fabrics in solid colors without design to avoid the difficulties in matching patterns. If you use patterned fabrics, be sure patterns match and are centered on similar pieces. Materials 50 inches wide are easier to use than narrower widths. Your pattern may be homemade or purchased, made of muslin or paper. Accent seams of the finished slipcovers with welting or use a corded, brushed fringe or other ready made trimming. Apply trimming only on principal seams, not on back or sides of seat where tuck-in allowance is provided. Most tailored slipcovers have welted seams.

MEASURING

Most easy chairs require 8-9 yards of 36 inch material or 6-7 yards of 50 inch material and about 12 yards of trimming. The average sofa with three cushions takes 20 yards of 36 inch material or 12 yards of 50 inch material and about 25 yards of trimming. For a sofa slipcover, measure in exactly the same way as for a chair cover and simply add extra width for seat back and extra material for cushions.

Measure width of each piece at the widest point. Measure length of each piece along the line of the furniture to floor or edge of upholstery. If length is measured to the floor, enough is usually left for a flounce at the bottom. For greater accuracy, measure to edge of upholstery. Then if you want a flounce, add allowance for type of flounce desired. This also permits variation in fabric for body and flounce. Tailored covers usually omit the flounce or use corner pleated or box pleated flounces, while feminine and informal slipcovers use wide shirred flounces or skirts. Hem and pleat or gather flounces before attaching to body of the slipcover.

Allow 1 inch seam allowance on all pieces and 4 inch tuck-in allowance around sides and back of seat. Take the chair measurements as follows:

1. Measure outside of chair back along line of chair from top of chair to floor or to edge of upholstery.

2. Measure front of chair back from top of chair to inside of chair seat.

3. Measure inside depth of chair seat and distance to floor or edge of upholstery in front.

4. For an armchair, measure from inside of seat over the arm and down to floor or edge of upholstery. Add this measurement twice, once for each arm.

For a chair without arms, measure side from seat to floor or upholstery edge and double this measurement.

5. Allow for two extra pieces at the front of the arms and two side pieces on chair back above the arms. Add seam allowance on all four sides of each piece.

6. Allowance for cushion—Measure length and width at widest points. Take twice this amount for top and bottom of each cushion plus the length and width of a joining or boxing strip. This strip is 2 inches longer and 1 inch wider than the distance around the cushion to provide for seam allowance and opening.

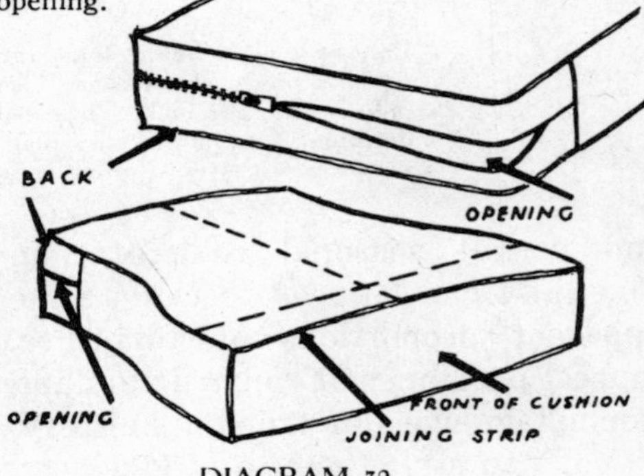

DIAGRAM 32

Measuring Cushions

7. Allowance for flounces—Depth is measured from upholstery edge to the floor, plus hem and seam allowances. Although the flounce usually comes to within 1 inch of the floor, it may be shorter if you wish. Sometimes, narrow ruffled flounces are used for a dainty, informal effect. Width is measured as follows:

For a straight flounce with pleated corners, take the distance around the chair and add 1¼ yards.

For a shirred flounce, allow twice the distance around the chair.

For a pleated flounce, allow 2-3 times the distance around the chair depending on how close the pleats are to each other. Plan placing of pleats so that the center of a pleat is at center of chair.

8. Add allowance for matching patterns. If design is large, add ¼ yard extra for each yard measured.

CUTTING AND FITTING

Cut the pattern from paper, muslin or worn out sheeting. Professionals always cut directly on the chair, but with care the amateur can make well fitted covers with a pattern. Plan pieces like the upholstery, placing seams wherever the upholstery underneath is seamed. Cut front first if the upholstery is patterned. Remember, the fabric is always laid on the chair lengthwise so that the selvages are at the sides. Be sure to indicate the straight of the fabric and see that the grain of the fabric is straight in each piece. Cut and label each piece.

Lay right side of fabric down facing chair so that the seams will be on the wrong side ready to baste together. Fit and pin each piece on the chair. Rounded edges may require small pleats at seams. Pin pleats and make darts to correspond on each side. Smooth each piece carefully, molding it to the chair, pin and baste. Remove from chair, stitch, press and fit. Use a medium long stitch, press each seam and fit on chair before joining to the next piece.

In order to remove cover easily, be sure to allow for an opening at one back corner seam of a chair cover, at both back corner seams of a sofa cover. Finish openings by attaching zippers or snap-fastener tape as in *diagram* 33. Or make a facing on back and extension on side, using snaps or buttons.

Attach trimming to edges of top and bottom of cushion cover. Then pin and baste boxing strip around front and sides to within 2 inches of back. Leave openings in back of cushions for zipper or snap-fastener tape, as in *diagram* 34.

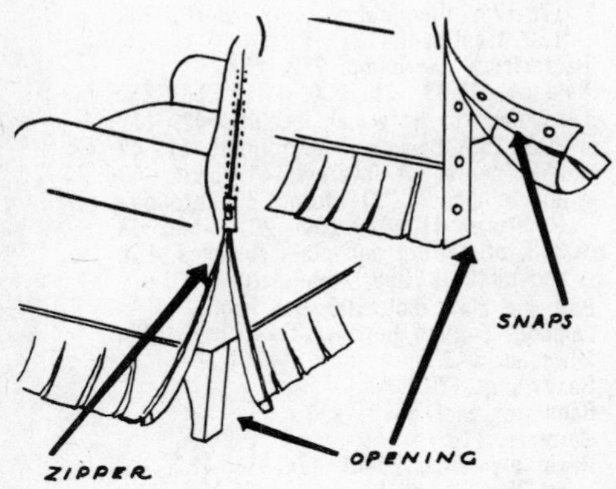

DIAGRAM 33
Opening in Back of Chair Cover

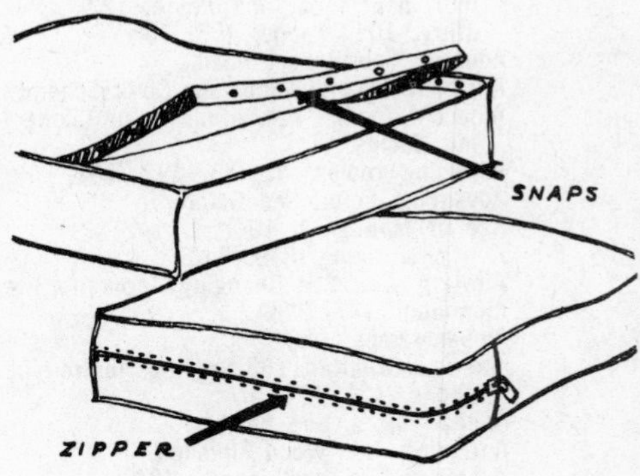

DIAGRAM 34
Opening in Back of Cushion Cover

Index

CAVALCADE OF

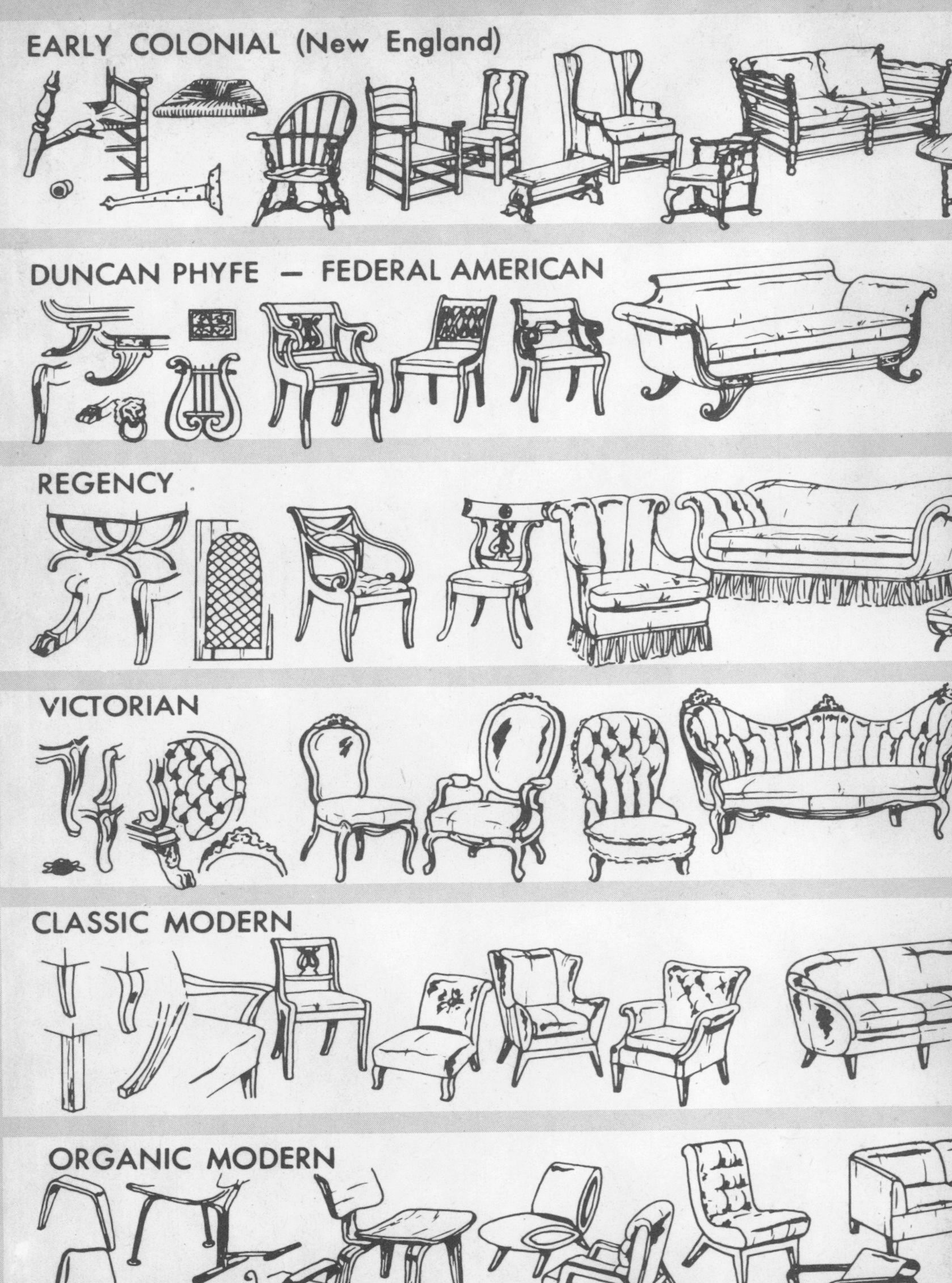

CONTINUED FROM INSIDE FRONT COVER